D1456820

THE WALK-ON METHOD

To Career & Business Success

31 Underdogs Who Became Extraordinary
(And So Can You!)

JIM RODDY

ISBN: 9798671609189

For more information on author Jim Roddy, visit:
www. JimRoddyCBA.com

To hire Jim as a keynote speaker, contact:
Jim@JimRoddyCBA.com

Follow Jim on Twitter:
www.Twitter.com/Jim_Roddy

Connect with Jim on LinkedIn:
www.LinkedIn.com/in/JimRoddy1

Follow *The Walk-On Method* on Facebook:
www.Facebook.com/TheWalkOnMethod

To order bulk copies of *The Walk-On Method*, email:
Contact@JimRoddyCBA.com

Special Thanks
Barbara & Evelyn Roddy
Research Guidance – Jon Saraceno
Transcription – Danita Evangeline White
Proofreader – Paul DeSante
Cover Design – CrossBay Digital Marketing
Website – Monocello Media & Communications

IN MEMORIAM

Zack Roddy
1986-2018

"Once a brother, always a brother,
no matter the distance, no matter the difference."

CONTENTS

Honorary Walk-Ons

Thank you for your support of The Walk-On Method

Victoria Abbott
Hunter Allen
Luis Artiz
Lance Bell
Brett Bennett
Tom Bronson
Paul Constantine
Jason Cowan
Derek DeNero
Matt Dockrell
Jason Dolak
John Dundon
Stephen Enfield
Rick Feuling
Michael Finazzo
Mark Fraker
Jim Freed
Jim Gerow
Velda Goodin
David Gosman
Thomas Greenman
James "Big Daddy" Henderson
Danny Hernandez
Brad Holaway
Edward Ip
Kirk Jackson
Jeremy Julian
Kopis
Juliann Larimer
Paul Leduc
Michelle MacKeith
Bruce Mann
Marsha Marsh
Colin Martin
David McCarthy
Melissa McGrath
Brady Nash
Sarah Nicastro
Mark Olson
Bob Perfetto
Lynn Skurla Perkins
Shannon Reichart
Tom Reichart
Jeff Riley
Justin Rivera
Chris Rumpf
Steve Silberman
John Tramontano
Vigilix
Zachary Wild
Ben Williams
Alexander Womer

"The Blueprint For Professional Success"

walk-on *noun* \ *'wŏk-ˌŏn , -ˌän* \
a college athlete who tries out for an athletic team without having been recruited or offered a scholarship

I published *The Walk-On Method* to share a life-changing lesson I learned the hard way – and to clarify a misunderstanding. In 2012, I published my first book, *Hire Like You Just Beat Cancer*, which offered team-building best practices from the perspective of a cancer-surviving executive (that would be me). I was 10 years cancer-free back then, but many of my business associates were unaware of my colon cancer surgery and chemotherapy because it's not exactly the topic one weaves into a conference call.

Shortly after *Hire Like You Just Beat Cancer* was released, one of my industry friends told me, *Now I understand why you're so driven and do everything with a purpose – you're relentless about every challenge. Now that I know you had cancer, I get why you are the way you are.* I politely thanked him, but I couldn't agree with him. I didn't wake up every day thinking about myself as a cancer survivor. Except for hiring-related presentations where I mentioned my book, I rarely thought of cancer, so it certainly wasn't a catalyst in my daily life.

Upon reflection, I realized I attacked cancer the same way I approached my role as a basketball walk-on at Gannon University, a Division II powerhouse in my hometown of Erie, Pa., from 1988-92. My walk-on attitude also guided me to launch and publish my own sports magazine (1993-98) and then rise the ranks from Managing Editor to Operations Manager to company President/General Manager at IT publisher Jameson Publishing (1998-2016). The behavior pattern I established at Gannon through four years of extreme commitment, hard work, perseverance, and resiliency is the blueprint for professional success – mine and yours.

That concept was intriguing and enlightening to me, so I scratched on a sheet of scrap paper the core elements of my walk-on behavior, which I eventually crafted into The Walk-On Method (which I'll detail later in this introduction and then illustrate throughout this book).

The Walk-On Method

Step 1: Take a Big Shot
Anybody can make a layup

Step 2: Make a Passion Statement
Prepare with Passion, Practice with Passion,
then Play with Passion

Step 3: Run Uphill
Takes longer, makes you stronger

Step 4: No Fuss, All MUS
Maximize Unique Strengths

Step 5: Make Them Throw You Out of the Gym
Never, ever, ever, ever, ever, ever, ever quit

All 5 Steps Are Within Your Power

Immediately I wanted to tell others about this formula so they could apply it to their lives. But I didn't think my walk-on and work stories would provide enough data to encourage others to change. They could point to what I did as an anomaly, the stars aligning, being in the right place at the right time. So, I decided to test my hypothesis: if I interviewed fellow former walk-ons about their college experience and their professional path, would I learn that The Walk-On Method paid uncommon dividends for them, too?

After five years of internet searches, outreaches via email, phone, and social media, and interviews with former walk-on student-athletes, the answer to that question was yes. An overwhelming yes. While each walk-on's individual path was unique, the mindset, skills, and behaviors developed and the outcomes achieved after college were similarly remarkable. Ordinary people will accomplish extraordinary feats when their energy is properly channeled.

Our walk-ons applied The Walk-On Method first to college football, basketball, rowing, golf, or track & field, and then they parlayed that behavior pattern into success in business ownership, engineering, coaching, law, finance, broadcasting, medicine, insurance, film, management, education, banking, acting, and ministry. These former walk-ons were behaving subconsciously, unaware that scrambling to make a college sports team and fighting to keep their roster spot was foundational to their life's work. Going the extra mile in their profession is second nature, and they wonder why others don't take that same (and seemingly obvious) path.

Most people don't realize they're in control of their career trajectory. We're advised by family and friends to play it safe, follow a well-worn path, or choose the most financially prudent option. We're encouraged to seek immediate rewards for our efforts and "look out for number one" because nobody else will. When we read a media account of a successful person, their accomplishments are often painted as a one-in-a-billion anomaly, a lightning strike of genius or opportunity. This book destroys those myths one walk-on success story at a time and reveals this important reality: your professional success is within your control. Repeated (and bolded) for emphasis: **Ordinary people will accomplish extraordinary feats when their energy is properly channeled.**

I'm predicting the only name you might recognize among our featured walk-ons is the late Sam Wyche, the former NFL player, coach, and broadcaster who led the Cincinnati Bengals to Super Bowl XXIII in 1989. Everyone else we profile has flown below the radar, living what poet Henry Wadsworth Longfellow wrote: *The heights by great men reached and kept / Were not attained by sudden flight, / But they, while their companions slept, / Were toiling upward in the night.* Before introducing you to our walk-ons and their inspiring stories, let's provide detail to each step of The Walk-On Method to help you apply it to reshape your future.

Step 1: Take a Big Shot
Anybody can make a layup

Don't sell yourself short when setting your next career-related goal. Don't contemplate what you *really* want and then aim for something far less just to play it safe. Anybody can do that. Instead, Take a Big Shot. That's what Colleen Healy did (Chapter 10: "We Have To Create An Uncharted Path"). The Connecticut native accepted a scholarship to play basketball at Division II New Haven and enjoyed a productive start as a freshman, leading her team in minutes played and ranking second in points. But at the semester break, she packed up all her belongings, drove home through a blizzard, and announced to her parents she was dropping out of school because her goal was to play for Division I power UConn. After a year sweeping floors and filling water bottles as UConn's team manager, Healy suited up for the Huskies, serving as a key reserve guard for three NCAA tournament qualifying teams. After graduation, Healy moved south to pursue a career in medical sales, advancing to senior positions at two multibillion-dollar companies over 22 years. Always striving to take a bigger shot, she left the medical field in the rear-view mirror to become a consultant and co-found a leadership organization where today she speaks to corporations and student-athletes across the United States.

Step 2: Make a Passion Statement
Prepare with Passion, Practice with Passion, then Play with Passion

Don't wish that your dream will come true. It's also not enough to give your all only when an opportunity presents itself. *Walk on* to your dream. Walk-ons of course Play with Passion, but first they

Prepare with Passion and Practice with Passion. Former Georgia Tech football walk-on Sean Bedford (Chapter 1: "You Can Always Do More") is an example of that. Lacking size and athleticism, he spent extra time in the weight room, practice field, and film room. He even watched extra film when he was on the scout team so he could better mimic opponent moves in practice. When Bedford earned a starting position at center, he would study and memorize the favorite moves of each first-string *and* second-string opponent. After graduation, Bedford applied his walk-on attitude when he was wait-listed for law school, hitting the books harder than anyone else to finish in the top 10% of his class. Now a patent attorney, he possesses a "leave-no-stones-unturned" approach to every case.

Step 3: Run Uphill
Takes longer, makes you stronger

We're taught to avoid obstacles and seek the path of least resistance. But walk-ons lean into the difficulties of their situation and embrace obstacles, knowing on the other end of the experience they'll be battle-tested. The kid who starts in the mailroom and works his way through the organization is far more prepared for a leadership position than the anointed child of the company owner. When you encounter a career challenge and see everyone around you shrinking to avoid the situation or wishing the moment will pass, show courage and jump headlong into the problem. Convert it into an opportunity or a victory. In other words, when you see a hill, don't slow down to walk and sure as heck don't stop. Run Uphill. A shortcut may reduce your immediate pain, but you will miss the long-term benefit of gaining strength fighting your way up that hill. After a stellar three-sport career in high school, Chris Doering (Chapter 3: "It Was The Path I Needed To Be On") had a long list of college options to choose from. But none of them was a football scholarship from his dream team, the University of Florida Gators. Undaunted, Doering chose a walk-on role at UF, worked his way up the depth chart, and earned that scholarship his junior year. Through that experience he improved so much that he was selected in the 1996 NFL Draft and played in the league for ten years. After football, he joined the mortgage industry just in time for the Great Recession of 2008. Instead of bailing, he fought through the financial crisis to establish his own business. Doering delegated as his company grew which enabled him to pursue a sideline career in television broadcasting. Undaunted after initial rejections, Doering works today as a TV analyst for the SEC Network.

Step 4: No Fuss, All MUS
Maximize Unique Strengths

Two parts to this step:
- No Fuss means control your emotions (especially the negative ones) as you seek to advance your career. Got passed over for a promotion you thought you deserved? Shake your head for a moment in private, then resolve to work harder and perform better. Chagrined that your pay raise was lower than you hoped? Instead of retaliating by coasting, complaining, or doing the minimum, work overtime to improve your company's numbers and build your skills. Need to have a difficult talk with a co-worker or client? Ignore the pit in your stomach and initiate that conversation. Frustrated that you're working late while friends are going out? Get over yourself. Any amount of energy spent rueing your lot in life is energy wasted.
- All MUS means Maximize Unique Strengths. Most of our walk-ons were shorter, skinnier, or slower than their more gifted scholarship teammates. So, they figured out the special ability or attitude they brought to their team and maximized that to benefit the whole.

As a teenager, Paul Woodside (Chapter 8: "If You Don't Believe In You, Why Should Anyone Else?") was burdened with a paralyzing stutter. Ignoring his impediment, he walked into the West Virginia University football office in August 1981 to speak to a coach about playing for the Mountaineers. After struggling for 20 minutes to express himself, Woodside and the coach stepped onto the football field – where he shanked his first attempts so badly the coach accused him of playing a practical joke. Woodside relaxed, began making his kicks, and because of his uncommon mental toughness and work ethic, developed into an All-American. When other WVU specialists would get their work in and then hit the showers, Woodside would run the stadium stairs for two-and-a-half hours, even in nasty weather. Today he counsels prospective college and professional kickers as the owner and lead instructor of Before U Kick: Seeing Beyond Uprights. Woodside trains his pupils on technique, but his focus is helping them establish a special attitude.

Step 5: Make Them Throw You Out of the Gym
Never, ever, ever, ever, ever, ever, ever quit

After his freshman season as a walk-on for the Wake Forest men's basketball team, Alan Williams (Chapter 26: "It Takes Commitment And Grit To Get To the Other Side") was told by his coach he wouldn't have a spot on the team next year. That off-season, instead of transferring or hanging up his sneakers, Williams kept showing up in the weight room. And at the track for cardio work. And the gym. And when walk-on tryouts were held in the fall with the Demon Deacon coaches looking for a much taller player, Williams showed up there as well. His relentless effort was recognized and earned him a roster spot the next three seasons. Williams continues to seize opportunities today. He's co-president of a food products company, founder of a leadership organization, a two-time author, and a motivational speaker. His talks focus on the importance of teammates and tenacity, sharing many examples from his walk-on experience at Wake.

When Megan Lightfoot (Chapter 5: "Your Actions Perpetually Inform People About Who You Are") first visited the UCLA rowing office to ask about trying out for the team, she was told by a coach "you're probably gonna quit." Instead of giving in, Lightfoot ramped up her commitment. She endured grueling workouts on indoor rowing machines, spending hours learning stroke fundamentals and treating blisters. Several other walk-on candidates quit, but Lightfoot kept showing up. She ignored the soreness, mental fatigue, the salt water in her face, and every other tribulation to make the team and eventually earn a partial scholarship her senior year. After graduation, she attained a Doctor of Law degree then became a family law attorney with a firm in Northern California. She is aptly suited to handle the emotional turmoil of family law thanks to the steely resolve she developed as a walk-on.

All 5 Steps Are Within Your Power

The beauty of The Walk-On Method is the only person who can stop you from taking any of the five steps is you. It takes no special skills or knowledge to Take a Big Shot or Prepare with Passion. No advanced degree is required to control your emotions (No Fuss) and maximize your unique strengths (All MUS). If you want to increase your knowledge, skills, and competence, and if you want to change the trajectory of your career, start thinking and acting like a walk-on.

The Walk-On Method isn't just a mindset shift. It starts there, but it's followed by action. Let's get to work learning from our featured walk-ons.

CHAPTER 1

"You Can Always Do More"

Sean Bedford
Georgia Tech, Football
Attorney

The story of Daniel Ruettiger walking on to the Notre Dame football team was so compelling that Tri-Star pictures made the movie *Rudy* about him in 1993. You know how it goes – the scrappy kid overcomes numerous obstacles and ultimately earns his way onto the field for one play his senior year, sacking the opposing quarterback, then being carried off the field.

What if instead of overcoming repeated rejection to make *one* play, I told you that Rudy had also endured two knee injuries, developed into an all-conference player, and then after completing his undergraduate work earned his law degree and was hired by a leading international law firm? That's the success story of Sean Bedford – a kid who couldn't get Notre Dame to return his phone call, so he walked on at Georgia Tech, the team Rudy Ruettiger faced way back when.

Bedford was a dedicated and decorated student-athlete at Buchholz High School in Gainesville, Fla., in the mid-2000s. He was second-team all-state for football in 2005, one of Florida's top discus throwers in 2005 and 2006, and all-area in football, track, and weightlifting as a senior. A star in the classroom, Bedford was elected student body president and was named Scholar-Athlete of the Year by the *Gainesville Sun*. He was surrounded by athletic talent as well. Buchholz won three city championships and two district titles in football and a team state track championship during Bedford's high school career.

But when recruiters visited the school to assess potential players, Bedford was overlooked. His dedication was off the charts, but others had superior raw athleticism. "I had teammates who were more heavily recruited," Bedford recalled. "But they were often content to get by on natural ability. Some of them did the bare minimum and rarely showed up to offseason workouts. Some had a very 'me first' attitude, which isn't compatible with success in football. I would get paired with these guys whenever coaches and recruiters came to watch them work out because I could hold my own with them in the weight room. Even though I usually outperformed the more heavily recruited guys, assistant coaches from those schools would ignore me, dismissing me as just another high school football player who didn't really stand out."

Undaunted by those assessments, Bedford still dreamed big. "I grew up in a big Irish Catholic family from the Midwest, so the thought of going to Notre Dame was very romantic to me. It was my dream school and something I'd set my sights on early in my high school career. I must have called their office 40 times, but never got a response. I sent them at least five packages with all my tapes, stats, and contact information, but I never heard back."

The rejections hit Bedford harder than any opponent ever had because he wanted to play major college football so badly. "From the time I was in elementary school, college football was the goal," he said. "All I ever dreamed of was to play in a major college football game. Honestly, what bothered me more than the coaches who said, *I don't think you're good enough*, was the lack of even a courtesy call from most of the schools I reached out to. They could have just said, *Thank you for your interest, but we don't have a spot for you*, but they didn't even bother to write back. That always fueled my fire."

Bedford was never offered a Division I scholarship but, because of his grades, he did receive interest from coaches at Georgetown, Harvard, and Penn, among other universities. All great schools, but not exactly big-time college football programs. Bedford also looked at Georgia Tech in Atlanta because of his interest in their world-renowned engineering program – and to appease his mother. "I was pretty tired of applying to colleges. But, at my mom's insistence, I applied to Georgia Tech just before the deadline for automatic consideration for the President's Scholarship Program. A few weeks later, I learned I had been named a semifinalist for the scholarship. My semifinalist interview was conducted by a gentleman named Wade Barnes, who had played football at Tech and had a connection with Buddy Geiss, the wide receivers coach at the time. Dr. Barnes put me in contact with the coaching staff after I told him I would be interested in walking on. I was ultimately awarded a President's Scholarship, which gave me the financial assistance I needed to walk on. Georgia Tech was the first Division I school that was up front with me. They said, *If you come in and you work and prove your worth, there's a chance you'll get to see the field someday.* That was really all I needed to hear."

When Bedford joined the team for training camp in the summer, his career began in less-than-storybook fashion. In fact, Bedford describes his first two years as a struggle. "I came in as a defensive end and was promptly told *not* to play defensive end because I was too short. They moved me inside to tackle and told me I needed to gain some weight because I was too light. I had to go from about 220 pounds to 275 over the course of a single summer. Somehow, I managed to do that in about two-and-a-half months by eating roughly 10,000 calories a day and working out three times a day."

Bedford never had the chance to fully adjust to the new position because of two knee injuries his redshirt and freshman seasons. "All I did in my first two seasons was practice with the scout team, so I didn't play or travel for away games," he said. "I had two knee injuries and hadn't played a down. I wasn't feeling great about the direction things were headed."

During the off-season, Georgia Tech changed head coaches. Chan Gailey was let go after the 2007 season and was replaced by Paul Johnson, who had revived Navy's football program in large part because of his spread option offense. At first, it appeared to Bedford that his third year on the team could be summed up as "new coach, same role," but then he caught a break that was years in the making.

"At the start of fall camp, I was told I would be on the scout team defense again. But after one of our first practices, Coach Johnson singled me out for my effort and encouraged others to approach practice the same way. The next day before practice he asked me if I had ever played offensive line. I told him I had played center as a freshman in high school. He just kind of nodded. Later, in the middle of the team stretching period, he grabbed me and said, *You're a center now. Instead of kicking their butts on the scout team*, he said, *why don't you come and try to beat them out?* He pulled me out of my warm-up line to practice snaps with the backup quarterbacks and sent one of the equipment managers to get me an offensive player's jersey. I was suddenly practicing and traveling with the varsity team from that point forward."

Bedford didn't see playing time right away – but he was definitely a giant step closer to realizing his childhood dream of playing in a major college football game. He was essentially a third-string center and took the field briefly for games vs. Mississippi State and Miami.

Before we get ahead of ourselves and get to the upside of Bedford's college career, understand that he considered hanging up his cleats that sophomore season – twice. "The two moments that were most difficult for me – and I don't know if it was by coincidence or by divine providence – were immediately followed by the biggest sparks that motivated me to keep going. The first challenging moment was actually the day before I was singled out at practice for my effort and work. That was the day I found out that I was going to be on the practice squad again. At that point I was thinking, *Well, I've given this my best shot. It's time to start transitioning football to the back burner and start thinking about life after football.* As an aerospace engineering major, I always knew I had to put school first. I was mentally prepared to start phasing football out of my life, but then Coach singled me out at practice, switched my position, and gave me a shot, which reignited my love for the game."

"The other difficult moment came the week before I finally got to play in my first game. I lost my aunt and uncle in a span of three days – my aunt to a prolonged battle with breast cancer, and then my uncle suddenly died of heart failure just two days later – in the week leading up to our game against Mississippi State in 2008. I was very close with my aunt and uncle; they had always been like an extra set of grandparents to me. I was a mess that week and didn't want to play. Although I was on the varsity team at that point, I still didn't think football was really going to work out. I wanted to come home and attend the funeral, but my family insisted that I stay. In their minds, there was a chance that game could be the good news they needed to take their minds off a tragic week. They were right – Coach put me in the game, and we scored a touchdown on my first drive. I felt like this was what I was supposed to be doing."

Bedford received another unexpected opportunity during spring drills his junior year when Tech's starting center couldn't practice due to an injury. Bedford clicked with the first team that spring and won the starting job in the fall. And what a team Tech had that year! The Yellow Jackets finished the 2009 season 11-3, winning the ACC Coastal Division, the ACC Championship game vs. Clemson, and were chosen to play in the Orange Bowl, where they lost to Big Ten runner-up Iowa, 24-14. Among Bedford's teammates were future NFLers Demaryius Thomas, Jonathan Dwyer, Stephen Hill, Anthony Allen, Derrick Morgan, Morgan Burnett, and offensive lineman Cord Howard, who started at guard next to Bedford.

Bedford was named the first-team all-ACC center that year and retained that honor as a senior in 2010. Tech skidded to a 6-7 record his final season, but Bedford received numerous accolades for his performance. He was a candidate for the 2010 Outland Trophy (for college football's best interior lineman), a candidate for the 2010 Rimington Trophy (for college football's top center), a finalist for the Lowe's Senior CLASS Award (which recognizes outstanding student-athletes for their work in the community, classroom, character and competition), and was the first ever recipient of the Burlsworth Trophy, which is presented to college football's most outstanding player who began his career as a walk-on.

"It might be a cliché, but I truly believe that luck is the intersection of preparation and opportunity," Bedford said. "I capitalized on my situation because I put myself in a position where I was ready. When I got that opportunity, I was prepared to make the most of that chance. You never really know when your chance is going to come, but if you prepare every day and you work as hard as you can to get yourself ready for that opportunity, it doesn't really matter when it comes. You can't figure out when the stars are going to align; you can only prepare for it."

Bedford's never-give-up/keep-on-working attitude has paid off for him after his days at Georgia Tech. "Those lessons carried over to law school. I was rejected by a number of schools and was wait-listed at the law school I ended up attending (University of Florida). That drove me to say, *I'm going to prove you wrong.* I ended up being one of the last five people who qualified for our class and ended up finishing up in the top 10%."

Bedford said his walk-on experience enabled him to view law school hurdles as motivation, not career-killing hindrances. "I thought, *This has happened before. I've shown people before that they were wrong. I know I can do this if you give me the chance – that's all I need to be successful.* I wasn't daunted by what initially seemed like rejection because it wasn't the first time I had been told I wasn't good enough. It fueled me and didn't deter me in any way.

"I also felt I had an advantage over a lot of my peers in law school because my undergraduate workload forced me to develop good study habits. Between football and my major, I was used to running on little-to-no sleep. I was ready to do whatever was necessary to take care of my work and get the job done. The thought of covering every base to prepare and going a couple days with maybe an hour or two of sleep wasn't going to prevent me from doing what I needed to do.

"One of the realities of being a walk-on is that, if you want to be part of the team, you don't really have the option to say *No,* or *I don't want to do that.* You just have to suck it up and do whatever you're asked to do, regardless of how hard or intimidating it might be. That's a lesson we can take anywhere in life. I think walk-ons, generally, aren't afraid to go after big things.

"At Tech, I was outweighed by virtually everybody I went up against, so I felt I had to put in extra time in the weight room, extra time on the practice field, and extra time in the film room. After a week of game preparation, I would invite other offensive linemen over on Thursday nights and watch extra film of our opponents. I didn't consider myself ready for a game unless I could tell you the entire two-deep roster for the opposing defense and the favorite pass rush move of every guy on there. I tried to learn everything about them, except maybe their girlfriends' names. I wanted to know everything I could about the opposing team before we lined up because I knew that was the edge I needed to be successful.

"I'd closely examine tape even when I was just on scout team so that I could emulate the opposing players as best I could. In 2006, we were playing Virginia and Chris Long (second overall selection in the 2008 NFL draft) was their star defensive end. So, I studied him closely to see what he did in various situations, how he'd try to hold the point against the run, what he reacted to, and what sort of pass rush techniques he liked to use. I think that's partly why I was able to catch the coaches' attention on scout team. I took my job seriously and paid attention to details even though I probably wasn't going to get in the game."

Bedford continues his preparation today as a registered patent attorney, and that's helped him during his tenure at Alston & Bird, an international law firm based in Atlanta with well-recognized practices in intellectual property, litigation, corporate law, and tax law. Bedford has litigated before district and appellate courts across the country and the International Trade Commission and has worked with a wide variety of technologies.

"My walk-on experience made me realize the importance of attention to detail and thorough preparation. Patent litigation can hinge on nuances in complex technology and disclosures buried in dense technical documents. You have to consider the entire universe of references, so when you're involved in litigation, it's important to take note of every detail in the patent, every inventor, every inventor's history, the relationships between the parties, who else might be connected to this in some way, and what problems the patent solves within its particular area of technology. You can't work in this field without paying very close attention to detail. The 'leave-no-stones-unturned' approach I developed as a walk-on has helped me immensely, and I believe it can help anyone find success."

In addition to his law practice, Bedford has stayed involved with his alma mater. He currently works as the color commentator for radio broadcasts of Georgia Tech football games. "There's nothing quite like college football – it's a special part of my life, and I suspect it always will be. I don't get to put on the pads anymore, but I still love breaking down game film and getting myself mentally ready for each week's game."

Even though he's years removed from being that lightly recruited high schooler and overlooked scout team walk-on, Bedford says that time continues to shape him today. "Being a walk-on taught me that when you reach the point where you think you can't work any harder, or you think you're doing as much as you can, you can always do more. Adopting that approach has been the difference between success and failure for me. If you have enough breath left to complain, you're clearly not working as hard as you *possibly* can, because if you were, you'd be out of breath. There's always more that you can do.

"I think the people who are willing to do what others aren't – the people who endure through whatever hardships or challenges present themselves – are the ones who succeed. They take a challenge and turn it into an opportunity."

CHAPTER 2

"Appreciate Your Role On The Team"

Ronald Burt
Duke, Basketball
Associate Director/Analyst

The 1991-92 NCAA national champion Duke men's basketball team was stacked with talent. The Blue Devils' roster featured national player of the year Christian Laettner, All-Americans Bobby Hurley and Grant Hill, future NBA draft picks Cherokee Parks, Brian Davis, Antonio Lang, and Thomas Hill … and self-described "runt" Ronald Burt, the team's only walk-on.

In high school, Burt wasn't on any school's recruiting radar, Division I, II or III. "My high school (Gould Academy) was a fairly small private school in Maine, and we weren't a basketball power by any stretch," he said. "It was more of a skiing and winter sport school. We were one of a few schools in the country that actually had a ski jump and a biathlon range on our campus. Our class schedule changed in the winter time to allow the kids to get to the slope earlier. So, it was a very, very good ski program, but not much of a basketball program."

Burt eschewed the snow and became a gym rat, but because of his size (he weighed 150 pounds as a senior), he never seriously considered playing collegiately. He received a partial academic scholarship from Duke, enrolled there as a mechanical engineering major in 1988, and by happenstance connected with the men's basketball program. "One of my best friends when I got to Duke ended up being a basketball manager, and through him I got close to the guys on the team. I had a chance to play a little bit with them pre-season and after the season during my sophomore and junior years when they needed an extra body."

College basketball got real for Burt after Duke won the title in 1991. Two Blue Devils transferred out of the program, leaving the Duke roster at 11 including the incoming recruits. Coach Mike Krzyzewski believed 12 players was optimum for an efficient practice, so he opened the process to add a walk-on that fall. "I spent literally the entire summer working out hard from a conditioning standpoint," Burt said. "I figured I would come in and try to impress him with effort and energy as opposed to ability alone. When you're a national champion and you're returning most of the team, you're not looking for a walk-on to come in and contribute from a talent standpoint. You want someone who can contribute from an attitude and an energy standpoint. I think a combination of the stars aligning and me putting in the work and the effort to get myself prepared to take advantage of the opportunity led to me being a walk-on. I made sure I was on top of the part that I could control. It was actually one of my earliest lessons that success favors the prepared."

So when Burt made the team, did he celebrate that he was going to be part of one of the most storied programs in college basketball history? "I was scared as hell," he said. "These guys had just won a national championship and I didn't want to be the guy that screwed it up. You definitely don't want to be the guy that hurts Bobby Hurley. There were a few times when we collided in the drills and I thought, *Oh my goodness! Did I just ruin the season?*" The coaches made clear to Burt what his role was. "They said, *The two main things you can do for this team is push the blue unit (second team) so that we can have an effective practice, and then push Bobby so that he's ready for the game.*"

That season Duke won its final 13 games, seven of them over nationally ranked opponents, including 20-point drubbings of #6 Michigan and #20 North Carolina. So can you imagine how the Duke starters hammered the second team day after day in practice? "Yeah, they beat us pretty bad," Burt said. "Because I was a senior and older than the other guys on the second team, I was able to dig into them and make sure that they were playing hard even though we knew practices were designed around the 'starting seven.' Those guys on the second team were All-Americans in high school that wanted to be a part of the 'starting seven.' So, I took some pride in saying to the blue team, *Alright, let's beat them today. Let's see what happens if we beat them today – if we beat them at one drill today.* We never did, but it helped to keep the practices competitive. It was probably annoying at the time, but I think the overall effect of it was appreciated."

The coaching staff used Burt's consistent high energy to push the first team as well. During a stretch where Hurley was injured, Duke moved Grant Hill to play point guard, which meant he'd go nose-to-nose with Burt in practice. Well, maybe we should say toe-to-toe with Burt being only 6-feet tall and Hill standing 6-foot-8. "There were one or two sequences where Grant kind of took it easy," Burt recalled. "The coaches said, *Hey, Ron's ready. Why aren't you?* I kind of did a dumb thing and got up in Grant after that, and then I lost count of the number of times he dunked on me in that practice."

Burt said despite getting torched in practice regularly and seeing very little playing time – he registered only 10 points and eight assists across the 36-game season – he knew he was a key contributor to the team. He credits Krzyzewski for articulating and valuing everyone's role. "One of the things that K did masterfully was preach roles and responsibilities, not just to the guy who has the role, but to the other 11 guys on the team," Burt said. "They all had an appreciation for what my contribution was to the team, and that helps you stay engaged. K would say, *Ron is supposed to do this, and Bobby is supposed to do this. And we need all of you guys doing your job for us to be as effective as we want to be.* If the other 11 guys didn't give a damn about what I did, it would be hard for me to stay engaged. When you have 11 other guys on you saying, *Hey, why aren't you doing what K wants you to do to help this team get better?*, it's easier to stay engaged even if you're not playing in the games."

Burt has carried into his professional career the lessons of embracing your unique role in order to fulfill your responsibility to the team. Today he's an analyst at Standard & Poor's, a financial services company that publishes financial research and analysis on stocks, bonds, and commodities. Burt enjoys his job, but it's not what he had pegged as a career during his days taking engineering classes as an undergrad. After Duke, Burt earned his MBA from the University of Massachusetts in 1995 which led to an internship at Sallie Mae and a career in banking. In 2000, he received a master's in finance from the University of Rochester and a job offer from Citibank to work on Wall Street with their investment banking group. He worked in the investment sector until 2008 when the Great Recession rocked the banking world.

"I saw the collapse coming in 2007, and I tried to manage it as best I could, but it was brutal," he said. "I applied for a position in data analytics at S&P, and they said, *Actually, we want you to look at this other job because they really, really need support and help.* When they say, *We think the highest and best use of your skill set in this company is with a particular group,* I listen. All the moves I've made career-wise are probably fifty percent what I can do, what I think is best for me, and fifty percent is opportunistic.

"I think that's one of the things I've been able to hang my hat on throughout my career, and it's one of the reasons I ran away from an engineering career that didn't have enough interpersonal aspects to it. I appreciate the entire process that leads to the end job we're trying to accomplish, and I appreciate my role in the process, the people around me, and their roles in the process. At S&P there's a lot of cross-group functionality needed to get something accomplished. It's not just me having to deal with the publishing team. It's also working with the back-end team in IT that actually inputs data into the system. For me to effectively get done what I want to get done, I have to have a great appreciation for the other people that play a role in me delivering that product or service." Burt says that perspective was cultivated by Krzyzewski during his walk-on experience. "He started everything out with this whole concept of five fingers spread apart meaning five guys doing things individually. They don't have as much impact as if they come together in a fist. You're able to strike a greater blow with a fist than you can with an open hand. The complementary aspect of that is for the team to be as effective as you want it to be, each one of those fingers has to be appreciative of their roles and responsibilities in informing that fist.

"The other thing K talked about a lot was passion – developing a passion for whatever it is that you're doing. He said to us back then, *Let's make our passion winning. A great crossover isn't our passion; running the play right isn't even our passion. Our passion is winning.* Once we defined our passion, everything we did individually contributed to that. It focused everybody that nothing else matters but the things that contribute to winning. What I've tried to do professionally is find ways to develop a passion around what it is that I'm doing. Part of the reason why engineering didn't work when I was leaving Duke is because the environment was dry – it didn't have enough interpersonal interaction and was a little bit too technical for me. There was one job I looked into that was going to be basically watching a machine. It's hard for me to develop a passion around that.

"The way we described it in banking was we were 'deal-oriented.' Getting a deal done for a client was an exciting thing and we focused everybody's energy around the execution of the deal. You're basically the quarterback for all those pieces, and I took a lot of pride in being able to get all those different pieces to come together. Where I've struggled the most throughout my career is whenever I lose passion for the end result. If I don't really care about what the end result is, it shows up in my effort, and it shows up in just my general fulfillment about the job. But when I'm able to develop a passion around what it is that I'm doing, it makes it almost not work anymore."

Just like Krzyzewski did with him during the national championship run, Burt counsels younger employees about the importance of sacrifice to achieve the collective objective. "It's difficult because people really want individual recognition. I hate it when companies recognize people for only doing their individual job because it's very difficult to impress upon people that the recognition is about the overall product success and not your individual success. You should see it as exciting if the team wins, not if you score 40 points and the team loses. I'm not always successful in getting people to see it that way. I stay focused and I try to lead by example in that regard. Every successful person that I've ever worked with, every teammate that I've ever had, they saw it the same way."

Burt said his year as a walk-on – he received little individual attention but earned a national championship ring – helped cement his team-first thinking. But you don't have to serve as a last-off-the-bench guy to embrace these concepts. "A lot of people at the end of the day still say, *Yeah, it didn't work, but I did my part so I'm okay.* And I try to explain, *You know if the company fails and they start having to lay people off, you won't feel so good about whatever it is you felt you did individually.* I'm not saying it's not a good thing to be focused on your individual role, but at the end of the day the first thing that should matter to you is the collective objective."

Ironically, that team-first approach led Burt to earn individual recognition as a member of a legendary college basketball team. And he still receives appreciation from a man many consider the greatest basketball coach of all time. "I still get a personal birthday card from Coach K every year," Burt said. "It surprises me every time that I get it."

CHAPTER 3

"It Was The Path
I Needed To Be On"

Chris Doering
University of Florida, Football
Former NFL Wide Receiver; Owner, Chris Doering Mortgage;
Studio Co-Host, SEC Network

From a distance, Chris Doering's life appears to be a scripted storybook. He was all-state in three high school sports in 1991, starred for his hometown University of Florida football team, won three SEC Championships there, and then enjoyed a long NFL career before launching his own business and picking up a side job as a football analyst for the SEC Network.

Was this guy born on Easy Street or what? Hardly.

Despite his scholastic success in the Gators' backyard, Doering had to fight his way onto the Florida squad as a walk-on wide receiver, which he says motivated him to triumph well beyond the football field. "The walk-on route drove me," he said. "It helped channel inside of me the motivating factors that prepared me for what I was going to go through in my NFL career, in my post-NFL career, my broadcasting career. All these things stem back to this experience of having to walk on. If I hadn't had to walk on, who knows if I would have been complacent with that idea of, *I got this scholarship. It's what I dreamed of.* I wouldn't necessarily have had that perseverance in the face of insurmountable odds. Those things are very relevant in my daily life even today."

Let's dig into the non-storybook version of Chris Doering's life from the start and see what lessons we can learn from him. Doering was all-everything at P.K. Yonge High School in Gainesville: all-state in baseball, basketball, and football, plus he was MVP of the 2A state basketball tournament. "I tell everybody I had the greatest senior year in the history of senior years – I was even the lead guy in our musical theater production. I couldn't have had a better experience as a senior."

Doering's only disappointment that year was Florida never offering him an athletic scholarship. "My parents were both graduates of the University of Florida, so I attended all the games since I was a little kid. I always had it in my mind that I was going to play for the Gators and then go on and play for the Miami Dolphins and have this big contract and I'd never have a real job – all the different things that you think as a kid. But the one thing that I always *knew* was going to happen was getting a chance to play for the Gators. P.K. Yonge is run by the university's College of Education, and it's located across the street from the campus, so it's virtually a part of the university. It was a natural transition in my mind. And they knew who I was because I went to their football camp. I expected the Gators to notice me and give me a scholarship offer, but that never came."

Doering was offered a preferred walk-on spot from both Florida and rival Florida State, and he seriously considered joining the Seminoles. "I felt like Florida had let me down and not fulfilled their part of the bargain that I had dreamed up in my head, and so I was a little bitter with them," Doering said. "My dad and I went to a Florida State baseball game here in Gainesville and saw all those Florida State folks doing the tomahawk chop. I just couldn't see myself ever doing it. It was so anti my upbringing that I knew that I wanted to play for the Gators."

Doering knew he'd be facing an uphill climb as a walk-on against Gators on scholarship. Head coach Steve Spurrier had been hired in 1990 and was beginning to attract All-American talent, especially at the skill positions. "Most coaches don't want to give walk-ons an opportunity – they see it as a double-edged bad sword for them,"

24

Doering said. "If you give a walk-on an opportunity over a scholarship guy, you did a bad job in evaluating his talent and giving that other guy a scholarship. Second, you missed out on a guy who was right in front of your nose who you probably should have given the scholarship to. I was fortunate that our coaches didn't really care either way. They wanted the guy in there that was going to play the way he was coached and did the things he was asked to do. They loved guys who were in great condition and loved to compete. I was well-prepared in terms of being in great shape, and I just loved the competition every single day of practice, just showing up and trying to prove people wrong."

Doering redshirted as a true freshman in 1991 and served as a little-used backup receiver the following season. At the start of camp prior to his redshirt sophomore in 1993, Doering had worked his way near the top of the depth chart – and Spurrier rewarded him with a scholarship. "I was so excited because I felt like it was part of the validation that I had been looking for," Doering recalls. "I felt like I needed to run upstairs and sign that scholarship paperwork before they took it away from me."

Doering quickly became a fan favorite when he capped a Florida comeback victory at Kentucky in week two of the 1993 season. The eighth-ranked Gators had thrown seven interceptions and trailed UK by three, 20-17, when they began their final possession with 90 seconds to play. Florida moved the ball to the Wildcat 28-yard line and faced third down with only eight seconds remaining. That's when future Heisman Trophy quarterback Danny Wuerffel found Doering streaking down the middle for a game-winning touchdown. "Coach told me right before the Kentucky game that I'm going to start," Doering recalled. "So here I've gone from being a walk-on to getting a scholarship and now I'm starting in an SEC game. Then in the beginning of the fourth quarter, I catch my first career touchdown so I'm thinking, *Golly, this is the ultimate for me because I caught a touchdown pass for the Gators.* Little did I know I'd catch the game-winner which really has immortalized my name in Gator history."

Doering's game-winner sparked the Gators to a 10-2 season record, SEC championship, and #5 national ranking after clubbing West Virginia in the Sugar Bowl, 41-7. And the phrase "Doering's got a touchdown" lives on decades later on YouTube and in the hearts of many Gator fans. "One of the great thrills for me today is every time I'm among Gator people at different events, many of them come up to me and say, *I can tell you exactly where I was when you caught that pass against Kentucky!* And they tell me the whole story about what happened. I think I appreciate their stories probably more than anybody else probably could because of my history as a Gator fan growing up, and being through the ups and downs."

When Doering was done at Florida, he had etched his name in the Gator record books, ranking among the all-time leaders in career receptions (149), receiving yards (2,107), touchdowns (31, also an SEC record which has since been tied by Alabama and NFL star Amari Cooper) and single-season touchdowns (17 TD catches in 1995, which set an SEC record back then). A senior team captain, he was named first-team all-SEC and second-team All-American.

He was done as a Gator, but Doering's football career wasn't over. He was selected in the sixth round of the 1996 NFL Draft by the Jacksonville Jaguars before landing as a rookie on the Indianapolis Colts practice squad, eventually cracking Indy's active roster by season's end. He suited up for seven different NFL teams between 1996-2006, totaling 42 receptions, 476 receiving yards, and three touchdowns. "I loved what I was doing, and I was getting paid a tremendous amount of money to do it, but I don't think I had the same passion about the NFL as I did about playing for the Gators," Doering said. "I don't think it meant quite as much. I was always one of the guys who was right on the edge of being either on the team or one of the last to get cut. There's a lot of pressure that went along with that. I got to the point where I just wanted to know that I was going to be on the team."

Doering recalls the moment he first yearned for a life beyond football. It occurred during the fourth quarter of a 2004 preseason game kickoff against the Philadelphia Eagles. "I'm a 6-foot-4 skinny dude who wasn't all that fast, so I was never well-suited to play on the kickoff team. I wasn't great covering kicks. I wasn't physical at tackling and blocking. But in the NFL, if you don't start, you have to be a special team's player. I'm one of the oldest guys on the team and most of the older guys all had their shoulder pads off, and they're chilling. Before the kick I look to see who I'm going to block, and it's this 250-pound dude that runs about a 4.6 40 (yard dash). I think to myself, *There's got to be a better life to live.* I was wishing I was back in Gainesville. They kicked the ball, and this guy identifies that I'm the one that's going to block him. And instead of trying to elude me, he just runs right through my face – my head's ringing and I'm feeling all kind of miserable."

Doering had no post-football plans, so when he hung up his helmet he was open to almost any opportunity. In 2007, a friend recommended Doering give the red-hot mortgage industry a shot by starting a branch in Gainesville. Despite little knowledge of the business, Doering jumped at the opportunity … and then the Great Recession of 2008 hit. "The first three or four years were miserable, and I was struggling financially," Doering recalled. "When everything was crashing in the housing market and imploding the mortgage industry, I would have given anything to be back out there on the front line of the kickoff team and let those guys run through my face. The pain that I was experiencing in this new world was way more than what I had experienced in playing football. Fortunately, I had this drive to be successful and stay in it. By me staying in and everybody else getting out, I was able to grow the business after experiencing the most difficult underwriting period in the history of the industry."

Doering credited his walk-on attitude with seeing him through the hard times and keeping his commitment high. "I was able to block out the distractions on the periphery and really focus on what it is that I wanted. I love the idea of faith. Faith is that idea of believing in something that we have no tangible proof that it is actually going to happen or that it exists. I think there are a lot of people who don't have that faith. We live in a disposable society where, if something isn't working, we'll just quit and go and do something else. I'm fortunate because at a young age I had something that meant enough to me that drove me to go do whatever it takes to achieve the goal. I loved visualizing myself as a Gator receiver like Cris Collinsworth. I loved playing catch with my dad. I would sleep with a football. I would throw the ball to myself in the house. It was an obsession. Playing at Florida meant so much to me that I was willing to work that hard for it.

"I feel sorry for people who have never discovered what's within them that lights their fire, that creates that passion, that creates that urgency. We were designed to be challenged, and through those challenges we grow – the challenge motivates us and stimulates us. The time you relax is where you become complacent. You're backsliding. You're not getting better; you're getting worse."

After the recession waned, Doering was able to build his business to the point that he could hire staff, delegate some responsibilities, and return to football as a television analyst. "I took this mentality that I had from playing football where to fulfill a goal you surround yourself with successful, like-minded people who are motivated and driven. I've had people who've worked with me a long time because they share that vision with me."

Doering saw himself as a TV color commentator but was initially overlooked by ESPN and the SEC Network, so he worked weekends for Westwood One Radio. Undaunted, he kept pressing to have meetings and stay in front of the TV decision makers hoping they'd give him a color man assignment. Instead he landed a plum job as an in-studio analyst for Friday night and all-day Saturday SEC coverage, shows that attract far more viewers than an individual game. "It wasn't the path that I thought I was going to take. It wasn't the timeline that I thought I was going to take. But it was the path I needed to be on, and it ended up working out better for me. I loved doing the studio job more than I loved doing the in-game analysis. I didn't even know that that was possible."

Doering plans to continue to stretch himself both personally and professionally no matter what obstacles get in his way. His walk-on experience continues to fuel him to be extraordinary. "I was constantly told I was making a bad decision, and I wasn't good enough to be playing at Florida. I had coaches telling me I was too slow and I was too skinny. There are very few people who overcome the fear associated with putting yourself out there, putting yourself in an uncomfortable situation. After I got done playing in the NFL and got into the real world, I realized that the majority of people are willing to be average. They're really not interested in doing anything that's going to require more work, and they won't take the first step to put themselves out there. Failure is a natural and a necessary part of succeeding. I had plenty of failures throughout my football playing career and since. Those things helped me develop that expanded capacity that allowed me to ultimately succeed."

CHAPTER 4

"Learn To Be A Servant"

Rev. Darin S. Maurer
Stanford, Basketball
Executive Director & Minister

To fully understand Darin Maurer's walk-on experience, we need to view it through the prism of his life story – from age five through today:

- His parents' turbulent marriage ended in divorce, resulting in Darin moving with his mom and brother from Oregon to Honolulu where his aunt and uncle were stationed with the Air Force.
- One of the few kids in his school not of Asian descent, Darin, who is white, feels like an outsider, so he pours himself into basketball in an attempt to fit in.
- He bonds with a fellow non-Asian basketball junkie, a slender black classmate named Barry. Well, everyone at Punahou School called him Barry, but you know him as Barack Obama. President Barack Obama.
- Even as seniors, despite their dedication to the game, Darin and Barry can't crack the starting lineup for Punahou's state basketball championship team.
- In college, Darin's prayers are answered (literally) when he walks on to the Stanford basketball team as a sophomore.
- He maintains a spot on the Cardinal roster for three years – earning a full scholarship as a senior – because of his drive and commitment to run his coach's system.
- Today Darin is fully committed to obey God and counsels others to live a Bible-based lifestyle.

Let's unwind this story by first diving into Maurer's high school days to understand how he and his now-famous friend, the future President, were bound together by basketball and race. "If you grew up as a white or black person in Hawaii, it was harder to go through your childhood," Maurer recalled. "Basketball became a way for Barry and me to get along well with others. I think that he actually learned a lot about dealing with people through basketball because the game is the great equalizer. You can either play or you can't. So, it's not whether you're white or black or Asian or Hispanic or anything. We just really found a lot of joy and excitement and comfort, I guess you could say, through basketball together.

"We literally lived for basketball from seventh to 12th grade. We were the two basketball junkies in our school, and everyone else thought we should get a life and have more aspirations than basketball. But that's what we cared about and, really, all we wanted to be good at was basketball. We played one-on-one and trained and went to basketball camps together. We did other things like golf and go to the beach. He says he learned to play basketball in my driveway."

Maurer and Obama would drive themselves all over the island of Oahu to find a game, including regular trips to the University of Hawaii to play pick-up against players college-aged and older. "I remember one guy yelling at us, *Get off the court. You don't belong here.* It would have been really easy for us to quit and never even show up again. But we kept putting ourselves in that position where we would have the harsh treatment because we knew that was what would make us better. With all that passion and time spent on basketball, you would have thought for sure we'd have been starters on our high school team."

Despite those extra efforts, Maurer and Obama saw only limited playing time as seniors – in part because several teammates were elite athletes who would excel in college and the pros, including NFL running back John Kamana. The seniors went their separate ways when they left Hawaii to attend college, but Maurer's love for the game didn't wane. Playing college basketball was still his dream, so as a freshman at Stanford he would jump into pickup games with the Cardinal scholarship players. Maurer was improving to the point where he could keep pace with everyone else on the court, so in the spring of his freshman year the varsity players recommended he get a look from their coaches. Then Maurer looked to a higher power.

"I get a call from Dick DiBiaso, the Stanford head coach, and he said, *We can't offer you a scholarship or guarantee you even making the team, but I'd like for you to try out as a sophomore if you're interested.* I didn't have the heart to tell him that I didn't even start for my Hawaiian high school team. I told him how much I appreciated the opportunity. Then I went over to the church at Stanford – it has this high Gothic ceiling, a very high open space. I looked up and said, *God, if You are there, this would be a great time to show Yourself. If You put me on the team, I'll tell everybody that You did it.*" Shortly afterward, Stanford women's basketball star Angie Paccione shared with Maurer a copy of *Handbook on Athletic Perfection* which integrates faith with athletics. That book was life-changing for Maurer. "Training with that book's input from scripture gave me peace for the first time believing that Jesus' death and resurrection had paid the penalty for my sins. My confidence soared, and so did my game."

On the first official day of practice for the 1980-81 season, after the varsity wrapped up their workout, Maurer took the floor with about two dozen other kids hoping to make the Stanford roster. After an hour of skill tests, 15 players were dismissed from the gymnasium. "I did well at the drills because of all of the basketball camps and all the other stuff that I had done with Barry Obama," Maurer said. "Then they had us play pick-up ball for the last hour-and-a-half before telling us to go home and wait by the phone. Right around midnight coach calls and says, *Is this Hawaii Five-O?* That was his nickname for me. I acknowledged that, and he says, *Book 'em Dano. You made the team.*"

Maurer kept the promise he made at the Stanford chapel and committed his life to God. Just days after officially joining the team, he organized a prayer meeting with some of his teammates to mourn the passing of a fellow student-athlete. "Coach called me into the stands before practice and he says, *Dano, we did not put you on the team to start a prayer meeting.* I told him that God put me on the team. He said, *Well, Dano, when that decision was made, I was in that meeting and Coach Russell was in that meeting, but the good Lord was not in that meeting."*

The coaching staff admired Maurer's hustle and drive, but they didn't commit to giving him much playing time. In fact, they promised zero playing time. "Coach told me, *You'll never play here, but you can help us in practice. We'll give you food and we'll give you shoes.* I thought that was just great. My dream came true. I was on a college team." Technically DiBiaso broke his promise that season when he inserted Maurer into a game – for two seconds. "The real reason that happened is Coach DiBiaso knew my parents were in the stands for that game visiting me. He tried to get me in the game with a couple minutes left, but play never stopped until two seconds to go, the whistle blows, and I get to go in. Well, that was more than I ever bargained for. I was thrilled."

As a junior, Maurer was tasked with increasing his intensity to push the scholarship players even more. "Coach said, *Show up every day as if you're going to start.* So, I went with the mindset that I would play but knowing in my heart that I never would. I practiced with that kind of focus – like a starter." Maurer played four games that season ("only during garbage time" he said) as the Cardinal finished 7-20 overall and 2-16 in the Pac-10.

That spring, Stanford made a change and Maurer felt he had to make one as well. DiBiaso resigned and was replaced by Dr. Tom Davis, who had just led Boston College to the NCAA Elite 8 (and would later become the University of Iowa's all-time winningest coach). Maurer's change of plans was tied to finances. Only one year away from graduation and the real world, Maurer informed Davis before returning to Hawaii for the summer than he would need to hang up his sneakers. "I told him that I can't play next year because I had to go get a job this summer and I wouldn't have time to train. He had been seeing me play in pick-up games with the varsity, and he says to me, *We'll give you a full scholarship.* I was stunned. It was amazing to have a walk-on experience and not even dream of playing more than a couple seconds a game and then, all of a sudden,

I have a full scholarship. He told me, *It doesn't really matter how good you are. If you run my system, we'll be successful.*"

Back home, Maurer threw himself into every pick-up game and summer league that he could. He improved so much that when he returned to campus, he was competitive with the recruited players. "Our first day of practice, we had two-a-days and I'm one of the starters in the morning. By the second practice that day I wasn't starting any more, but for one brief moment I was a starter – and I hadn't started anything since my sophomore year of high school. And that was just our JV team. There's a Bible verse in Philippians (4:13) that says, *I can do all things through Him who strengthens me.* I had written in my Bible next to that verse that I will start for the Stanford basketball team. And I wrote that a couple years back right after I had been told I would never play. God followed through on that for me in my life." Davis had previously stated to his team he considered a starter anyone who advanced to first substitute on the depth chart. Maurer achieved that and more, traveling with the team, playing significant minutes, earning a varsity letter, and receiving not only his scholarship but also the Palo Alto Club's *Off The Bench Award.*

Maurer saw action in 19 contests that year. For his Stanford career, he played 24 games, scoring 21 points while making 6-of-12 field goals and 9-of-14 free throws. He officially logged 96 minutes on the court across three seasons. In the Cardinal's final game of the season, an 88-75 home win vs. Oregon State, Maurer was on the court with the ball as time – and his surprise collegiate career – expired. "I was able to finish the season as the one who dribbled out the clock. The whole thing was just a gift from God."

After graduation, Maurer joined the staff of Campus Crusade for Christ and with his wife Allison (they were married while assigned to assist the CCC workforce at Stanford) served as missionaries to Yugoslavia for a year. Still the basketball junkie, Maurer played on a club team in Belgrade when he and his wife weren't working. He then enrolled at Dallas Theological Seminary, graduating from there in 1994 with highest honors. Today Maurer serves as the Executive Director of LOGOS Leaders Outreach, a Houston-based ministry non-profit he launched in 2008. Maurer says lessons from the Bible along with his walk-on experience taught him to never give up.

"Two times at Stanford I called home saying I want to quit. Walk-on life is just hard. You're not getting to play, you're at practice all the time, and even one time a guy got mad and threw the ball at me. You're not appreciated. I feel Christ gave me the ability to deal with all that and not quit. And then I got to see the benefit when it started working out and I got to play more. Sometimes in my ministry now, things don't go well with discipling. I disciple about 60 guys, and a lot of these are businessmen with pressures and with a temptation to quit. We talk about what you need to do is keep showing up. Show up in your marriage. Show up at your job. Just show up in anything. If you don't quit and instead you keep showing up, that gives God a chance to work things out. That was what I started doing as a walk-on. You need to have the resolve to do what you're supposed to do, what the coaches want you to do, even if it's not appreciated by everyone. If I ever stripped a guy in practice, that was monumental for me. If I ever got one steal, if I ever had a coach say, *Way to go, Darin*, that was my big accomplishment.

"Back then, being obedient to the coaches was my goal, and being obedient today is still my goal. Jesus said, *If you love me, you'll obey me*. I'm obedient in a sense of serving others, like serving my children and my wife. I really consider myself a servant leader. To be Christ-like for me is not getting my way, but it's dying for others. That's a form of obedience."

Maurer said he fully embraces (and teaches) servant leadership today. His Stanford basketball experience introduced him to the concept, plus his favorite pastoral Bible passage (Philippians 2: 3-5) emphasizes that belief. "*Do nothing out of selfish ambition or vain conceit. Be humble and value others above yourself.* As a walk-on, you're not the one who gets the praise. The servant is not the one who gets acknowledged. Your success is when others do well. So, you learn to be a servant as a walk-on. You learn to consider other's needs as more important than your own. All that training was poured into my life later for sure.

"I got a three-year training program in what it was like to be a servant. I'm constantly drawing upon that experience now when things get hard."

CHAPTER 5

"Your Actions Perpetually Inform People About Who You Are"

Megan Lightfoot
UCLA, Rowing
Attorney

During their on-campus recruiting visits, scholarship athletes are treated like royalty by the coaching staff. They're escorted through the athletic facilities, meet the training staff, tour available housing, and enjoy a good meal (or two). Megan Lightfoot wasn't extended that hospitality by UCLA when she met with a rowing coach in the summer of 2005 about walking on to the Bruins. "I don't recall exactly what he said, but it was along the lines of, *We take walk-ons, but they never last, and you don't really seem like you have what it takes. You're probably just gonna quit, but if you want to come back and learn more about this, we do have an initial team meeting for walk-ons.*"

Sure, that coach wasn't super encouraging, but Lightfoot wasn't shaken because she didn't have a lifelong dream to compete as a Division I rower. In fact, before that meeting, her only exposure to the sport was watching it during the summer Olympics. A lifelong athlete (volleyball, swimming, basketball) from a family of athletes (football, track), Lightfoot showed interest in collegiate rowing at the recommendation of a friend who thought it could serve as a natural social network for her at UCLA. So when the rowing coach essentially told Lightfoot to jump in the lake (and preferably someone else's lake, please), she could have chosen the easy way out and looked for an on-campus community providing less resistance. Instead, she ramped up her commitment to make the team. "It really bugged me that he dismissed me so easily," Lightfoot said. "I thought I was really putting myself out there – I'm willing to try this new thing and I really think that I have a lot to offer."

When Lightfoot returned to campus in the fall to begin classes, she attended the first team meeting – and was immediately overwhelmed. "There were about 150 women at this meeting to walk on to the UCLA rowing team. I was just blown away. Some of these girls looked so much more athletic than me, so much taller. I'm 5-foot-9, but I'm not so tall that you would think, *Oh, my gosh, this girl is really going to be able to move a boat!* I was looking around and thinking, *Maybe he was right. Maybe this isn't really where I should be.* We heard basically the same message in the meeting that I heard in the office. *Yes, we take walk-ons, but if you don't know what you're doing, you probably won't ever make an NCAA racing boat. But we need people in practice boats to race against.* My reaction was the same. I was going to do this. I don't know why they think someone like me would not want to do this. I know that I have something that I can contribute here. That just kind of started the whole process for me."

"Process" is putting it lightly. Lightfoot and the other walk-ons endured grueling workouts on indoor rowing machines, spending hours learning stroke fundamentals and treating blisters. Mental barriers needed to be overcome as well because there was an obvious line between scholarship athletes and walk-ons. "All the girls who were recruited and who were already on the team, they had all the full team gear," Lightfoot recalled. "They had multiple pairs of sneakers, all matching, all UCLA. It seemed like they had a million different pairs of team spandex, long workout pants, short workout pants, team tank tops, team hats, team jerseys, sweatshirts – everything. And all the student-athletes had these very distinct UCLA blue backpacks, so like a mile away on a campus of 45,000 you knew that person was an athlete. We didn't even get a T-shirt as a walk-on, so it was very clear who was on the team and who was not during our workouts. I know it might sound silly, but working to 'earn' the right to have that same gear was incredibly motivating. To me, it represented a sort of badge of honor that could be earned by working hard enough to be one of the best. Earning a shirt that said 'UCLA Rowing' meant I belonged, and that was truly valuable to me."

Mental fatigue, muscle soreness, and the required time commitment caused several other walk-ons to give up before the newbies made it onto the water. But Lightfoot stuck it out, setting a goal for herself to make the pain worth enduring. "Eventually we got into the boat, and even with all the training, I had no idea what I was doing. It was just terrible. You're just getting splashed with salt water week in and week out. I had blisters everywhere. I was getting up at 5:00 in the morning. I told myself, *Megan, if you make the team, you just have to do this for a year. You don't have to come back after that. Just complete the year from beginning to end, try to race in a boat one time, and see what that's like.* Honestly, from where I started, that was a pretty huge hurdle to even make it into a boat. There was a whole class of recruited freshmen, and then there were all the older girls on the team as well that I had to compete with."

The UCLA team consisted of two Varsity 8 boats (eight seats per boat for the team's 16 fastest rowers), a Varsity 4 (four seats), and a Novice 8 boat for eight first-year rowers. "I had no shot whatsoever at the varsity boats, but I thought maybe I could weasel my way onto that Novice 8 boat. People kept quitting and some others got cut right before the first race of the year, and then somebody got sick, so at the last minute I got thrown into their spot. It wasn't the coaches thinking, *We gotta have Megan in there because she's going to make us so much better.* It was more like, *We don't really know who else to put in there. Maybe Megan can help, so get her in.* I was so nervous because I had built this moment up in my mind. This is my one race, and I'm not even prepared."

Lightfoot stretched that one-race accomplishment into an entire season. She stayed in the Novice 8 boat through the year's final race, feeling confident in her abilities until the post-season meeting with the coaches. "For whatever reason, they still didn't have faith that I was going to come back and that my commitment to the team was long term," Lightfoot said. "It was basically, *Well, if you come back, great. If you don't, have a nice life.* I thought to myself, *What do you mean? I just worked so hard all year. Why wouldn't I come back? Why would I just work for a year and not come back?* The whole time I felt I was proving to them that I can contribute and this team is better off because I'm here from a morale standpoint, from a work-ethic standpoint."

Lightfoot said she was intimidated to articulate her thoughts, so she let hard work do the talking for her. "I was always taught don't be flashy, don't oversell yourself, let the work speak for itself. Keep your eyes down, work hard, and you're going to get where you need to go. People are going to take notice. You just have to take one day at a time. I think that that attitude spiraled into get through the end of the year and see where you are. Get through the end of your sophomore year and then see where you are. Get through the end of your junior year. It snowballed into this mentality of 'work hard right now and then assess after you've put the work in whether it was worth it or not.'

"Stay composed and keep your mind inside the boat. Keep your mind inside of whatever task you are on. I taught myself to have a tunnel vision. You have to have that in times of high pressure or high stress when you're really trying to perform."

Lightfoot's challenge her sophomore year was to qualify for the Varsity 4 boat because the novice vessel was no longer an option for her. To start the season, she competed in a non-NCAA boat during meets but after "plugging away, plugging away, plugging away" as she described it, Lightfoot became a member of the Varsity 4 for one meet and stayed in that boat the rest of the year. Her effort led to a spot on the second Varsity 8 as a junior and then, as a senior, a position in the first Varsity 8 boat, selection as a team captain, and a partial scholarship. Perhaps the sweetest honor was earning the respect of the assistant coach who had doubted her years ago.

"The coach who I first met was my Varsity 4 coach. It took him a little while to come around to understand that I could contribute. He told me, *Megan, I really didn't think you were going to last. We just really didn't think that that was going to happen.* My reaction was,

I knew that. I'm still here, I'm having fun, and I'm trying to make sure everybody else is having fun while we're competing."

Upon graduating from UCLA in 2009, Lightfoot pursued a Doctor of Law degree from the University of Oregon which she earned in 2013. She also served internships with California U.S. Senator Dianne Feinstein and Hon. Mustafa Kasubhai of the Lane County Circuit Court in Eugene, Ore.

Lightfoot then became an attorney at Perry, Johnson, Anderson, Miller and Moskowitz where she currently practices family law. "When I interviewed for the job, I used my walk-on story to make the analogy that I know that I'm really inexperienced, and I know you're probably interviewing people who have many more years of experience than me. That's a similar situation I found myself in at UCLA, and here was the end result. There were bumps along the way, but I know that I can get myself to a pretty high level.

"They really liked what I was saying and the earnest way that I was saying it. Then, of course, they looked for action afterwards. *That's a great story. We really believe it. Now put your money where your mouth is.* I've learned that your actions perpetually inform people about who you are. You have to consistently work hard, be an open person to talk to, take ownership of your actions, and be a team player day-in and day-out. Slowly people will just make that assumption about you. You just have to put the work in every day for that to be the case."

Lightfoot said the most difficult aspect of her job is the "emotional turmoil" of family law. Family attorneys engage in cases related to highly charged situations such as divorce, child custody, child support, paternity, and domestic violence. Lightfoot said her walk-on experience trained her to keep her composure no matter how emotional a situation.

"I can't even tell you how many times my coach would scream that word – composure – when we were practicing, because staying composed under pressure and fatigue was a huge part of what rowing is really about. If you try to pull too hard or try to work the boat too hard, it's not doing anything except disrupting everybody else there. So, you have to have the mental composure and belief in what you're doing, and you have to trust that the person in front of you and the person behind you are going to pull as hard as you are. You can't fly off the handle and try to win the race on your own because it won't work. Staying composed and keeping your mind inside the boat, keeping your mind inside of whatever task you're on, that has been a huge lesson that I took away from my experience. It taught me to have a tunnel vision in times of pressure when you're really trying to perform."

Progressing from being among dozens of what's-her-name walk-ons to become UCLA team captain gave Lightfoot confidence that she applies in her profession. "At the outset of my rowing career, I didn't have a lot of confidence because I had no knowledge base or physical base to draw from. The same with being an attorney. I wasn't a paralegal before going to law school. I had never even worked in a law office. My parents are still married, so I don't even have any experience with divorce. So I read and listen to what everybody else is saying and take that knowledge in. Essentially, it's mimicking how other people do things. That's all rowing was – mimicking the girl in front of you the best that you can. Eventually all that will become an instinctive response. After doing that enough times, it's that muscle memory where I can actually say it back and then add some more information that I absorbed along the way."

Lightfoot hopes she serves as an inspiration to others like her grandfather Vernon "Vernie" Lightfoot was for her. Vernie overcame several obstacles to earn a football scholarship to the University of Missouri, suiting up for the Tigers in the 1942 Sugar Bowl. "He came from this really, really small town in Kansas and he didn't have any money. He played football and he kept working hard, and he eventually got that scholarship to Missouri. I grew up on that story – the classic Dust Bowl type story. He didn't do it for glory. He accomplished it because of hard work, and he carried the pride of his hard work with him the rest of his life.

"I didn't grow up during the Depression, but I think I'm shaped by working hard at something that other people I think are going to connect with and respect. I loved my time at UCLA and reflect with pride that I'm a Bruin and that I worked hard enough, and persevered past my own self-doubt and the initial doubt of my coaches, to have a unique four-year experience as a Division I collegiate rower.

"In 2017, we lost our family home during the California wildfires. I had kept all my old UCLA gear in my parents' garage because I could never bring myself to part with it. I think I kept it to remember what my walk-on experience was like. One bright spot from this was when I returned to work, I realized I still had one of my most valuable rowing possessions there at the office: a UCLA oar given to the seniors. I keep the oar next to my desk not only as a great conversation starter with nervous clients but also as reminder to me of how hard I'm able to push myself – and how proud I am when I do."

CHAPTER 6

"I Had No Aspirations
To Be Average"

Brian Stablein
Ohio State, Football
Executive Director, JPMorgan Chase

Back when Brian Stablein played high school football, college recruiting was conducted via coaching visits and VHS tapes, not online like today. So, for major college coaches at that time, an athletic but skinny wide receiver at Erie (Pa.) McDowell High School in the northwest corner of the state wasn't worth driving out of the way for. It didn't matter that college football was in the Stablein family's blood with older brother Chris a backup quarterback at Ohio State.

In the summer of 1988, just weeks before the fall semester, Brian was resigned to hanging up his helmet and shoulder pads forever. "I was pretty much finished with football, not that I didn't want to play," he said. "Chris told me we should talk with (Ohio State head coach) John Cooper to see if I could play there. I told him, *If you think I can play there, you're out of your mind. I can't even get recruited.* But Chris had a good idea of my skill set, so he went to Cooper and said he felt he should offer me a preferred walk-on spot. John called me to his office and asked me did I want to walk on. I said, *Sure. Why not?* I ended up at camp as a preferred walk-on."

You might expect this story to play out that Stablein worked his way onto the Buckeye depth chart and made a play or two as a collegian before entering the workforce. Actually, after a redshirt season and four years as a reliable wide receiver and punt returner in Columbus, Stablein was an NFL draft pick and enjoyed eight

47

seasons in the pros with the Indianapolis Colts and Detroit Lions before embarking on a successful banking career.

How did he get there? With grit, preparation, persistence – and a sense of humor about his circumstances.

"My brothers and I had gone to Ohio State practices before to watch Chris. We're four boys all a year apart, so you can imagine how that went growing up – we made fun of things all the time. My brother Todd and I were laughing at these two players on the field because their job was to just run at the punters and scream at them. You know you're low on the depth chart if that's all you do. My first day of practice at Ohio State they needed help with special teams, and I hear, *Brian Stablein, come on down here.* I'm looking at the punters while I'm jogging down, and I'm laughing to myself because I was thinking, *I guarantee you they're asking me to run at the punters and scream at them.* And, sure enough, they said, *I don't want you to touch the ball. I just want you to run at the punter and scream.* If Todd was there, he would have been all over me. I was laughing out loud, and the other guys asked, *What are you laughing about?* I said, *I can't believe I'm that guy.*"

Stablein used his redshirt season to learn the Buckeye system and add 30 pounds of muscle to his 6-foot-1, 162-pound frame. "I wasn't a slow kid with no athletic ability," Stablein said. "I had a 40-inch vertical, and I could run a 4.47 40 (yard dash). I don't believe I was an overachiever at all, but I absolutely needed a redshirt because I wasn't strong enough to play at that level at that time. But by my second year, I was ready."

Ready both physically and mentally. "If you're a walk-on, you pack your own bag and you only have one set of pads. At practice you have no stripes on your helmet, you have no buckeyes (stickers). Those are the little things that motivate you. I think it kept me on edge. I focused on every sprint. I stayed at practice and in the weight room longer. Instead of understanding one position, I made sure I understood all the positions. People limit themselves by saying, *I only play 'X.' That's all I know.* What if the Z position gets hurt? What if the Y gets hurt? If you can only play one position, you can technically be better than someone else who plays another position, but the coaches won't put you in the game if you don't know what you're doing. I made sure I understood the playbook better than anybody else. We took a test each week on the game plan, and I didn't close my book until I drew up everything – just to let the coaches know. Most people took their test in 15 minutes. Mine took 45 minutes.

"People would call me a brown noser. I didn't care what they said. If they didn't want to take a rep, I'm taking their rep. I'll take 15 reps. I'll take all the scout team reps. It doesn't matter to me. They're going to call you a 'try hard' or 'brown nose.' I don't care. I'm not sitting back there with you when I have something to earn. I'm taking every rep, and I'll never complain about it once. If you want me to go five times in one-on-one because you don't want to go, I'll go five times in one-on-one. Then guys complain when I'm playing instead of them. Well, I blame you."

In the seventh game of the 1989 season at Minnesota, Stablein was named one of OSU's starting wide receivers because the coaching staff was looking for more consistency at that position.

"Bottom line, I'm nervous as hell. I'm now starting at Ohio State, nobody in the world knows who I am, and I'm not necessarily accepted. I'm the young guy with these older players, so none of the guys really know me all that well. The game was going 4,000 miles an hour. We go down 14-0. Then 21-0. I run a route and I'm wide open, but I drop what would have been a touchdown because I was nervous. I come out of the game and everybody is yelling and screaming at me. On the next play we give up a sack, and then Minnesota runs for a touchdown and we're down 28. I don't go back in the game the next series – they yanked me. My biggest fear was I might screw up. I did that and now I'm done. I'm not going to get another opportunity at Ohio State.

"Well, the guy who got benched which made me a starter, he goes in and he screws up a play right away. They put me back in. We ended up making one of the biggest comebacks of all time in college football history. We won the game (41-37). I ended up making two catches in the game and with a couple minutes left I made a diving catch for a first down on our winning drive. From there I never came off the field. It's really interesting how those things can happen. I made a big mistake and they could have thrown me out. Fortunately, I was able to calm down and make some plays in a big situation."

Stablein, who eventually earned an athletic scholarship, finished his Buckeye career with 96 receptions for 1,289 yards (13.4 avg.) and four touchdowns plus 37 punt returns for 276 yards (7.5 avg.). As a senior for the 1992 season, he caught 53 passes for 643 yards and two scores, helping Ohio State to an 8-3-1 record. Those numbers – and his versatility – started earning Stablein looks from NFL scouts. He was drafted in the 8th round (210th overall) of the 1993 NFL draft by the Denver Broncos. Stablein could call himself a pro, but he hadn't quite made it to the show.

"I went to Denver and I felt like a walk-on again because I wasn't getting a lot of reps for whatever reason. I got cut and went home to Erie. San Francisco worked me out in Three Rivers Stadium (in Pittsburgh) but didn't want me. I really didn't know where I was going to go. I went a week-and-a-half sitting at home with a resume ready to go so I could find a job."

Stablein caught a break when Indianapolis signed him as a practice squad player. This wasn't luck. Gene Huey, Stablein's first receivers coach at Ohio State, was now the running backs coach for the Colts, and he helped make the signing happen. Stablein didn't make the active roster and see the field until 1995, and he played the next three seasons for Indy. In 1998, he signed a free agent contract with the New England Patriots and moved his family to the Boston area, expecting to be part of head coach Pete Carroll's receiving corps. To Stablein's surprise, the Patriots cut him just before the start of the regular season.

"Cut time was four o'clock. Pete called me at 3:59. He's talking to me and I'm arguing back-and-forth. *Why did you have me move here? Why did you have me sign? I could have gone to five or six other teams. You should have just traded me.* While I'm on the phone, I get a call from (Detroit Lions head coach) Bobby Ross on call waiting. I take the call and he says, *I want you to come to Detroit. We have a flight for you at 5:20 out of Providence.* My first thought was I have a pregnant wife – do I even want to do this anymore? I tell Pete I'm going to go to Detroit, and Detroit signed me right away." After three years with the Lions, Stablein finished his NFL career suiting up for 87 regular season games and five playoff games. He caught 77 passes for 792 yards (10.3 avg.), scoring three touchdowns.

Soon after the 2000 season ended, Stablein used his relationships at Ohio State to land a job as a mortgage banker, working his way into banking management, business development, and a role as national purchasing director. Today he's an Executive Director at JPMorgan Chase where he has worked for nearly two decades. His walk-on experience has shaped him in many ways, especially building relationships and developing a consistently strong work ethic.

"There's a correlation between being a walk-on and treating people with respect no matter who they are," he said. "I wasn't a heavily recruited guy where everybody kissed my ass. I never developed the arrogance like so many guys do. I didn't feel I was better than them because I played at Ohio State and in the NFL. When I got to Ohio State, I was very appreciative of anybody who would talk to me – I appreciated anyone who knew my name.

"You can learn a lot from other people, and there's always more to learn. At the end of the day, if you work hard, if you apply what you've learned, and people like you, you generally have some success. Chase has been a phenomenal company to work with. I interact with the people here well and I work hard."

Stablein said his walk-on experience also helped him learn how to appropriately handle the day-to-day frustrations of the work world. "I'm coaching some folks on my team, and we laugh because you have to learn from the small stuff even though it might frustrate you. Day-to-day frustrations shouldn't stop you from doing your job. Stop making excuses for yourself. Put together a plan that you believe in, follow the plan, and tweak it as you go along. Quit making excuses that you're not meeting your goals because of little things that might be frustrating you. You're hired to do a job. Find out how you're going to do that job, and then go after it as hard as you can. It's like preparation mode for a game and creating game plans. I make a plan that I believe in and then I work diligently to get there. And if the plan didn't work, you can fire me. At least I tried. And I'm okay with that. I got cut a few times in the NFL. I hit some bumps in the road but I also realized it's not the end of the world. So, don't be afraid. Take some chances. Learn from your mistakes. Put a plan together. Believe in it and let it fly."

One of the areas Stablein has stepped outside his comfort zone is public speaking. "I'm very comfortable presenting today but I wasn't always that way. I've bombed in front of people, but I've always been willing to put myself in the situation to be able to present. As you grow in business, you're naturally going to be put into more leadership roles and you're going to be in front of more groups. If you screw up, you learn from it and that builds your confidence."

Stablein has expanded from presenting at internal Chase meetings and client engagements to speaking at national conferences. The competitiveness that was stoked beating out scholarship players on the field drove Stablein to master public speaking. "I had no aspirations to be average – none. I wanted to be the best on the field, and now I want to be the best in the room. I want to be the best at what I'm doing. If I'm in an entry-level position, I'm looking at the next rung and then the next rung after that and see how I get there. You always need to be asking yourself, *How do I apply myself to get to the next level?*"

CHAPTER 7

"Every Business Is A Team"

Brandon Landry
LSU, Basketball
Co-Founder/Co-Owner/CEO, Walk-On's Sports Bistreaux

Throughout this book, we've shone a light on former walk-ons and how the lessons they learned as student-athletes propelled them to professional success. In the case of Brandon Landry, we left the flashlight in our pocket. Landry has put the walk-on concept in bright lights as the co-founder, co-owner, and CEO of Walk-On's Sports Bistreaux, a growing chain of sports bars throughout the southern U.S. "Everything that we talk about at our company, it all goes back to the days of me being a walk-on and being on a team," said Landry, a four-year basketball walk-on at LSU. "I was in those shoes as a player asking, *What can I do to make this team better?* It's really the same thing today, except we're serving burgers and beer while walk-ons are throwing footballs and basketballs."

Before we talk about Walk-On's the business, we have to go back to Landry's basketball career – which almost didn't happen – to fully understand his success story. Never an imposing physical presence, Landry was cut from the Baton Rouge (La.) Catholic High School team his freshman year. He worked his way onto the club the next season and never looked back. As a senior, Landry was his team's Defensive Player of the Year and was named All-District, averaging 14 points, five assists, and three rebounds per game. "When I got cut, I wasn't going to accept that," Landry said. "I busted my tail and came back better the next year."

Landry had options to attend smaller colleges to continue his playing career, but he chose to go for the big-time and walk on at LSU. After making that decision, he had to work up the nerve to make his intentions known to first-year Tiger coach John Brady. "You're 18 years old and here you go walking into the head coach's office – you're nervous about how it's going to go," Landry said. "Getting the courage and not being afraid to walk through the door and introduce myself was the first step."

Brady pointed Landry towards LSU's walk-on tryouts which attracted nearly 60 students in October 1997. Just like high school, Landry was close to making the club but was cut again. "The guys who tried out were going to get a phone call by a certain time if they wanted you to come back. I never got the call. I ended up talking with one of the managers the next day, and he said they picked two other guys. Of course, I had that same feeling four years previous in high school. Once again, my mindset was the same. *I got to work harder. I got to play more. I got to get stronger. I got to do the things I need to do to make this team.* I was working on that when I got the call back a month later."

Midseason turnover on the LSU roster created an opening for Landry. A spot on the active roster wasn't available, but Landry was asked to be a practice player. He wouldn't dress for games or travel, but he'd participate in drills and scrimmages to help prepare everyone else. Landry jumped at that chance – literally. "I got a call on a Friday afternoon asking if I could be at the gym at 6:30 Saturday morning for practice. I was stoked. My dad's a sugarcane farmer, and November/December is grinding season – harvest season. I was on a tractor helping him out on that Friday afternoon when I got the call. I remember jumping up and down like a crazy 19-year-old. I think I was there by 5:30 the next morning. I was so excited just to get an opportunity to put on that uniform. But I was also scared to death not knowing one person there and going up against 6-7, 6-8, seven-foot guys," said the 5-foot-11 Landry. "I knew I might not be the best guy out there, but I was going to work harder than them."

Landry experienced the difference between intramural ball and major Division I competition right away. "At the rec center you may be the best guy on the court, but when you get out there against the scholarship guys, you're just fighting to get around them," he said. "Even just the physicality of going for a layup – it's no longer high school where you get touched or bumped and then get a foul call. I remember after the first couple practices, I thought, *Man – am I good enough to play with these guys?* It's a learning curve. Some people don't learn and they figure they can't do this. That wasn't in my vocabulary. I thought, *Okay, I have to figure out how the John Stocktons of the world play out here because we're the same size.*"

Landry recalls a particular one-on-one battle with 6-foot-2, 190-pound DeJuan Collins, who later enjoyed a 13-year pro career as a high-scoring guard in Europe. "He's 21 years old and a little bit bigger point guard with a filled-out body. After a walk-through, he asked to play me one-on-one, and, man, he took that opportunity to put me in my place. He was just pushing me around, backing me down every time he wanted. Here's a *point guard* having his way with me. I was so tired because of the beating he was giving me, that by the time I got the ball I couldn't do anything with it. That was an eye-opening moment that I had to get stronger and work out more."

Landry developed his game and his body, earning a roster spot as a sophomore for the 1998-99 season. He was told he could dress for home games but wasn't going to travel with the team for road games. "It took three or four games before they actually had a jersey with my name printed on the back," Landry recalled. "One of the coaches said to me, *Don't worry about it because your shooting shirt is never going to come off.*"

Coach Brady apparently needed that identification because he wouldn't refer to Landry by name during Tiger practices. "The first six months I'm on the team, he didn't know my name," Landry said. "Every time he would call me, he'd say, *Hey, walk-on, come over here.* I didn't let it get to me. I just loved the part where I would kick one of the asses of the starters and he'd say, *Are you going to let that walk-on do that to you?* He truly didn't know my name."

Landry saw game action only twice his sophomore season but received significant playing time that summer during LSU's team trip to Italy. With only six scholarship athletes available, Landry averaged 2.4 ppg and played 17 minutes against the Angolan National Team. He was hopeful to crack the rotation during the upcoming regular season, but that never materialized after more scholarship players arrived on campus and led LSU to a 28-6 record and the NCAA Sweet 16. Landry played in eight games, his only scoring being three-pointers in routs of Grambling (112-37) and Alabama (93-60). He still takes pride in his shot against the Crimson Tide. "At Alabama, our bench was probably three feet from where the student section starts, and the students were on my butt the whole game. I told them, *When I get in there, I'm going to shut you all up.* I get in with about four minutes left, and they hit me with a pass on the baseline. I hit a three and did the 'Shhhh!' sign all the way down the floor looking right at them."

Landry played seven games as a senior, the Tigers slipping to a 13-16 mark and no postseason bid. For his career, Landry registered eight points over 17 games, shooting 2-for-9 on field goals, 2-for-8 on threes, and 2-for-2 from the foul line. The stat line doesn't show the further development of his relentless attitude and that on the end of the LSU bench is where the idea for Walk-On's was brainstormed. Landry and fellow walk-on Jack Warner, after visiting top-rate restaurants and sports bars during road trips, recognized the need for a similar concept back in Baton Rouge. During a flight home from the University of Tennessee, Landry and Warner sketched a restaurant floor plan on the back of a napkin. Three years later, on Sept. 9, 2003, Landry and Warner opened the first Walk-On's near LSU's Tiger Stadium.

Landry said the walk-on attitude was infused in the Walk-On's culture from day one and still thrives today. "Our tag line is 'Walk-On's: Because Everyone Needs a Little Playing Time.' It has a double meaning, but it speaks the truth. Everyone plays a part on a team. I played only 10 minutes the year we made it to the Sweet 16, but I was a big part of that team and I did so much to make that team better that year. I knew everything that I had done was a contribution that made that team better. If I wasn't on that team, I don't know if they would have gone that far even if I didn't play much. That was my mentality.

"We preach in our restaurants today that one of the most important guys on our team is our dishwasher. He's our walk-on. He's our guy. He sits at the end of the bench and doesn't get all the fame, doesn't get all the glory, doesn't hang out with the pretty girls drinking martinis, but, at the end of the day, if he's not back there busting his tail and making sure that every dish is coming out sparkling and that every glass is clean, then they can't serve that food. They can't serve those drinks. He's our guy that's playing 10 minutes a year but doing all the dirty work behind the scenes to make our company better.

"One of the first interview questions we use in our company, whether you're applying to be a dishwasher, a bartender, a server, or a manager, is, *Have you ever been a part of a team? Have you ever played on a team?* It doesn't matter if it's a football team, gymnastics, cheerleading, or croquet – we don't care. Understanding the value of teamwork and working together is so important. It's not about the individualism because every company, every business is a team, and if you can't play together and understand the dynamics of teamwork, it doesn't work."

That approach has worked for Landry as Walk-On's has expanded from a single-location restaurant to a chain with a national reputation. Walk-On's began sponsorship of the Independence Bowl beginning in 2017, two years after NFL Super Bowl XLIV MVP Drew Brees of the New Orleans Saints joined the company as a co-owner and partner in 2015. Landry has received several professional accolades along the way including Louisiana Restaurant Association Restaurateur of the Year, Baton Rouge Young Businessperson of the Year, and Baton Rouge Sales and Marketing Executives Marketer of the Year.

Walk-On's success sounds like a storybook fantasy, but the reality is that the concept almost never got off the bench. "We got turned down by six banks when we did our first restaurant," Landry said. "If the seventh bank had never said *yes*, we would have gone on to number eight. It was going to happen because I believed in the idea,

I believed in the concept. That's just my way of thinking. To be honest with you, it was a natural transition from what we went through as walk-ons to what we did in business."

Remember how coach Brady couldn't recall Landry's name? It turns out Walk-On's helped the guy known as "walk-on" earn some name recognition. Landry said of Brady, "I saw him recently and he said, *Hey Brandon, I should be getting some royalties off of your restaurants now because I called you 'walk-on' first.*"

Landry is quick to credit legendary Tiger coach Dale Brown, who won 448 games and advanced to two NCAA Final Fours coaching LSU from 1972-1997, for making Walk-On's possible. Brown, who Landry calls "an unbelievable guy," coached Jack Warner his freshman season (1996-97). Brown believed every member of the team was important – and he wasn't shy about preaching that.

"Coach Brown had a bunch of McDonald's All-Americans on that team, and Lester Earl was the number one freshman in the country," Landry said. "Jack told me that coach Brown started the first team meeting saying, *Lester Earl – stand up. Everybody knows who Lester Earl is, right?* And all the players say, *Of course.* Then he says, *Jack Warner – stand up. Does everybody know who Jack Warner is?* They had no idea who he was. Brown says, *You're right. He's a walk-on. Lester Earl is the number one recruit in the country. Now they're both on this team. This is a team. If I see any one of you guys treating Jack Warner any differently than Lester Earl or Lester Earl any differently than Jack Warner, you're off the team and Jack gets your scholarship.*

"He set the precedent that day that they were a team, and everybody was a part of it. I think after 30 years of coaching he understood everybody plays a part. And it's everybody's contribution that's going to make this team better."

CHAPTER 8

"If You Don't Believe In You, Why Should Anyone Else?"

Paul Woodside

West Virginia University, Football
Owner, Before U Kick: Seeing Beyond Uprights

Paul Woodside's college football career started as a "joke" in 1981 but ended with All-American honors and a lifetime of lessons to be applied. Okay, it wasn't literally a joke, but one of the assistant coaches at West Virginia University thought it was.

After graduating from Falls Church (Va.) High School, Woodside wasn't sure what to do next. Even in early August of that year, he wasn't enrolled in any college and didn't have a job lined up. A severe stutter was an impediment to moving forward, and being a kicker meant few coaches were paying attention to Woodside on the field. What was supposed to be a casual drive to visit his sister and brother-in-law on Aug. 8, 1981, became a turning point for him.

"To get from Virginia to Pittsburgh, I had to drive through Morgantown (W.V.)," Woodside recalled. "That's when I went into the football office unannounced and said, *I'd like to try out.* It took me about 20 minutes to say it. I had no personal confidence whatsoever. Because of my stuttering, I was really insecure, really awkward, nothing made sense. The only part of my life that made sense was to kick a football. So, when I walked into the offices, there was a secretary there and I asked to speak to a coach to see if I could kick. The only coach there was Donnie Young, and he asked who I was and why I was there. That's where it took forever to speak."

Woodside handed the coach a card explaining his stutter. "I'm thinking it would buy time and he would be patient with me. I just wanted to kick – that's really all that I know how to do, and I wanted to show him that I can kick. Eventually we went down to the field and because I had just gotten out of the car, my first couple of kicks were not the best. Coach asked me, *Is this an April Fool's joke? Did one of the other coaches put you up to this?* But then I started to kick like I could, and he walked up to me and said, *If you'd like to walk on, you can.*

"I went up to my sister's house and called my mom and told her I was going to West Virginia. She had to drive from the D.C. area to take my stuff to West Virginia because practice started on Aug. 11. At that time, I didn't know the expression, *You don't know what you don't know.* I didn't know that I should be afraid or scared or nervous. You have high school seniors who already know by October what school they're going to. They've already applied and been approved and admitted. Back then, I didn't know that you should have done all that. They basically walked my application to admissions when I went back, and that was it. I guess everything else is just history."

Woodside's big leg and non-stop work ethic helped him see the field as a freshman that fall, first only for kickoffs but eventually as the Mountaineers' full-time placekicker. He scored 34 points that year (8-for-12 on field goals, 10-for-11 on extra points) capped off with four field goals vs. Florida in the nationally televised Peach Bowl. "I found out afterwards that some of the people who were involved with the football program at my high school watched the game and they started to cry," Woodside said. "Some other people were saying, *No way – that can't be the same guy.* They were calling the house just to verify that it was me. Everyone was excited because it was so unusual. Nobody really knows anybody that that happens to."

Woodside blossomed as a sophomore, leading the team in scoring with 116 points. His 28 field goals (in 31 attempts) set the NCAA Division I record for most field goals in a season, earning him All-American honors from the UPI (second team) and Associated Press (third team). His junior year was even better as he was named a first-team All-American by *The Sporting News* after connecting on 21-of-25 field goals and all 32 of his extra-point attempts. He repeated as a first-team All-American as a senior, hitting 15-of-21 field goals and all 28 extra-point attempts. He led WVU in scoring for the third consecutive year, set a school record with a 55-yard field goal vs. Louisville, and kicked the game-winning field goal in a 17-14 win over national power Penn State. Fourteen years after graduating with several NCAA and school records, Woodside was inducted into the West Virginia University Sports Hall of Fame.

Woodside was awarded a scholarship after his freshman season – and that actually might have been the only part of his career that didn't exceed expectations. "There's the expression, *Ignorance is bliss*. Well, ignorance is also stupidity. A couple of weeks before the spring term, I got a phone call from Coach Young, and he said, *Hey, we really like you, but we don't have a scholarship for you*. So I said, *Well, then I'm not coming back*. I got a call back 10 minutes later and he had a scholarship for me. In hindsight, I realize what an idiot I was. Why would I think that, let alone say that? That certainly did not go with who I was at the time. It was just a reaction – I wasn't even thinking. I didn't know he was going to call me. I wasn't thinking about a scholarship. I don't know where it came from, but I got the scholarship."

Woodside also earned the respect of his teammates because of his work ethic. Many of the team's other specialists (punters and kickers) would hit the showers before the offense and defense finished practice, but Woodside would stay and work. "Even if it was November and 30 degrees out and the other kickers were done, I would run the stadium stairs for two-and-a-half hours. The other guys would go inside the sauna. I was like, *No, I can't do that*. I wasn't trying to earn brownie points. It just didn't feel right to leave. So, I would run the stairs and these offensive linemen who could squat five times my weight would look up and they appreciated it. It's amazing how much they would block on my kicks and how they would hold people out. If you work, the fun will take care of itself.

"You don't recognize in the moment all the benefits of doing that. I wasn't thinking, *I'm going to do this because it's going to make me mentally tough.* I'm not thinking about that when I'm working out while other people are having fun and going to the pool. I'm not thinking this is going to make me a better teammate. I'm just doing what I love to do. But, in hindsight, you can look back and see that's where you develop a mental toughness to perform."

Ever since, Woodside has been passing on the lessons he learned as a walk-on – and he's received national publicity – as the owner and lead instructor of Before U Kick: Seeing Beyond Uprights, where he trains prospective college and professional kickers and runs football kicking camps. (By day, he's a UPS delivery driver in Alexandria, Va. "I basically do that so I can do this," he says.) Among Woodside's past pupils are college kickers Tyler Durbin (Ohio State), Chris Blewitt (Pitt), Nick Weiler (North Carolina), Alex Frubank (Virginia), and Nick Novak (Maryland, NFL).

Of course Woodside trains kickers on technique, but his main focus is their attitude. "What's really hard for me is that a lot of athletes don't want to work. They want to get ranked and recruited, but they don't want to work for it. I always saw work as a gift – living a dream. I don't see myself as 'old school' but I say to them, *I'm just wondering why don't you want to do this? If you say you love this sport, then why aren't you doing anything and everything possible? Why aren't you going beyond what I say and coming up with stuff on your own to make yourself better?*

"What's natural to someone with a walk-on attitude is foreign to other people. They want to dismiss it as, *Well, I just don't have the talent. I'll move on and do something else.* There has to be a measure of talent, of course, but it might be undeveloped or under-developed. I'm trying to get athletes not to be arrogant or cocky but to believe. You have to believe it before you see it. If you feel insecure and your head's down and your shoulders are slumped, it isn't going to happen. If you don't believe in you, why should anybody else? To me, that's the walk-on story."

Woodside intentionally makes his kicking students uncomfortable to eventually build their confidence when they're under pressure on the field – or in the game of life. "The first thing they have to do is get out of their control zone and step out with faith in themselves. When they do that, they're developing a series of victories that gives them confidence. It's not my intent to rattle them or get under their skin. I know how college football works. I know it's a fast game, it's an unforgiving game. The standards you set set you. Your standards have to be higher than those that are expected of you.

"For example, in a camp we had a whole bunch of football players kicking 40-yard field goals. I said, *You miss it, you chase it.* They said, *What about using these balls here?* I said, *No, you have to chase that one ball we're using.* We attempted 23 40-yard field goals until we made one. That accomplishment became a matter of our will. Attitude is more important than technique. If we get the athlete to buy into what we're trying to do, then the technique thing will take care of itself.

"We do some crazy physical stuff: pulling benches and running up hills and flipping tires. I'm not getting them to buy into me. I'm getting them to buy into themselves at a deeper level so when they need to 'cash that check,' the money is there and it won't bounce. They can't see it at the time. They're like, *Why do I need to run up the hill in the rain?* You're paying yourself a dividend. At some point – you don't know when it's going to happen or how it's going to happen – you know you'll be ready when it happens. John Wooden said opportunity is something you prepare for in advance because once the opportunity is there it's too late to prepare for it. A multivitamin is supposed to be taken every day. You can't take 31 multivitamins at the end of the month. You can't make up for the work that you haven't done. It's a lost opportunity, lost time, lost advantage."

Woodside also preaches that short-term success doesn't afford you the opportunity to relax. "One of my guys who was in the NFL at the time sent me an email that he was just offered a contract extension for more money. I said, *Good. Train like you just got a pay cut.* When I got my scholarship, I said, *Good. You got the scholarship to help the family out. But you have to get better.* A lot of times the scholarship guys think that they are a pedigree as compared to a pound dog, a mutt. But the pound dogs are the ones that are always more loyal, and they're always going to be there for you. The one area where truth remains in sports is you're judged on your performance. If you don't perform, it's on you. If you do perform, it's because of you. You're judged by others if you change the scoreboard. Be it your teammates, your coach, the fans – all they really care about is if you change the scoreboard. It doesn't matter if your ball is in end-over-end or a spiral. As long as it gets through the uprights, then in their minds it's a success.

"If the uprights are your judge, then your standards aren't high enough. So, there's failing vs. a failure. I'll tell the kids if somebody with your talent was sitting in the stands watching the game, that's a failure. If you miss a kick, that's a failing. That's a missed kick; don't take it as a personal identity. Debrief yourself. *What did I do wrong?* Missing the kick on a Friday night or a Saturday or Sunday afternoon, that's the realization of the miss. It occurred somewhere else along the way either from lack of preparation, lack of trust, lack of discipline, lack of focus – whatever it is, it's realized when the ball goes left or right of the upright.

"I'm trying to get the athletes to understand, do you wash a car or do you detail it? It sounds trite, but those are simple words that create a standard. The idea is to have the spread of your best kick and your worst kick be really tight. If your best kick is a 50-yard field goal and your worst kick goes sideways into the stands, then you have a problem mentally and physically."

Woodside's passion for maximizing potential hasn't waned in the nearly 40 years since he boldly walked into the WVU football office asking for an opportunity. And he doesn't plan on letting up – ever. "If I don't work, basically stick me in the earth because I'm done."

CHAPTER 9

"Ask More Of Yourself"

Dr. David Marden
Cal State-Chico, Track & Field
Physician/Medical Center Director

The stereotypical walk-on is uncommonly industrious with laser-focused commitment. Fueled by self-confidence, they're determined to overcome any obstacle placed in their way to achieve their dream. That doesn't describe David Marden when he arrived on the Cal State-Chico campus in 1982. His college choice and his decision to run track weren't part of any grand plan. "I kind of just showed up in school because I didn't have a place to live anymore," Marden said. "Chico State just happened to be what I could get into because I didn't get my college applications out in a timely manner. Back then, Chico State was considered more like the number-one party school in the country. It had a reputation of being a great social environment."

Marden was likely to follow the partying path, but his freshman year roommates changed his course. "I ended up with a couple of athletes in my apartment, and that's where me thinking of running track kind of started," he said. "I literally walked out to the track, found out who the coach was, and told him that I had run in high school. He knew nothing about me."

That coach was Larry Burleson, a former Green Bay Packer under Vince Lombardi and the brother of Dyrol Burleson, one of the first Americans to break the four-minute mile. Larry Burleson fit the mold of an old-school coach, and though he allowed Marden to participate, he didn't give the freshman any breaks. "I really felt like the guy didn't like me," Marden recalls. "I felt I didn't exist. I was just another kid on his team – there wasn't anything special about me. He was a combination of mean and grumpy and old, even though he wasn't that old. He was a believer in hard work and pushing the team harder and making things happen. And that was a perfect formula for a kid like me. That part was missing for me. My grades weren't that great the first year at school, and I was just kind of floating."

The youngest decathlete on the team, Marden recognized "everybody is bigger and better" and, lacking self-motivation, his being harangued by Burleson was exactly what he needed. "It was a soul-searching experience, but I didn't realize it at the time. At the moment I was thinking, *Maybe this isn't for me. Maybe I need to move on.* And I didn't know what 'moving on' meant. I wasn't necessarily trying to overcome something. I was tapping into something. I wasn't using my full capability. I realized, *Well, gosh, if I'm going to be good, I need to work out a lot, and then I'm going to have to deal with a lot of pain.* I had to train, make a commitment, and sacrifice. That's where my brain was.

"It led to a self-observation of *What could I be doing better?* My answer to myself was, *Well, maybe having a schedule where you actually get to sleep and don't stay up until after three in the morning would help. Maybe if you actually go work out and run and do things above and beyond just what's asked of you.* You need to ask more of yourself rather than just waiting for everybody else to tell you what to do. Before, I was grasping at how to just keep treading water. Then once I figured that out, the other steps fell into place.

"I didn't understand what that path was until I started creating some of those inner discussions of how to approach things. And it wasn't some chip on my shoulder. It wasn't *I need to show people* or whatever. It was even more simplistic than that. It was that people had said to me for years, *You have such potential,* so what's missing? And I saw what was missing: I wasn't putting forth enough effort. I started to tap into 'the harder I work the better results I get,' and the better results I got came from when I wanted to work hard.

Up to that point, that wasn't normal for me. That wasn't a regular occurrence in my earlier life."

Once Marden began applying himself fully, he started leaving the competition in the dust. When his career as a Wildcat concluded, Marden was a three-time Division II All-American decathlete and the school record-holder in that event. He was later inducted into the Cal State-Chico Athletics Hall of Fame.

An exercise science major, Marden parlayed the lessons he learned on the track to the classroom and beyond. He decided to test himself academically and pursue a career as a physician. "Going into medicine, my thought process was I was going to outwork people. I'm going to stay up longer than other people. I'm going to study longer. I'm going to overcome somebody else's talent or somebody else's genius, or somebody else's skill by outworking them."

He converted that mindset into a reality. "I surprised myself because initially I didn't think of myself as doctor material. I didn't think of myself as bad, but I thought that wasn't a level that was achievable for me. When I started applying myself and becoming more successful, I thought, *Why not?* There was no reason I couldn't apply the same principles from track to school to life to parenting to medicine – whatever you want to do. Now, sometimes it really works well and sometimes it doesn't. Sometimes other things are out of your control. I taught myself to lower my fears and not let fear keep you from moving forward, working hard, and realizing your potential."

Marden is now the owner of Embrace, a medical center for advanced gynecology and women's wellness in Bristol, Tenn. Marden is board certified by the American College of Obstetrics and Gynecology and is considered a pioneer in minimally invasive bioidentical hormone replacement solutions. He is also a Clinical Associate Professor in the Department of Obstetrics and Gynecology at the Edward Via College of Osteopathic Medicine and an Associate Professor in the East Tennessee State Department of Surgery and Family Medicine.

Persistence is now a hallmark trait of Marden, and a famous quote by Calvin Coolidge helps spur him forward. Coolidge, the 30th U.S. President, wrote: *Nothing in this world can take the place of persistence. Talent will not: nothing is more common than unsuccessful men with talent. Genius will not; unrewarded genius is almost a proverb. Education will not: the world is full of educated derelicts. Persistence and determination alone are omnipotent.*

"That eloquently says what I could never put into words. I wish I would have seen that much earlier in life because I would have identified with it and might have been able to skip a few steps. I think I would have been less worried about people more talented than me. I would have been less worried about people that were smarter.

"Everybody has a journey to go on, and that was the right balance and approach for me. I found that there are many different ways people can do a great thing. Sometimes you just need to take a different approach."

CHAPTER 10

"We Have To Create An Uncharted Path"

Colleen Healy
University of Connecticut, Basketball
CEO, Consultant, & Motivational Speaker

UConn has served as the gold standard of women's college basketball since its first of 20 Final Four appearances in 1991, winning 11 NCAA National Championships. When recalling the greatest players who suited up for Basketball Hall of Fame head coach Geno Auriemma, fans will mention Diana Taurasi, Rebecca Lobo, Sue Bird, Maya Moore, Breanna Stewart, and Jennifer Rizzotti among others.

Nobody will mention Colleen Healy. "Why should they?" said Healy, the first walk-on to earn a scholarship under Auriemma. "The impact I had on the UConn women's basketball program is small. The impact wearing a UConn women's basketball jersey had on my life is immeasurable."

Healy's walk-on story transcends accolades, trophies, statistics, and the game of basketball itself. It's about grit, authenticity, and never letting others define your potential.

An all-state athlete in softball and basketball scoring over 1,000 career points at Windham High School in Willimantic, Conn., Healy became the first in her family to attend college when she accepted a scholarship to play both sports at the University of New Haven, a Division II school about 90 minutes from her home. Her choice to attend UNH was more of a default vs. a decision. "We never discussed college as an option for me. That's not the fault of my parents. Neither of them went to college. They hadn't traveled down that path. As a result, there was no map for me. I was not a great student on top of it. I experienced great difficulties, particularly in math. It wasn't due to a lack of effort. I really tried which stung even more. So, I learned how to use my sense of humor to get me through embarrassing moments. I chose University of New Haven because they were willing to give me a scholarship. We didn't have a college fund. New Haven gave me a shot at an education and to play softball and basketball at the collegiate level. I thought I 'made it' with that offer and I took it."

Healy developed her skills playing against the boys in her neighborhood. "We all went to St. Mary St. Joseph School and walked to and from school together first grade to eighth. The boys were like my family. In sixth grade, the boys could try out for basketball and the girls could try out for cheerleading. I went to basketball tryouts so we could all walk home together when it was over. I happened to have gym class that day, so I changed into my gym clothes and I was shooting around with my buddies before tryouts. The coach walked over and asked, *Do you want to try out?* I didn't even think it was an option. But when he asked, I didn't think twice about it. I tried out and became the first girl to play on the boys team. That experience prompted me to try out for the lead role in the school play in eighth grade. The play was *Fiddler on the Roof*, and I decided I wanted the role of Tevye, a Jewish milkman. I have to give SMSJ credit: they were pretty progressive for a Catholic school. They allowed me to play basketball on the boys team *and* they let me have that role. It was such an influential and life-changing message to me as a young girl. If you deserve the part and you're willing to take the risk, you can earn it."

Not everyone was supportive of Healy achieving her goals. "An employee at my high school told a teammate of mine, *Colleen's not good enough to play in college. She will never pass a class in college.* At first it hurt my feelings that an adult would say that about me. But you spend your life proving people right or proving people wrong. Rather than shattering me, I used that comment to fuel me to prove them wrong." Healy would walk a few blocks to play pick-up basketball against the Eastern Connecticut State University women's basketball players or ECSU male students – whoever was on the courts.

At New Haven, Healy started her freshman year strong, leading the team in minutes and ranking second in scoring for games played during the winter semester of 1989. But her life would change in November. "I received a phone call from my dad to come home for a funeral because my half-brother Keith had passed away. His body was discovered floating in the Connecticut River. We didn't know the circumstances behind his death. It was assumed to be drug-related. He was just 27 years old. Keith had made the mistake of getting involved in drugs, and he paid the ultimate price. I didn't judge him for his mistakes. I felt guilty for the life I had and the one he lost. There was no doubt in my mind that participating and providing value as a young athlete was the positive distraction I needed. I knew I was as susceptible as anyone else to go down the wrong path. Sports required me to walk a certain line. To be clear, I was no angel, but I wanted to play sports, so I did my best to conform to the requirements. His death woke me up. I decided it was time to write my own story. I would learn from his mistakes and live a storied life in his honor.

"Several weeks later, after we lost to the University of New Hampshire, I decided it was time to find my new path. When we got back on campus, I packed my car with as many of my belongings as I could and started the long drive home. My car died on the highway – there was actually a small engine fire. It was a blizzard, the roads were sleet and slush. I was still in my travel dress outfit from the game. I got picked up by a couple who was driving to UConn, which was fine because I had friends who played for UConn and I could stay with them for the night.

"Eventually I got to the UConn dorm and I called my parents. I had to tell them that not only did I quit school but my car was also dead and on fire. You can imagine they did not take that very well. The next day a friend drove me home, and I'll never forget the conversation in our kitchen. I had a scholarship. I had an opportunity that nobody in my family ever had. I had a free college education and yet, as an 18-year-old, I took it upon myself without any guidance to leave school with no plans. I just knew I had to take a different path. I just knew I had more in me. I walked to my room crying, and I'll never forget my father coming in and saying, *Babe, why are you doing this?* I said, *Dad, I don't want to be 30 years old and wonder if I was good enough. I don't want to watch the Final Four and wonder if I could have played with them. I have to know.*

"That was enough for him. My dad never missed one of my softball games, home or away. He never missed a basketball game, home or away. He was tough. He was engaged. He was my number-one fan. I didn't know what some of my other teammates' parents looked like. They were never there. Dad was always there. Dad had grit. He quit school at the age of 16 to make money. He worked his way up from the mailroom to the boardroom. He got his GED at 33, and was overseeing 12 departments at the Pratt & Whitney engine plant by the time he retired. He was a nose-to-the-grindstone, get-it-done kind of person, rolling up the Lucky Strikes in his Fruit of the Loom T-shirt. He's made of something beyond blood and bones. He worked hard and said if you work hard good things will happen. So, I was going to follow his lead. I learned to respect a strong work ethic. I wanted to be like Dad, without the Lucky Strikes. He was there for me, and that one moment when he said, *You have to do what you have to do*, I knew that as long as I had him, I would be okay."

Within 48 hours of arriving home, Healy enrolled at ECSU, whose campus entrance was across the street from her living room window. She played softball that spring, helping the Warriors win the Division III national championship as their starting left fielder. But her ultimate plan was to go north seven miles and play basketball at UConn. "I had played pick-up ball with the girls at UConn, and I thought I was good enough to compete. That summer I worked at the UConn basketball camp with the youngest kids and led the talent show for the campers. Coach Auriemma knew me through camp.

"That summer I called Coach Auriemma on my parents' rotary phone to ask him if I could transfer to UConn and try out for the team. He said, *Well, you know you have to sit out a year for transferring and after that you can try out, but there's no guarantee to it. You want to be the manager?* Three months prior to Coach A's offer to be manager, I earned the title of 'national champion' and before that I was a scholarship athlete and starting point guard at the University of New Haven. Coach was offering me a manager job with no guarantee that I would ever participate in collegiate sports again. My answer was yes. Sometimes you have to be willing to risk it all to make a dream come true. Next semester, I was a manager filling water bottles, sweeping the floors, turning the lights on."

But no scholarship meant Healy was racking up expenses she couldn't cover. "My parents had to dig into their 401(k) to cover those semesters. When I was in high school my dad made a deal with me. He said, *For every A you get, I'll give you $100.* I thought, *Now we're talking!* In high school, dad's wallet was secure, but the season I served as manager I did everything I could to increase my odds to making the team the following year. That included becoming a better student. Coach was not going to take a chance on me if I was dragging the team GPA down. That year away I never missed a class. I took such great notes that classmates wanted to borrow them. I became a Dean's List student. Dad couldn't afford me anymore. I no longer needed that monetary motivation. I told Dad to keep his cash. I tell kids today, *If you want your parents to take a risk on you, then you better put in the effort to prove you are worth that risk.* My parents took a risk on me when I left New Haven and ECSU. They invested in my future. I never took that for granted. The way to repay my parents for that risk was to put the work in to achieve good grades."

Healy was the manager for the 1990-91 club, the first women's basketball team in UConn history to advance to a Final Four. Healy officially walked on for the 1991-92 season as a sophomore, recording seven points, three steals, and two assists in 39 minutes of action across 15 games.

"Growing up, I was a scorer. For my team to win, I needed to contribute on the scoreboard. When I made the team at UConn, coach made it very clear if I was going to get on the court I better learn how to play defense. He didn't need another scorer, or a kid

73

who 'thinks' she can score. He could use a kid that would take pride as a defensive specialist. So, I learned my new role. Forcing me to adapt in order to contribute prepared me for life after basketball. The ability to adapt in order to succeed in corporate life has been a huge asset."

Healy played in 28 of UConn's 29 games her junior year, scoring 39 points, the most important of them at Georgetown on Jan. 30, 1993. In that game against the Big East Conference leader, the Huskies lost multiple players to foul trouble, including freshman point guard Jen Rizzotti, who two years later would be named Associated Press Player of the Year. "We ran out of players," Healy recalls. "Coach had no choice but to put me in the game."

Healy checked in with 38 seconds to play and the Huskies trailing, 78-77. "Jen grabs me, her eyes welling up with disappointment. Jen didn't like to lose, and she really didn't like to be out of the game where she could prevent us from losing. She grabbed my arms and looked me in the eyes and said, *You win this for me!* So, I go in the game with no timeouts left and it's our ball on the sideline. I fake right and run left toward our basket, catch the pass, make my layup and get fouled. The team goes crazy because we got the lead and Georgetown's best player fouled out with that play. I go to the line with us up by one. I miss the foul shot. They take a timeout and get the ball out at half court. I hang back at the three-point arc. They toss the ball at their point guard close to the half-court line. While the ball was in the air, I rushed at her. Trying to protect the ball, she steps into the back court and it's a turnover. We pass it in, they foul me, I hit the next two foul shots, and we win by three. The newspaper headline read *Walk-on Rescues Huskies: Healy Responds with :38 to Play*. It was a pretty amazing moment. I recalled all of those dark days looking down at the court when I was a manager, wondering if I would ever play again. It all paid off in that moment.

"Georgetown is one of my proudest moments on the court, but Coach Auriemma put me in my place right away. After the game he said, *You're not going to be an offensive target, just so you know, kid.* I knew that. I just continued to work hard. But that was the moment where it all was worth it because now I'm part of that UConn record book."

For Healy's efforts, Auriemma awarded her a full scholarship her final two seasons. "That was his way of rewarding my dedication. I also believe he saw me as an underdog. He could relate to the underdog because he was once one himself. People forget that. Nobody expected for Coach Auriemma and (assistant) Coach (Chris) Dailey to create a legacy of winning at Storrs. I think he appreciates kids who show up and give it everything, sweep up the floor, get hit with screens all day long, maybe never take a shot – just to be a part of something. I wanted to show that if you invest in me, you made the right decision. I needed him to believe in me, and then I needed to prove him right."

"When I speak to kids today, I say, *You never know when your day is going to come. You watch time and time again, whether it's March Madness or college football where the starting quarterback gets hurt, and now you're that quarterback who gets to replace him. Are you ready to go in the game and make an impact?* I was prepared mentally and physically to do that. I didn't go in thinking, *I'm going to win this game.* But every day I worked hard to make my teammates better. They in turn made me better. My teammates respected me. They believed in me which made me believe in myself. It's contagious that way. I was prepared when the moment came because of the work I put in and the encouragement of my teammates and coaches.

"Confidence isn't built in warm-ups; it's built in the work we put in every day. We tap into that confidence in those pressure moments because we know we put the deliberate practice in to prepare for that moment. If you want to get the 'butterflies' under control in pressure moments, tap into your memory bank of all those hours you put in for this exact moment. Say to yourself, *I have prepared for this. I put the work in. I have played this outcome over in my head. It's my day to do it.*

In Healy's senior season, UConn finished 30-3, winning the Big East regular season and tournament championships before falling in the 1994 Elite 8 to eventual national champion North Carolina. Healy played in 19 games, scoring 15 points. For her three-year UConn career, she saw action in 62 games and scored 61 points on 19-of-49 shooting from the field, 2-for-11 on three pointers, and 21-of-32 on free throws. She graduated from UConn that spring with cum laude honors.

As we mentioned at the outset, Healy's walk-on story goes deeper than numbers and NCAA tournaments. "I'm thankful for the opportunity to play and for the scholarship, but the greatest gift I ever received from my UConn experience is the sisterhood of my teammates. I needed to be a part of that sisterhood at UConn. I needed to be part of that team, more than I ever knew. The older I got, the more I realized what a life-changer it was. I'm a fan of my teammates' lives and accomplishments after UConn – they're family. They still demand and want my best. I love them for it. My contribution to UConn women's basketball is minimal. UConn women's basketball's contribution to my life is immeasurable.

"There was a fire inside of me after the loss of my half-brother. I guess the fire was always there but without the direction. I didn't have a map, but I knew I had to change paths. At New Haven I just said, *Wait a minute; this is my life. If people will take chances with me, they will not be wrong.* I had to take the risk first. So that decision changed the trajectory for me. ECSU and University of New Haven were great schools academically and athletically. They just were not my path. I had more to give academically and athletically. I wanted to see what I had in me. I wanted to see how much more I could push myself."

That approach has never changed for Healy. After graduation, she continued her athletic aspirations qualifying for and running in the Boston Marathon and competing and finishing the Lake Placid Ironman three times. Professionally, Healy worked the next 22+ years in the digital health information, education, and consulting sectors ascending to Senior Medical Science Liaison in her 13 years at Merck and then to Senior Director, Medical Education during a decade-plus run at WebMD/Medscape. In 2019, Healy and wife Missy West, a basketball player at Duke and National High School

Athletic Hall of Fame inductee, co-founded ORCA Leadership. Healy and West speak to student-athletes across the country through their Beyond The Game Academy. The academy is a combination of on-court fundamentals combined with in-classroom workshops for student-athletes. "The life lessons sports participation offers are distributed equally for all kids that wear a uniform," Healy says. "You don't have to be the best player on the team. If you can find a way to contribute to the team, you will gain the benefits of the experience. We bring an awareness of the benefits beyond the points scored and the time on court with the objective to keep kids in the game.

"That's also true in corporate America or any career you choose. We're extending our workshops to corporate teams where we discuss similar concepts but at the professional level: opportunities, resilience, contribution, and accountability. As individuals, we have the ability to craft our given jobs into meaningful careers. We just need to become aware of the tools to do it. It's never too late to live your best life or to figure out how to bring out your best self."

Healy said she built her career on principles and work ethic learned through a lifetime of sports participation bookended at UConn. "In a consulting or sales role, you better know your industry and serve as a resource. Clients need to trust you will deliver, and you must be authentic. My job is to make my clients look good for having chosen me to collaborate with. That means I need to deliver. If a client bets on me, I'm going to prove them right. It doesn't matter which company I'm working for. Collaborators and customers receive my best because it has my name on it. One of my friends toasting me at my wedding said, *Colleen is 100% or she's not in at all.*"

Healy said another important career-related lesson she learned from her playing days was to constantly test yourself against – and learn from – those who possess stronger skills. "Surround yourself with people who are more talented than you. People you can learn from. And, hopefully, you can contribute to their growth with your unique skills as well. When I was in grammar school, I was trying to keep up with high school boys. When I was in high school, after practice, I would go over to the Eastern Connecticut gym and would play against college kids. And at UConn, I was playing against All-Americans every day. I was always trying to compete with, mingle with, associate with the best. I didn't do this for status purposes. I did it to learn and build confidence. I figured, *If I can hold my own with this group, I can hold my own anywhere. If I can finish an Ironman, I can handle this next presentation on very little sleep to an unfriendly audience.* I had been filling a reservoir of resilience that I could dig into anytime things became difficult. Those who were faster and stronger raised the bar for me and made me work harder. I was okay treading water among the best.

"Growing up, I thought I would be the big fish in the small pond, but I'm so grateful I took the risk to be the small fish in the big pond. We're all little fish in the big pond of life. And sometimes you have to swim with sharks. I was willing to swim toward the sharks at a young age – I took a risk to be a part of something special and it has paid dividends."

Healy said another lesson learned at UConn was that sometimes what appears to be setback or a failure can turn out to be a positive. "I broke my nose at a home game against St. John's – I was bleeding and the whole place was hushed. The team doctors walked me off the court to be examined. After they fixed me up, I ran back into the gym from the tunnel and Coach Auriemma told me to go in the game again before I could sit down. I jumped over the chairs and Gampel went crazy. We realized the next day that I had broken my nose, so for the next few games, I had to wear a custom-fit facemask for protection. Our next home game was against Stanford. This would be the first nationally televised women's game on CBS and it was a sellout crowd. I not only had this hideous mask, I had black eyes to match. What terrible luck, I thought. I went in the game for defense, and the facemask had me all over TV. Robin Roberts (formerly of ESPN, now a Good Morning America anchor) was calling the game. *The sparkplug Colleen Healy is in the game,* she said. *Healy, the one-time manager now a walk-on.* I didn't score a point and yet when I got home the phone was ringing off the hook. If I hadn't broken my nose and ended up wearing that hideous mask, Robin Roberts wouldn't have mentioned my name. No reason to. I didn't do a darn thing out there. Sometimes what seems on the surface to be bad luck could open up opportunities we could not have imagined otherwise. My broken nose ended up being a lucky, albeit painful, break.

"Bringing that to my professional life, I've had some tough years in terms of sales, but I never gave up. I do not give up on people. In return, they do not give up on me. I've had my share of good luck, but you can't rely on luck alone to be successful. I can honestly say, with great pride, there is rarely a day I go to bed saying I could have done more. I give my best each day. The day's outcome may not be what I had wanted, but I can sleep better knowing I gave it my best regardless of the situation and the circumstances.

"Take risks to make your life better. Work hard with integrity, every day, and good things will happen. They may not happen in the timing you hoped for. You may not achieve the results you expected. But good things will happen when you give your best every day. Sometimes, magical things will happen, like at Georgetown. The magical moments of my life far outweigh the difficult times."

In her speeches at schools, NCAA events, or corporate gatherings, Healy regularly delivers that message. "I grew up seven miles down the road from the UConn campus. Sometimes to get to where we need to go, we have to create an uncharted path. When that path is uniquely yours, there is no map. I would not suggest my path to others. I do suggest the tools I leveraged can serve as a compass for others to create their own path, their own journey, their own story. Straight lines don't make for good storytelling anyway."

CHAPTER 11

"You Never Know When A Bad Thing Is A Good Thing"

Joel Nellis

Wisconsin, Football
Teacher, Coach, & Author

After graduating in 2001 from James Madison High School in Madison, Wisc., home city of the University of Wisconsin, Joel Nellis wanted in the worst way to be invited to the Badgers preseason camp. An all-conference and all-city defensive back in high school, Nellis had already secured a spot in the UW program as an invited walk-on but participating in drills before school began wasn't a given for non-scholarship players.

Nellis knew the program well because the father of best friend Jason Palermo was the Badgers' defensive line coach, and Nellis was eager to a wear a Wisconsin uniform because he had already experienced game days behind-the-scenes at Camp Randall Stadium. The summer of '01 turned out to be a brutal physical test for every football player in the Midwest with temperatures regularly exceeding 90 degrees. Many sports fans will remember that Pro Bowl lineman Korey Stringer of the Minnesota Vikings died of heat stroke that summer after his team's second preseason practice.

Nellis would not be invited to Wisconsin's camp, a decision he described as "devastating" at the time, but now he looks back on it as "a blessing in disguise."

"I didn't realize how unprepared for college I was," Nellis said. "When I joined the team, I realized how weak I was and how bad of a football player I was. I couldn't even give a good scout team look. I honestly told the scout team coach, *Hey, I'm not trying to get out of reps, but is there a way to put me in places where I don't have to do a face-to-face block?* They were trying me at tight end, and I was going up against senior defensive linemen. It wasn't pretty."

Nellis said that even pre-game drills with his veteran Big Ten teammates were a struggle. "We're out doing the warm-up drill called 'pat-and-go' where you're just catching balls from the quarterbacks. I'm there for the first time and I'm getting yelled at during pre-game because I wasn't catching the ball with my hands. I was letting the ball hit my body. Before the second game, coach told me, *Don't even come out for pat-and-go. Just come out with the rest of the team.* I'm a couple games in and I realize I'm not even giving the scout team a good look, so how is this going to play out? How is the rest of my career going to go? Jason and his dad had provided me this opportunity, so I thought, *Alright, man. I'll stick it out for the year.*"

At that point Nellis also realized if he had been invited to participate in preseason camp – which was even more physically demanding – he might have hung up his cleats then. "At first when I didn't get invited to camp, I thought my career was over. I didn't see until later that was the best thing that could have happened because I might have quit at camp. I lived in Madison, and the seminary where the team had camp was only a mile from my home. I could have walked home if I had said to myself, *Forget about it – I'm out.* I actually might have quit had I gone to that camp. I'm so glad I didn't, but I didn't know that at the time. My dad likes to say, *You never know when a bad thing is a good thing.* He's right. You never know when a bad thing is a good thing in terms of the long-term process."

Just because Nellis adjusted his attitude about his situation didn't mean everything was going to become easy for him going forward. After redshirting in 2001, he participated Wisconsin's next preseason camp, but playing time was still in the distance. "When you're warming up for a game and you look and you see 11 people ahead of you, and that's what you see all the time, you think, *Wow*

– am I ever going to get there? Honestly, I was just trying to survive. I was trying to make it through the season and not get destroyed by the defensive line."

Nellis said he had to determine what unique strengths he could bring to the team and maximize those. "I had to figure out how I was going to carve out a niche. Everyone is there for a reason. The other guys were recruited because they're strong, they're fast, they're smart. My thing was going to be understanding the playbook and knowing that if they put me in, at least I wasn't going to make a mental error. And I was going to try my hardest. You were going to get my best effort, and I was going to know the assignment."

Nellis also seized the opportunity to build the foundation for a coaching career. "I knew I wanted to coach in some capacity when I was done and thought this is going to be the best platform for me to do that. So, whether I make it onto the field or not is not going to be my main goal. My goal was to learn everything I can through this whole process."

That's not lip service from Nellis. He actually welcomed the new recruits with open arms – and an open playbook – even if they were slotting ahead of him on the depth chart. "The coaches were honest with me, and I appreciated that. They would tell me, *We have this guy coming in as a scholarship player. He's going to get reps ahead of you.* I knew how complicated our system was. I knew how hard it would be for them to transition regardless of how many stars they had next to their name. I knew that whatever high school they came from, they probably weren't ready for the type of detail and intensity and everything else that was about to come their way. So, I treated it like it was a coaching position – I wasn't going to withhold information from them. In fact, I was going to make sure that they *didn't* get yelled at."

Along the way, Nellis improved not only his football IQ but his strength and skills. He earned a scholarship for his final two seasons, playing in 18 games and recording one solo tackle and three assisted tackles on special teams. He graduated with a 3.8 GPA and a degree in Physical Education, earning Academic All-Big Ten honors as a senior.

So what does Nellis point to as his biggest accomplishment at UW? "I survived. I made it through all five years," he said. "Anyone that's a part of that team is a part of that team. The fact that you finished puts you in a different category from everyone else who just showed up for a shorter period of time. And I can keep going back to those five years and say I gave everything that I had. Maybe to everyone else that wasn't a success, but to me that was a huge success. Anytime I need to, I can go back to those times and say, *I did this. I put in five years of effort. I didn't miss any sessions, and I know there's a reward at the end. I know that I can do that.*"

Nellis appreciated his opportunity so much that in 2016 he co-authored the book *Walk-On This Way: The Ongoing Legacy of the Wisconsin Football Walk-On Tradition* with sportswriter Jake Kocorowski and Badger legend Jim Leonhard, a walk-on who played 10 seasons in the NFL at safety. The book chronicles the ongoing legacy of the Wisconsin walk-on program by featuring 50 former UW walk-ons.

Nellis also shares his walk-on lessons with the students he teaches and coaches at Brookfield Central High School, a suburb of Milwaukee 70 miles east of his hometown of Madison. Nellis is a longtime phys ed teacher at the school and was named varsity head football coach in 2019, leading the Lancers to the playoffs his first season at the helm.

"I talk with my kids all the time that you have to keep working whether someone's looking or not. I can relate through my own experience. The guys that are back-ups and working hard, I tell them I appreciate all the hard work that they've put in, and I've been in that same spot. I know it might be hard to hold on to but just know that this lesson is going to carry on with you for a long time. I tell them, *Let me tell you what I found: you're going to be glad you sacrificed everything even if you weren't a bigger part than you thought you could have been, and it's going to help you down the road in life – even more than the guys that play*. I tell them my experience, and they're thankful what they're doing will serve a purpose in their life.

"I think it's important for them to understand that everything is long-term, especially in this social media age where everything is so quick. An initial defeat is a bump, not a scar. It might not turn out how you envisioned it early on, but if you stick with it, good things are going to happen. You just don't know when. The timing is always uncertain. It may not happen when you hoped, but that doesn't mean it's not going to come true."

CHAPTER 12

"See What's A Need And Go Do It"

Todd Svoboda
Kentucky, Basketball
Senior Engineer

In the spring of 1992, Todd Svoboda had just completed a banner junior year at Division II Northern Kentucky University, leading the men's basketball team in both scoring (18.1 ppg) and rebounding (10.9 rpg). A starter and scholarship player since his freshman season, Svoboda had already passed the 1,000-point mark (1,114) and was on track to become the first 1,000-point, 1,000-rebound player in school history his senior season. Additionally, the basketball coaching staff gave Svoboda flexibility in his schedule to play tennis where he captured the Great Lakes Valley Conference championship at no. 5 singles. An excellent engineering student as well, Svoboda received the GLVC's Richard F. Scharf Paragon Award as the conference's outstanding male student-athlete in terms of academics, athletic achievement, character, and leadership. With all those accolades – and standing 6-foot-8 – Svoboda was literally the big man on NKU's campus.

That is until he decided to give it all up to attempt to walk on to the storied men's basketball team at the University of Kentucky. He wasn't guaranteed much when he transferred to UK, just the opportunity to *hopefully* carve out a spot as a role player.

Svoboda was part of a cooperative five-year engineering program between NKU and UK where students could matriculate for three years in Highland Heights, then go south for two years to study in

Lexington. "It was a tough decision," Svoboda recalled about his choice to transfer. "I was fortunate to be on scholarship at Northern Kentucky, and I was my coach's (Ken Shields) first recruit, so there was a special bond that I had with my coach. But Northern Kentucky didn't have a full engineering program, so coach always knew academically I could transfer to UK to finish my degree which was the ultimate reason I left."

Shields was crestfallen but helpful, reaching out to Rick Pitino's staff at Kentucky and recommending Svoboda get a shot to make the team. Svoboda was promised a look but not a spot on the roster. That summer, he enrolled in classes at UK and met with a Kentucky strength and conditioning coach who recommended a running program to help him keep up with Pitino's high-octane, up-tempo style.

Svoboda said his fellow chemical engineering classmates were the most skeptical of his idea to walk on to the team. "They said, *You're going to be missing too many classes. We can barely keep up without missing class.* But Svoboda's most trusted advisor – his dad – was 100% behind him. "My father was a tennis player at Purdue, and he majored in chemical engineering. He said, *Todd, if you don't try this, you'll never know, and you may regret this later.* I got to know some of the UK basketball players that summer, and they were very welcoming. It just encouraged me to go out there and do my best with what God has given me and just see where it goes. If I didn't try, I wouldn't know, and I may be sitting here today saying, *Man, I wish I had done that.* I look back, and I'm glad I gave it a try."

But there were signs during the preseason that Svoboda's status as a Wildcat was shaky. "I remember during the team pictures, they took half the pictures with me and half the pictures without me because at the time they didn't know if I would be on the team. I wasn't discouraged – it gave me more determination to do what I could."

Svoboda was proving himself among the UK All-Americans and improving himself at the same time. His commitment to conditioning enabled him to lower his mile time to under five minutes. "By the time the season started, I was running a 4:57 mile as a big man. I thought to myself, *I may not be the most talented out here, but I can outwork everybody else.* The guy ahead of me in my position was Jamal Mashburn, a future NBA lottery pick. He had a move that even when I knew it was coming, I couldn't stop it. But I said in my mind, *I'm going to outwork him. Even if I don't play in games, I'm going to be pushing him and helping him get better.* Those were my thoughts to help the team and give me a chance to make the team.

"Before practice one day, not too long after those team pictures, I was told Coach Pitino wanted to see me in his office. I ran up there and he said, *Todd, you made the team. You're not going to start, but you've worked hard and you've had an impact on some of the other players here. You're welcome to be on our basketball team.* He pretty much gave me the option to continue or leave the team; either would be okay with him. Well, there was no doubt in my mind what choice I was going to make. If I made that team, I was going to be on that team. I thanked him for the opportunity, ran back down to practice, and the guys could see it on my face that I made the team."

Svoboda went from averaging 18 points a game at Northern Kentucky to scoring 24 for the entire season at Kentucky. He played 38 minutes across 13 games, collecting 17 rebounds and connecting on 10-of-16 field goals, including a right-wing three-pointer in the final seconds of Kentucky's 106-81 NCAA regional win over Florida State, sending the Wildcats to the 1993 Final Four in New Orleans.

In part because of the enthusiasm he showed on the bench, Svoboda became a favorite of the UK fans in Rupp Arena – plus all the other arenas in the Southeast Conference. "It was funny how the crowd really got behind me. When we would get a big lead, people would start chanting, *We want Todd! We want Todd!* At Mississippi, they were chanting it so loud, Pitino walked down the bench and said to me with a grin on his face, *Todd, tell them to shut up.* I said, *I can't, coach,* and then he said, *Well, then go in the game.*

"I had several fans tell me, *Todd, you're doing what I always dreamed of as a little boy.* I didn't take that lightly. I knew what having 'Kentucky' on your jersey meant. People saw how much I enjoyed being on the team even though I wasn't playing or starting. I was definitely one of the biggest cheerleaders on the bench."

After the season, Pitino told Svoboda his impact on the club went beyond towel waving and garbage-time points. "I remember Coach Pitino saying he didn't think we would have made it to the Final Four without me on the team. Every person had their role, and I had that role of doing whatever needed to be done and encouraging the team. Could I play and score? Yeah. I was 6-8 and I had a 36-inch vertical. But my role during my year on that team was to do different things that a lot of people didn't see. I was fine with that. I didn't pout on the sidelines because I wasn't playing. I said, *What can I do to help this team?* That's all I tried to do: see what's a need and go do it."

Soon after graduating from UK in 1994 with his five-year degree in Chemical Engineering, Svoboda parlayed his diploma and his walk-on attitude into a successful 18-year run at Lexmark. While at the company, he earned his Six Sigma Yellow Belt (2008), was named North American Consultant of the Year (2013), and earned a spot twice as a member of the Achievers Club (2013 and 2015). He also received a patent – #3,500,616 if you're keeping track – for Toner Mass Control by Surface Roughness and Voids. Over time, he filled several different roles at the company. "Lexmark gave me the opportunity to do quite a few things. All the ink that goes into the Lexmark cartridges, at one point I was over that production. We had several facilities around the world, and I was the lead for taking that from development to full-scale production. I had the opportunity to start facilities in the Philippines and in Mexico which really helped broaden my career. I did research and development for ink-jetting as well as the laser components that go into laser cartridges and laser printers. I worked with big companies like Dell and also with smaller niche companies that didn't have their own capital to invest in the technology we had. I worked on consulting for the sales team in the field where we'd go to Fortune 500 companies and talk to C-level executives to help match the technology and ask the right questions."

Svoboda jumped from Lexmark to the East Kentucky Power Cooperative near his home in Winchester, Ky., and has worked as a Senior Engineer for several years. When he first started at the co-op, he had to gain confidence in a new role with a new team – just like when he transferred from Northern Kentucky to UK.

"To me, building confidence is a gradual process. When I saw my strength and conditioning coach for the first time at Kentucky, he said, *When you're running two miles in 12 minutes, come see me again.* When I first got there if he would have said, *I want you to run a sub-five-minute mile,* I may have been discouraged. The process worked in steps. That first goal he set – I thought I could do that. When you reach that first milestone and know that it's achievable after you put in the hard work, you build confidence. Over time, it gives you the overall confidence to say, *I can do this.*

"When I took this new job, I asked myself, *What are some of the steps I need to take?* If you look at everything, it can be overwhelming. First, I need to know some of the people, know who to talk to so I can do my functions. Even in engineering problems I try to simplify things from a complex situation and say, *Let me break this down into more simplified pieces that are achievable and then go from there.*"

Svoboda said NKU's process when he transferred away has served as a blueprint for self-improvement throughout his career. "When I left, Coach Shields asked me, *What did we do well and what could we improve on?* He was looking for continued improvement. I remember that vividly – it was like an exit interview. He wanted to get better. I observe those behaviors now, and you can tell the people who want to get better and the people who are okay with staying at the same level. I want to improve. I want to do the best that I can. I'm not necessarily saying I want to be the CEO – not everybody can be the CEO. I want to improve in my career and make the people around me better, and my team better, and my superiors better. That's kind of the attitude I took from Kentucky into work."

Even though Svoboda now has decades of professional and engineering experience, he still seeks mentors and encourages others to do so. "I like to be mentored – I like to find somebody to guide me. Whether you're on an athletic team or in business, always look for somebody better than you and do what they're doing. In business, there are a lot of things you can mimic; you don't need to reinvent the wheel. Tailor things to your own liking, but a lot of information to help you move to the next level comes from just watching, observing, or listening to your mentor and others."

Svoboda stresses that all professionals should be active in their self-development. Just like he didn't wait for the Kentucky coaches to tell him what role to play, employees need to seek out answers to understand where they can be best applied. "I'm not afraid to ask questions. I've had the feeling where I don't know an answer or I don't know what people are talking about. Sometimes in the past I kept quiet during the meeting and afterwards I would talk to somebody to help me. I've learned to ask questions in the moment because the majority of the time others have the same questions. The answer would clarify what the person is saying and help the team be completely aligned."

As Svoboda said, not everyone can be the CEO, so find the right role for yourself in your organization. To do that, he applied the same methodology from his walk-on days. "I didn't change my approach because it works. People respond to you and accept you better when you're asking how you can best help them and the team. They know they can trust you. They know you've got their back because you're going to do what needs to be done for the team."

CHAPTER 13

"I'm Going To Define My Life As A Competitor"

Yogi Roth

University of Pittsburgh, Football
Broadcaster, Podcaster, Filmmaker,
Speaker, Moderator, & Author

Before you can blink your eyes twice while reading Yogi Roth's website (YogiRoth.com), you'll surmise he's a passionate storyteller about the human side of sports. So, let's allow Roth to tell his remarkable tale to you, starting with his days in the late 1990s as a wide receiver and two-time all-state defensive back at tiny Lackawanna Trail High School in even tinier Dalton, Pa. (pop. 1,195), near the city of Scranton:

"I remember my story like it was yesterday. I didn't start playing football until eighth grade, but I absolutely fell in love with it and I started to have success. My freshman year in high school I was starting, but on some document I was listed as a senior. I started getting letters and calls from coaches at schools like Bucknell and Columbia. The first letter I ever got, I thought, *I'm only a freshman and they think I can play? I'm going to go do this thing.* That's when I committed to play major college football. I never got a ton of support from those big schools, but I was going to test it out.

"By the time I was a senior, I knew I could compete because I went to a lot of summer camps, including one at Notre Dame. I would get in line first for every group drill and go at whoever was against me. It would get heated. I knew I could play at the highest level of college football, but when coaches are looking at a 6-foot-4 receiver and then me at 5-foot-11, I knew who was going to get the scholarship. Emails were just getting going, and I sent one to a recruiting analyst. I said, *I don't understand why I'm not getting any offers.* His response was, *Yogi, you're a good player but you need to be realistic about your ability.* That set me off because all it did was look at my measurables. It didn't look at my heart. It didn't look at my soul. It didn't look at my love for the game. I saved that email – I didn't think that was right to say to a kid who had a dream. I was lucky enough to stay strong enough to say to myself, *I don't care what you say. I'll just try even more.* And that's what I did.

"The night I saw Pitt beat Notre Dame in Pittsburgh (37-27, Nov. 13, 1999) was the night I decided I was going to go to the University of Pittsburgh. I didn't know one thing about Pitt. I didn't know what kind of academic institution it was. I didn't know what the dorms would look like. I just knew I wanted to play in that environment. I told my dad when we were driving home, *I'm going to walk on at Pitt.* I just needed Pitt to give me a chance."

After being named PA Small School Defensive Player of the Year, Roth was added to the Panther program as a preferred walk-on. "The first day I got on campus, I ran around looking for my locker thinking I'd be number 30 or number 80 or something like that. I looked through the 30s and I couldn't find it. I went to the 80s and I couldn't find it. I went to the equipment manager and said I was looking for my locker. He said, *Who are you?* I thought the equipment manager would know all the players, but he had no clue who I was. I told him my name, then he looked back a few pages on his list and said, *Oh, your locker is 106.*

"I remember saying, *What?* I had been playing football for a long enough to know that nobody has triple digits on their jersey. Locker number 106 was way back in the corner, way back in the hood. That's where they put all the walk-ons. When I got back there, I looked at my cleats; they were two sizes too big. I looked at my helmet and it had a lot of head space. I looked at my pads and they were way too big for me. And I said to myself, *I wouldn't want it any other way.* That was the moment where I said, *I'm going to define my life as a competitor.* And I just went to work.

"My first week, I got in a fight with (junior wide receiver and future NFL draft pick) R.J. English. I was playing defensive back in a blocking drill, and he grabbed me to stop me from making plays. He said, *Don't try to be a hero.* I freaked out and pushed him right back. I said, *I'm here to compete, but if you want to throw down, let's throw down.* I had to stand up for myself. I was not going to be that walk-on that you pick on every day. R.J. came up to me that night in the dorm room hall and he said, *I respect your work ethic.* That was great. That was sweet. Then I knew that those were the little things that you do in order to make it. I learned how to beat other guys with my hustle. I'd be the first guy out there and be the last guy to leave.

"Our second game of the season was a Saturday afternoon game at Bowling Green. I was supposed to travel because I was the backup holder, but on Thursday of that week J.D. Brookhart, my wide receivers coach, told me someone else was taking my place and I wasn't going to travel. I knew the minute that I dropped from two-deep on the depth chart, I was going on the scout team. One of my goals as a true freshman was to never play one snap on the scout team. (Defensive coordinator) Paul Rhoads wanted me on the scout team because he knew I could give him a good look, but I knew the minute I got over there I would be forgotten. After Coach Brookhart told me I would not be traveling, I responded that my parents were on their way to Bowling Green and that I could help the team as a wide receiver. He must have talked it over with the staff, and later that day I found out that I would, in fact, be traveling. While my parents never made the trip to Bowling Green I did, and I never played a snap on the scout team in my career.

"For that trip, they had me room with (future NFL wide receiver) Antonio Bryant. He's an All-American from Miami and I'm a walk-on from Dalton – not necessarily comparable backgrounds. We stayed up until three in the morning talking about each other's story. At the end he says, *Yogi, I'm going to make sure you play tomorrow.* He goes for three touchdowns (on nine receptions for 180 yards). It was full domination. After every touchdown, he'd run to the sideline and say, *Yogi, that was for you.* At the end of the third quarter (with Pitt leading 34-3) I saw him on the headphones talking to coach

Brookhart in the booth. He's pleading his case: *You got to put him in.* Then he says to me, *Come on. Coach Brookhart wants to talk to you.* I hustled over there, grabbed the phone, and I put it to my head, and I can't hear anything. *Hello? Hello?* I couldn't hear anything because I had my helmet on, and I didn't know you can't talk to someone on the headset with your helmet on. He said, *We decided you're not ready yet, so you're not going to play even though Antonio has been pleading with me all game long.* I said, *That's cool, coach. No problem. Are you going to guarantee me a scholarship?* He said, *It's the end of the third quarter. What are you talking about?* In my warped mind I was thinking only about how can I compete to be a part of this thing for real and get a scholarship and legitimate playing time. Coach said, *Alright, you want to play, go play.* The few snaps I played I had R.J. and Antonio cheering for me. The quarterback audibled the one snap I was supposed to make a catch on – I was so mad. I ended up playing in the final game with West Virginia, but I didn't go on the scout team for a snap all season.

"Walk-ons don't have training table, you sit on the third bus, you're the last guy to do anything, you don't get all the reps. To be honest, I loved that. I embraced it. You were just going to continue to fuel me. After every season and after spring drills every year, I walked into the coach's office and I'd say, *Coach, can I meet with you?* He'd know what I was thinking. *Can I have a shot? Did I earn a scholarship?* He'd say, *You're not there yet.* I'd walk in there with crazy confidence every time.

"I can remember the day I got the scholarship. I walked out in the locker room and the players are so jacked they're screaming and yelling. To me it wasn't even a big deal because I was already a Division I player. I think it is 100% more valuable to earn a scholarship as a student-athlete in college than being named a scholarship student-athlete in high school. There are 20 kids on every football roster that have a scholarship and they have not earned it every year, every rep. They don't work hard enough. They don't love the craft with every ounce of them. And there's a walk-on that could and should take their spot on scholarship."

Roth saw action in 32 games during his Pitt career totaling 15 receptions for 133 yards (8.9 avg.) and eight punt and kickoff returns for 53 yards (6.6 avg.). "Back then, I couldn't imagine turning on the television on Thursday night, watching other teams play on ESPN, and knowing I didn't try to play at that level. That's a vivid and powerful memory for me. I needed to take that shot. In our town, I can remember some of my own coaches saying, *Yogi, you should go to a small school, man.* That's what everybody else did. I was just never going to subscribe to that, and I'm never ever going to.

"As a walk-on you're tested. Do you want to do this for free? Do you want to put in the same amount of work as the people who are getting the scholarship? It shaped me in a way that allowed me to take a chance in life and work at beating everybody.

"After I graduated from Pitt (in 2004 with a degree in Communication and Rhetoric), Coach Brookhart was offered the job as head coach at Akron. He offered me multiple roles on his staff from coaching to player personnel to the media. It was awesome. It was more money than my parents ever made. I thought at first, *I'm on my way.* But in my mind, and this isn't a slight to him or their program, it wasn't a big enough swing for me. It was a great opportunity, but it wasn't a big enough risk, so I turned it down. I didn't have a better-paying job lined up. I just turned it down and started doing radio and TV in Pittsburgh for Pitt games. After doing that for a season and a half, I felt myself settling into that role. I needed to take a big swing – I needed to work in a major city, a major market. I needed to work in Los Angeles.

"I was offered the opportunity to come out to USC (University of Southern California) to work in personnel there. Two weeks in, (head coach) Pete Carroll asks me to coach, and I jumped on board with that. Four years later, I had a master's degree (in Communications Management), got promoted to assistant quarterback coach, and then I had a chance to go to the University of Washington as one of the youngest full-time quarterback coaches in the country at age 26. I knew what that meant. It means you're on your way. Again, I thought there was more out there for me to go do. And, again, nothing against the football coaching profession – I love it – but I had to take a bigger swing. I left coaching entirely which made no sense to people in the profession. I didn't have another job lined up. But it didn't feel right. And I have always trusted my feel, my instinct."

Roth hit the big time in various media roles, most notably in broadcasting on the Pac-12 Network, Fox, ESPN, Turner, Sirius XM, and Bleacher Report. He has also directed, produced, and starred in over 20 films and has multiple podcasts: *The Season of Sam* with USC legend and current NFL quarterback Sam Darnold, *The Yogi Roth Show: How Great Is Ball, Ted & Yogi's Pac-12 Adventure*, and *The Pac-12 Perspective*. Roth is the author of the book *From PA to LA* and co-authored with Carroll *Win Forever: Live, Work, and Play Like a Champion*. He's also an active speaker and moderator, presenting to colleges, keynoting at conferences, and on tour with brands such as Nike, Capital One, and Dignity Health. He has also interviewed well-known athletes and entertainers including Joe Montana, Wayne Gretzky, Will Ferrell, Drake, Jerry Rice, Larry Fitzgerald, Russell Wilson, Elgin Baylor, Terrell Owens, Metta World Peace, Rob Riggle, Jared Goff, Gary Vaynerchuk, Melvin Gordon, J.J. Redick, and Robin Roberts.

"I carried the walk-on experience with me into every audition, into every booth, into every book, into every story that I am a part of – no doubt," Roth said. "That is part of my ego. That is part of my soul. And I don't think it will ever change. I set a goal and then I'll bust my tail to accomplish it.

"If your dream doesn't scare you, it's not big enough. If it doesn't make you feel a little uncomfortable, it's not big enough. I needed to play on Thursday night on ESPN. Coaching in Akron at 22 years old, it wasn't a big enough swing. Continuing to coach major college football at 26 wasn't enough. Whatever my heart and gut has said, no matter who supported it and who didn't, I stayed with that. I've always taken the biggest swing in my eyes – it's almost like I needed to be uncomfortable. I needed to be far out. I needed to take risks. I needed to live uncomfortably daily.

"What I've learned as I've gotten older is we can control the decision, but we can't control the outcome. I can control the goal, I can control the vigor that I approach every task with, but I can't control the outcome. I want to call a national championship game on a broadcast; I can't control that. But I can control that I prepare for the Arizona spring game like it was the national championship. I try to set the bar from a work ethic standpoint for anyone who comes into my work environment or into my life. At Pitt, I felt like I was always the one who set the temperature for work ethic. I wouldn't have to say anything. I just set it by catching more passes, running more routes, and being more diligent in the weight room.

"I don't look at anything I've done and say, *Wow! Congratulations!* I'm proud of myself and my career, but I don't sit back and say to myself, *You've arrived.* Because as a walk-on kid you can get beat out, and they're always trying to beat you. I feel like I'm just getting warmed up."

CHAPTER 14

"Just Keep Plugging On"

Bernie Floriani
University of Virginia, Basketball
Owner, State Farm Insurance Agency (Gurnee, Ill.)

When Bernie Floriani's golf game went sideways at the University of Virginia, it put him "in the right place at the right time" and sparked an experience that has benefited him for decades. Floriani was a decorated two-sport star at Dover (Del.) High School, earning honors in both golf (two Delaware state individual junior golf championships and two team state championships) and basketball (all-state honorable mention after averaging 17 ppg as a senior in 1986-87). He accepted a partial golf scholarship to Virginia and kept in shape by playing intramural basketball and pick-up games in the winter. Until fate intervened.

"My sophomore year, my golf game wasn't quite working out," he said. "I loved basketball and I continually played pick-up until I heard about the JV team at Virginia – I didn't realize colleges had junior varsity teams at all. I tried out for the team, made it, became a starter, and was a big contributor. The great thing about it was we got to play games in the main arena on the main court and sometimes in front of the University of Virginia coaches who would be hanging around the gym. That's how I got noticed by (head coach) Terry Holland and his staff."

The Cavaliers needed a practice player to go nose-to-nose with their starting point guard, future NBA 11-year veteran John Crotty. Floriani was their man. "Our JV coach said to me, *Bernie, Coach Holland would like to know if you would like to join the team. I was* really blown away. I wasn't expecting it at all. I'm thinking to myself, *This is Terry Holland. This is the University of Virginia. This is where Ralph Sampson played. They've always been a highly ranked team in the 80s. This is the ACC.* All those things just blew me away. With high school and JV games, I played in front of very limited crowds, and then all of a sudden I'm going to play in the ACC. Wow! How could I say no?"

Joining the varsity during the second semester of the 1988-89 season, he didn't exactly receive red carpet treatment. "I'm 5-foot-10, 155 pounds and they gave me number 43 – it fit like a dress on me. It had no name on the back, but all the other players had their name on their jersey. My locker was generic; everybody else's was personalized. That first year I didn't travel to any road games. I was thrilled to be part of the team, but in a lot of ways I felt not totally part of the team."

Floriani said he was accepted by his new teammates – "I wasn't exactly threatening anybody's playing time," he said – but occasionally he received "walk-on treatment" from them. "Intramural basketball was played at Memorial Gym; everyone called it 'Mem Gym.' One guy on the team would call me and some other bench players 'Mem Gym.' As a walk-on, you can be disrespected like that and that didn't feel good. At the same time, it was a motivator. There's no shame in being a walk-on. There's a lot of honor in practicing hard every day, trying to make the team better, being a good teammate on and off the floor, and maybe helping the GPA of the team. There's honor in that."

Floriani fully embraced his role as a practice player and didn't back down to Crotty, who graduated as Virginia's all-time leader in assists. "He was very skilled and unbelievably competitive," Floriani recalls. "Over two-and-a-half years in all the practices, I can remember only two times that I ever picked his pocket (stole the ball). One time I picked his pocket and I had the whole court in front of me to go lay the ball in. At half court, he tackled me from behind. Not just a bump; he literally tackled me. That guy was a competitor, so in practice I had to bring it every day. I had heard the phrase, *The team is only as strong as the weakest link.* So, if I happened to be one of the weakest links, then I'd better get as strong as I possibly can on and off the court to help the team be stronger."

Despite a high number of bumps and bruises and low amount of playing time, Floriani would stay after practice to help teammates improve their individual game. One of those players was all-time UVa great Bryant Stith, who became a three-time first-team all-ACC forward and Virginia's all-time leading scorer before being selected in the first round of the 1992 NBA draft. "He used to pick me out and we would play one-on-one with one dribble. I would ask myself, *Why does he want to play with me?* Maybe he was trying to build up his confidence. Maybe he thought I was the only one who would spend extra time with him in the gym. Maybe it's because I was only 5-foot-10 and he was trying to work on getting the ball up quicker. What struck me was this was the best player on our team, and somehow he was finding a way to make one of the worst players on the team help him get better."

During his second season of play, Floriani felt like a full-fledged member of the Virginia program most of the time but was reminded occasionally that he was still deemed expendable. He was excited for a Cavaliers NCAA first round game and his mom and brother had traveled south from Delaware to watch him take the floor. But after a walk through the morning of the game, Floriani heard disappointing news. "Our team gets back on the bus to go to the hotel, and as I'm walking down the aisle of the bus, somebody taps me on my leg and it's (assistant coach) Dave Odom. He says, *Bernie, I just want to let you know you don't need to bring your basketball shoes to the game. You're not dressing out. We only have so many seats on the bench.*

"There are times when you really feel you're a part of everything, and there are times when you feel like an outsider. You feel bad for a moment, but you just keep plugging on, keep working hard, and just be grateful for the opportunity. I think that's the thing that has always worked for me. Be grateful for what you do have with the opportunity that you've been given. Just suck it up and take it as part of your role."

After Floriani's junior year, Holland retired and assistant Jeff Jones was elevated to head coach. That summer Jones called Floriani into his office and shocked him with the offer of a full scholarship. "His reasoning wasn't so much because of my basketball ability as it was how good of a teammate I was, he told me. There was one example that he cited where one of our players had gone out of town and had flown back into Washington, D.C. which is about two-and-a-half hours away from Charlottesville. The player called me and said, *Hey, Bernie, I need to get a ride back because we have a team meeting.* When a teammate calls, you have to go help them out, without hesitation. That was just my thinking. Coach Jones said, *You know, Bernie, I don't even know if I would have done that. I really admire that.* That one act of being a teammate may very well have earned me a scholarship."

Floriani played only 17 total minutes that final season, but he capped his career with a memorable performance on UVa's Senior Day vs. ACC rival Maryland on March 2, 1991. "A week before the game, the coaches told me, *Bernie, we have five seniors but, unfortunately, we made the decision you're not going to be one of the five that's going to start because we really need to win the opening tip and we're going to start Bryant Stith in your place.* Man, I was bummed out. But I accepted it. We go back into the locker room after our first warm-up, and the coaches are going over the matchups. After they name four matchups, they say, *And Bernie, you're guarding so-and-so.* I'm like, *What?* Then I think to myself, *Maybe I should start stretching out.* My adrenaline shot through the roof. All the other guys on the team were excited because I was given this opportunity. We go out for that final warm-up just before the game, and I'm walking on cloud nine. I get announced as part of the starting lineup, and the crowd goes wild. I'm just so pumped up. Bryant Stith isn't on the floor for the jump ball, but can you guess who the ball goes to?"

It bounces to Bernie.

"I curled up in a standing fetal position because I'm scared to turn it over, and I just yell out, *Crotty! Crotty!* and I hand the ball to him. After we go up and down the floor a few times, I catch the ball on the wing, foul line extended, and when my swing leg came down, I just went up for a jumper and nailed it. I yelled out so loud but I couldn't hear myself – the crowd was crazy loud.

"When I came out of the game, I sat down and Jeff Jones walked down to the end of the bench to give me a high five. I had tears flowing. He asked, *What's wrong?* I said, *Man, that was just the best thing ever.* He gives me this man-hug and a head butt. I'll never forget it. He gave me a chance and it worked out. We eventually lost the game, but you know what? We were winning when the seniors came out. That was a day that started out bad but ended up as one of the most unbelievable experiences of my life."

Floriani can stake claim to an unforgettable Senior Day as well as an unofficial NCAA record for shooting percentage. In 11 career games over 22 minutes, he never missed a field goal (4-for-4) or a free throw (4-for-4). For his career, he registered 12 points, three assists, two rebounds, and one blocked shot.

Floriani says the walk-on experience isn't just great for nostalgia. Every day in business and in life, he applies the skills and attitude he honed during his days on the UVa hardwood. In 1997, Floriani became owner of a State Farm Insurance Agency in Gurnee, Ill., branding himself as "Bernie from Gurnee."

"One of the lessons I learned as a walk-on is if you bring hard work and passion into something, it generally will pay dividends. It doesn't mean that it *is* going to pay dividends; you're not guaranteed anything. But, generally, it will pay dividends down the road in some way, shape, or form. It may not be immediate gratification; it may be something that comes to you later."

Floriani said his walk-on experience increased his empathy for others, and that has factored into how he communicates with employees, customers, and even strangers. "Knowing what it's like to feel invisible as a walk-on – that's a big thing for me. When you're in a room or meet people for the first time, you need to recognize them as a person. We are all the same. No matter what level they are in business, or what their position is, just recognize them and try to make a connection with them no matter what their situation or their status.

"There are times as an agent when I have to tell people bad news. My experience helps me to relate to them. When I was told I wasn't dressing for that NCAA game, that could have been done differently. It could have been, *Bernie, sit down here for a second. I have to tell you something. I have bad news. We're really sorry about this. We feel terrible.* It would have taken 30 seconds to make me feel at least decent about the bad news."

Overcoming adversity as a walk-on provided Floriani with early training for the business world. When things don't go right, he says entrepreneurs need to suck it up and prepare for whatever may come your way. "Everything doesn't go perfectly when you're running a business. I hoped when I opened my State Farm agency that I'd put my name out on a sign and there would be a line at my door. Well, that didn't work. You have to work for everything. You have setbacks almost daily, especially in sales. What I can take from my walk-on days into the business is preparation. As a walk-on, we played on teams where people are better, and you get to observe how they prepare, how they perform, and how they get better. How do they handle success and how do they handle failure?"

Those lessons are especially true for Floriani today. In 2014, he began experiencing muscle weakness that was eventually diagnosed as ALS (amyotrophic lateral sclerosis), a progressive neurodegenerative disease that affects nerve cells in the brain and the spinal cord. Floriani can still talk, but he's confined to a wheelchair. "Taking what I learned as a walk-on and applying it to my career and to my business, I think we can just go ahead and make that jump into life. A lot of things I learned as a walk-on and developed as a walk-on are helping me today. I feel like an underdog. I never give up. I always had that hope of getting in the game in my playing days, and I never gave up on that hope. Part of it is doing the best that you can with what you have. I wasn't gifted with height or size or unbelievable athletic ability, but I have an attitude that's way bigger than all that. With ALS, I just have to roll with it, just like I had to roll with being a walk-on.

"There were a lot of good things about being a walk-on and, in a weird way, there are a lot of good things about having ALS. You see a lot of people providing their love and support and care, and it just puts life in perspective. I've been able to experience a lot of good that's come out of people because of my situation. I've become more open talking about it, which feels great. Opening up about it has helped me out tremendously. I think that's part of the walk-on thing. There are hardships and setbacks that come your way. Success comes when you're able to work your way through them to overcome them or work your way around them and still continue to go on."

"I'd be lying if I said I didn't wish I was 6-foot-7 and could jump out of the gym when I was younger. But there are things we can control and things we can't. I don't look back and regret it at all. Maybe I regret that my golf game wasn't better at the time, but that opened the door for me. Every walk-on has big dreams. And I think we're all walk-ons because we all have big dreams."

CHAPTER 15

"A Leap Of Faith"

Sarah Alexander
Dartmouth, Rowing
Professional Triathlete & Independent Strategy Consultant

Sarah Alexander had a plan. She always knew she would attend college and pursue a professional career, and she knew she wanted to make an impact. Alexander's academic and professional successes have been made possible by lessons learned through her athletic pursuits; most importantly, that great things can happen when you have the courage to take a leap of faith.

"Throughout middle school, my skating coach and I were constantly nagging my parents to let me skate full-time because all of the girls I was competing against were home schooled and were training five to six hours a day," Alexander said. Despite splitting her focus between academics and figure skating, Alexander excelled in both. She was valedictorian at Laurel High School in Shaker Heights, Oh., a Cleveland suburb, and was accepted to attend Dartmouth College, an Ivy League school in Hanover, N.H. She also earned a silver medal at the Eastern Great Lakes Sectional Championship in 2004 and advanced to the national qualifier. "I was on the cusp of breaking into the top echelon of the sport. I knew if I went to college I couldn't continue to train with my coach or train enough. That would be the end of it. I wanted to see what I could do if I went all in, even if it was for just one more competitive season."

So Alexander deferred her Dartmouth acceptance for a year to skate full-time. "I'm an optimist at heart, and I'm deeply motivated to perform at the highest level of anything I do. I believe that I can do whatever I set my mind to. But that has to be paired with self-awareness. There's a point – and it's a hard point for every athlete – when you have to be realistic about what you're going to be able to achieve. I wasn't going to skate in the Olympics."

Alexander matriculated at Dartmouth in 2006. Desiring the experience of NCAA athletics, she had communicated with the cross country coach at Dartmouth about trying out for the team. But that's when Alexander took a leap of faith. "I was standing in the line to pick up my computer the first day on campus. The Novice coach for Dartmouth rowing walked up to me and said, *You're athletic and tall. Have you ever thought about rowing?* I had seen rowing in movies, but I didn't know much about it. I thought, *I guess I'll check it out.* I was actually thinking, *I'll try a practice, but I'm still going out for cross country.* However, after the first rowing practice, I was hooked. The sport seemed really challenging, and I loved the concept of a team sport."

Alexander quickly learned that to the recruited rowers, the walk-ons were outsiders. "The recruits rarely acknowledged walk-ons for much of the fall," she said. "In hindsight, I understand, because many walk-ons quit over the first few months of the year because of the sport's grueling demands. There was also a dynamic on the team that there was a major divide between the freshmen (Novice team) and upperclassmen (Junior Varsity and Varsity teams), even though we were all technically part of the same team – the Dartmouth women's rowing team. We practiced separately, ate separately, and for the most part, socialized separately until we were days away from the end of our freshman year and the upperclassmen finally 'welcomed' us into the team."

Instead of pouting about these dynamics, Alexander used them as inspiration to improve. "None of it upset me, but I was definitely motivated to seek my teammates' approval. I used the situation to make me better. I took extra time off the water to analyze my stroke with my coach, to watch elite rowers and see how they moved, and to strength train in order to develop the bulk and power needed to excel in the sport. I went to every practice ready to be a sponge. This was an approach that I took later to internships, my undergraduate and graduate studies, and to my professional career. As a walk-on, I learned humility and I developed the perspective that there's always more to learn, more room for improvement." Alexander's dedication to the sport paid off. She rowed for four years (2006-10), was named Varsity team captain as a senior, and earned several individual awards that year: NCAA Division I All-New England first team, team MVP, and the Dartmouth Women's Crew Award for Excellence in Leadership.

Her humbling experience as a walk-on influenced her leadership style as team captain and helped dismantle the wall between veteran rowers and newcomers. "When I became team captain, I instituted a big/little system on the team in order to make the freshmen – particularly the walk-ons – feel more welcome and to feel like valued members of the team. With the help of my fellow upperclassmen, we were able to change the dynamic moving forward between the Novice and Varsity teams. That's a contribution to the program that I continue to be proud of."

Alexander parlayed her experience as a student-athlete to become an effective leader after graduating from Dartmouth in 2010 with a degree in Environmental Studies. For three years, she worked at ICF International as an environmental consultant for federal agencies, assisting them with program management as well as research and writing for large-scale feasibility projects. She provided analysis on topics such as alternative fuel vehicles (i.e. electric vehicles) and energy efficiency.

"When I was captain of the crew team, I had to learn how to balance making sure that everyone was engaged in the team's goals while recognizing that not everyone on a 40-woman team can make the boat and acknowledging that everyone has contributions to make even if they bring different individual goals and levels of commitment," said Alexander. "I think that experience prepared me to be an inclusive manager and teammate in the office. That has helped me to gain the trust of teammates and managers alike and to progress professionally. The feeling of being an outsider provided me with empathy towards others."

After three years at ICF, Alexander left to pursue her MBA at the University of Chicago Booth School of Business, where she earned a merit scholarship and graduated in 2015. While in business school, she was co-chair of two groups: the Media, Entertainment, and Sports Group and the Triathlon and Running Club. If you haven't picked up on this by now, two keys to Alexander's success have been her work ethic and drive to lead others to achievement. She's not content to sit back and cross her fingers, hoping good fortune will come her way. "A mentor of mine always says, *Work hard. You'll get noticed.* That's a mantra I applied as a walk-on and continue to ascribe to today. Even when I was a senior, I never took my seat in the first boat for granted. I came to practice with the perspective that I had to defend my seat every day. My refusal to rest on my laurels is what pushed me to get better in rowing. It still drives me to continue growing now as a professional triathlete and as a businesswoman.

"That's how I've approached my career in consulting. Be a sponge, absorb everything I can, and keep putting myself out there. As a walk-on, there's an element of playing catch-up. You have to educate yourself and figure things out really quickly, otherwise you're not going to make it. A lot of people tend to think that's scary. And it is. I overcame my fear with curiosity, courage, and a desire to prove something to the world. You learn to be gritty in that process. My first few years as a walk-on, there was so much vulnerability. But I had to embrace that vulnerability as an opportunity to become stronger.

"For me, the decision to walk on to the crew team was, in a sense, a leap of faith. But it was one that I backed with confidence in my work ethic and determination. As my mom has reminded me, *What's the worst that happens if you try?* It's the only way to grow. Similarly, when applying to a job, you may not have all of the qualifications or complete confidence, but you still have to take courage and step up to the plate if you really want it."

Alexander operates on the premise that goals are only attainable if a person can stomach leaving his or her comfort zone and put in the work. That isn't just advice she gives to others; she's executing on that philosophy today with two businesses of her own. After graduating from business school, she seized an unexpected opportunity to race professionally as a triathlete. In addition to launching her professional racing career, she established Next Level Advisors to provide marketing strategy for SMBs (small to medium-size businesses). "I felt like a walk-on all over again when I decided to become a full-time professional triathlete, because I was competing against All-American runners and swimmers as well as women who had been racing professionally for years. Meanwhile, I just started committing to the sport at age 27. For me, succeeding required seeing obstacles for what they were and just focusing on what had to be done to overcome them. My triathlon coach and I talk a lot about achieving an almost imperceptible gain every day. Then, once a year or every two years, you all of a sudden look back, and you've made this huge leap. But that major progression is actually just a function of chipping away every day, getting a little bit better every day you practice, every day you come to work.

"I was starting at ground zero as a professional triathlete. I was a very small fish in a very big pond again as I sought to race the fastest women in the world. But all I could do is focus on what I could control. I've taken that approach with my school work, my professional work, and I applied it to my triathlon racing. I have to know that I left everything out there; that no stone went unturned in my pursuit of being my best. That's how I look at myself in the mirror; how I sleep at night."

That might seem like a surprisingly easygoing approach for someone with Alexander's resume. "It's funny because growing up I was very inflexible – I was super high-strung, very type A," Alexander said. "I remember thinking back in high school I had this plan of how things were going to go. I don't really know when it happened, but I feel like I've become more adaptable. It's important to have the ability to pivot quickly and not be so burdened by second-guessing yourself. You have to take the information you have and say, *We're going in this direction, and we're going to execute the process the best we can.*"

Alexander has continued to progress as a professional triathlete over several years of 25- to 30-hour training weeks. In 2017, her second year as a pro, she earned her first international podium and was on the championship-winning team in the Major League Triathlon Series. She has continued to earn podium finishes and is now pursuing the opportunity to compete at the hallowed Ironman World Championships, in Kona, Hawaii.

Moving forward, Alexander continues to have aspirations in the business world and is taking her triathlon career one year at a time. "Triathlon has shown me that of course there is value in planning. But it's also important to keep your eyes open for unexpected opportunities that life throws your way. I have confidence that the grit and resilience fostered as a walk-on will enable me to succeed regardless of the direction I take."

CHAPTER 16

"Love The Dirty Work"

Nick Berardini

Missouri, Basketball
Filmmaker & Writer/Producer/Director

Think the movie industry is all glitz and glamour, tuxedos and ball gowns, just like The Oscars? Documentary filmmaker Nick Berardini says you're mistaken. "The only thing worse than trying to survive practice as a walk-on is trying to be a professional filmmaker," he said. "Quite frankly, it's less glory and much harder."

Berardini would know. He was a four-year men's basketball walk-on at the University of Missouri from 2005-09, scoring just 13 points during his career. As a filmmaker, he's earned high praise for producing the documentary *Killing Them Safely*, which received positive attention at the 2015 Tribeca Film Festival and from Sundance Selects, but he knows documentary filmmakers take an arduous road to the red carpet. "There are a handful of people who make a very good living making documentary films. But for the rest of us, it has to be about the work. It can't be about the glory because that fades very, very quickly. It's mostly locking yourself in a room while everybody else is having fun and beating your head against the desk." So why would Berardini choose such a difficult line of work? For the same reason he chose to walk on at the University of Missouri.

As a high schooler, Berardini believed he had Division I ability, but he was inconsistent. Fortunately, he received exposure to college scouts attending Five Star camps and playing for the talented Illinois

Warriors AAU club alongside future Kansas University star and NBA lottery selection Julian Wright and future Duke All-American Jon Scheyer. The result for Berardini was an offer to be a preferred walk-on at the University of Dayton, his parents' alma mater. "I grew up going to UD games and I loved that environment and that atmosphere, so I was pretty set on wanting to go to Dayton," he said. "But right around this time, my AAU coach, Larry Butler, helped me get in touch with the assistants at Missouri. They just very politely, and I think not very seriously at all, invited me to visit." Berardini's response to the invite was *Why not?*

"My dad and I went, and we had no expectations. They were a top-five team getting ready for the season, and they weren't chomping at the bit to get me on the squad by any stretch. They were just were being nice – they were very casual about it. *Why don't you come down? Why don't you watch practice and get to meet everybody?* I got to meet a couple of the top 100 high school players they had signed for their next recruiting class, so it was fun. For my dad and me who had never really been around basketball at that level or even thought about being around basketball at that high of a level, it was a cool experience.

"After practice, after everybody had left, I just went out in my jeans and my leather jacket and started popping threes from about thirty feet. One of the coaches said, *You may be a little better than we thought. You know what? Why don't you come back for a game this year?* They probably figured what's the harm in inviting me to a game? In February 2004, I went down and saw them beat UNLV by over 30. It was an unbelievable atmosphere. The energy was great. The momentum was great. I was like, *Holy shit! You guys have the real deal over here!* It was around that point that they gave me a relatively confident indication that it might work out for me if I was willing to take a chance. But I'd have to lay it all out.

"For me it became sort of a no-brainer. I really loved UD, but Missouri had a phenomenal journalism school. I thought I'd go major in journalism and I'd get to play basketball in the Big 12 if I could hack it." So Berardini packed his bags for Columbia, Mo., with nothing more than a promise to have the opportunity to try out. His secret to making the team? "I kept showing up," he said.

In the preseason of his freshman year, before official practice and tryouts for walk-ons, Berardini participated in Missouri's grueling conditioning drills. He literally went the extra mile by attending a punishment workout. "All the scholarship guys got in trouble for something – somebody didn't go to a class or something like that. Coach (Quin) Snyder had everybody show up to run this hill we had outside – you know, the famous hill that every college has. He said, *Be here at 5 o'clock in the morning,* and I showed up with everybody else even though I wasn't officially on the team yet. I ran sprints with them and about died. I think that's when he first understood who I was and thought, *This kid is going to put in the work and the effort.*"

And that's exactly what Berardini did. He hit the weight room and developed his game outside of practice time, impressing the coaching staff enough to keep him on the squad. But as often happens in big-time athletics, Snyder resigned after a stretch of losses in early 2006 and was replaced by Mike Anderson starting with the 2006-07 season. Berardini had to win over a brand new staff – and he chose to embrace an additional role. "In Coach Anderson's first year, I was one of the oldest guys there, and there was a sense that I could help them fill a void in terms of experience and leadership. I could help the freshmen with understanding how hard you have to compete every single day when you're playing at that high level. I think I had a renewed sense of confidence not in thinking that I was going to get to play for this new staff, but more like, *You know what, I'm going to impress the hell out of them.*"

Berardini aimed to influence the staff to keep him on the roster, but he knew they weren't going to add him to the rotation. Ever. "I never had an expectation that I would play a meaningful minute at Missouri," he said. "I was pretty realistic about what my ability was. And my ability was never going to be a guy who Mike Anderson could rely on to get them to the tournament, which is ultimately his job. If they had asked me to go into a game to play a meaningful couple of minutes, I believe I would be far more likely to do something to help us win the game than to do something to make us lose it. But I knew I wasn't somebody they wanted to rely on for 10 or 15 minutes a game. I knew what my place was and I was really comfortable with that. I had more realistic goals like I really wanted to be considered a leader of the team."

Berardini said leadership is different when you're a walk-on. "I always saw my job as almost an extension of the coaching staff and to know when it's my time to speak. I had to make sure that if I'm giving somebody advice on the bench it's because I saw something very specific. I tried to be a guy that could be relied on especially during the games, because it was my job to know all the other team's stuff, to watch their tapes and be able to offer input about a player or when a specific play is coming."

Berardini was an emotional leader as well. In a *Columbia Tribune* article published his senior year, Berardini was described as "an enthusiastic, first-off-the-bench celebration machine." He said that came very naturally to him, not just because he's a self-described "big ham," but also because of his team-first approach to his role. "It was never about *I need to get mine*. I was always a person who cared about winning first. From the time I stepped into competitive sports, I wanted to win really bad. And so that enthusiasm was a natural part of it. Every play to me was life and death. Everything to me had that urgency because I was so desperate to win. I also knew not everybody can be that guy, but *somebody* has to be that guy. When a teammate takes a charge which leads into a TV timeout and everybody is clapping and going crazy, somebody's got to be first to go pick them up off the floor. And when practice is dull and coach needs somebody to get practice going, I'm going to get in somebody's face, knock the ball away, and start a little scuffle to try to pick up the energy level.

"I would do that in pick-up games especially with our younger guys. It was never dirty by any stretch of the imagination, but I would try to piss them off as much as possible. Say it's June and we're playing our seventh game of the day; I'm going to come after somebody and I'm going to treat that pick-up game like it's my Super Bowl because it is. This is the only thing I get out of this – I get the chance to make you guys better. So, I just took it upon myself to say, *I'm that guy.* I can be the guy who they can always rely on to compete. The scholarship guys can look at the guy who's getting nothing out of it except bloody noses and a couple of minutes every 10 games when we blow somebody out and see him still competing.

"That was the main reason I put up with all that crap as a walk-on. And I think the other players really respected that. That's why I could have a voice with the team, eventually, as an older player because they knew I'm not coming from any place other than I wanted to win. So, if I get in your grill, it's not because it's personal or I'm trying to take your minutes. It's because I want to win, and if I don't think you're showing up to win, I'm going to embarrass you or I'm going to pick a fight with you. We're going to compete."

The coaching staff fed into Berardini's role and used it to motivate the scholarship players. "There was an assistant who had this great Arkansas drawl," Berardini recalls. "He would be screaming at one of the scholarship guys, *You think you're going to play point guard in the pros? You can't even guard Nick Berardini!* I took a lot of pride in that. When I went in, I wanted to raise the level of competition not by pure talent, but by urgency. That was my job. The only thing I'd get out of it is the joy of going on the road and beating somebody that we're not supposed to beat, or seeing a guy that you helped get extra shots up at the end of practice, and he's making big shots in a big game. You get a sense of your moment, too, because you know what you've been doing behind the scenes. And you have to be inherently unselfish and all about the team to be that guy."

Berardini developed an acute sense of self-awareness through his walk-on experience. He understood his limitations, his role, and the actions necessary to remain part of the program. He's carried that into his work today as a filmmaker and contributing journalist to MSNBC, The Daily Beast, and The Intercept. "I'm a good storyteller now because I'm a very self-aware person. I didn't lie to myself about what I was there to do as a walk-on," he said. "I found it very easy to say, *If I'm the twelfth guy on this team and I'm good, our team is going to be good.* You have to understand the reality and the context of the situation you're in and find your niche."

Berardini sees parallels between his efforts to find his niche in the documentary film industry and the grit required for him to walk on at Missouri. "You have to take enough swings. You have to be entrepreneurial. You just keep your head down and eventually it just starts working. When you're walking on at a big school, you're always auditioning. They can get rid of you in a heartbeat and nobody would blink an eye. I think the attitude to never get complacent is crucial to the work I do now. The second you get complacent, somebody else is right behind you ready to take that opportunity. When you're a walk-on, you never forget that you're there of your own choosing. You're there because you wanted this life; you can't just want the glory. You can't just want the fun part where you run out on the court before the game and it's a sold-out crowd and everybody starts going crazy. You have to want it when it's July, it's hot, you're tired, and you're asking yourself, *Why the hell would anybody want to do this?*

"The students that I work closely with today, a lot of them are very talented; they want to get into filmmaking. They start wondering, *What am I going to do for a job? What's my life going to look like?* I tell them none of that matters now. You have to commit to the industry. If you think about going to grad school as a backup, you're not going to make it in the film industry. It's too difficult. Don't give yourself an out. You have to stick it out. You have to care about the craft.

"That's where my self-awareness about what I got into as a walk-on was really helpful. You have to enjoy the beat-down. It has to fuel you. If for you it's all about going to Sundance and shaking hands and going to some party and meeting some producer who tells you he's going to make you famous, you're going to have a quick stay in this business. When you have the wherewithal, you don't worry about where you're going to eat tomorrow. Sometimes I thought, *This is not what I had hoped for, but it is what I chose.* I think that sustained me through the really hard times. It should never cross your mind that you're going to quit."

Berardini said confidence, commitment, and perseverance – three key walk-on qualities – are paramount in the professional world as well. "You have to see it all the way through. Many people are going to try and not make it. You have to know you gave it a full, honest effort and you didn't quit early. If your intention is to try to have this life because you think you're going to get some validation out of it from people telling you how great you are, go work on an app. Go do something where you can make a billion dollars.

"Certainly there were times for me when it was fun to be on a big-time college basketball team. You're popular. It's fun to go run out of the tunnel before the Kansas game. I wanted to be the first one out and hear the crowd. But 97% of the time, you're doing the dirty work. That 3% of the time when there's some glory, it isn't enough to sustain you if you don't love the dirty work."

CHAPTER 17

"Where Do I See Myself In 10 Years?"

Austin McLeod
Harvard, Football
Attorney

Sacrifice short-term gain for a long-term benefit. Seek balance in your life. We've all heard that advice, but how many of us have the courage and discipline to execute on those principles? Austin McLeod does. He turned down a money-making opportunity to instead incur tens of thousands of dollars in debt so he could maximize his athletic and academic potential.

A highly decorated athlete and student at Hermitage High School in Henrico, Va., McLeod's honors could fill an XXL trophy case. On the football field, he was the Panthers' special teams player of the year and a second team all-district linebacker. When he didn't have his helmet on, he was Student Council Association president, junior class president, and a member of the National Honor Society, Spanish National Honor Society, and math honor society. Those accomplishments led to more awards including being named the school's male scholar-athlete of the year for 2005, being selected a National Football Foundation scholar-athlete, and receiving the *Richmond Times-Dispatch* Scholar-Athlete Award. And we should also note that McLeod received a Superintendent's Certificate of Recognition for being co-leader of an effort that raised over $74,000 for victims of the 2004 Indian Ocean tsunami – all before celebrating his 19th birthday.

Nearby William & Mary wanted McLeod to attend college there, so they offered him a scholarship that would cover all his expenses and then some. A combination of academic aid and athletic aid would overlap and result in a stipend for McLeod every semester – a full ride along with cash in his pocket to spend as he pleased. McLeod was set to accept that package and join the Tribe, but then his application to Harvard was accepted, so he and his family visited the campus in Cambridge, Mass., mostly for the experience of seeing the grounds of an Ivy League school firsthand. "I was intent on going to William & Mary," McLeod said. "But then when I was accepted to Harvard through regular admission, nothing to do with football, I went up there for one of their student weekends. It wasn't part of an official visit as a football player from a formal recruiting standpoint. I was really there almost as a courtesy – almost like a free trip. I had my mind set and had told my friends and family I was staying close to home, being a kid from Richmond, Va. But then I got to Harvard and I fell in love with it. I met a lot of great people and decided to give the school a chance."

But what about the finances? McLeod was informed he could earn a spot on the Crimson football team, but there would be no athletic aid. Instead of enjoying walking-around money, McLeod would have to find a work-study job, get some financial help from his parents, and take out loans to cover what his academic aid wouldn't. McLeod heeded the advice of a Hermitage High alum to take what appeared to be the rockier path. "She said, not to sound cliché, the Harvard experience would be priceless. Upon reflection now, that would probably be the one of most fortuitous pieces of advice I've ever received because I find I'm still benefiting from the experience – not just the degree but the connections that I made from the experience of going to that school. My path would have been a lot different if I had focused on the initial cost instead of the extended benefits. I looked at it as an investment because it's one of those things that no one will be able to take it away from you."

McLeod amassed $60,000 in student loan debt, but that wasn't the only pain he was feeling. As a freshman, McLeod was sidelined for eight weeks with a herniated disc. "It hurt to walk, stand up, sleep, sneeze, or even just breathe," McLeod said. He was banged up again as a sophomore when he suffered a foot infection and a broken hand. He saw action on the JV team and in a few varsity games, albeit with a cast slowing him down. Instead of succumbing to the injuries, McLeod stepped up. "At that time it really hit me football wasn't promised or guaranteed. So, that spring in practice, I took every opportunity to go as hard as I could, even when I was still on the scout team. I made a point not to fear the pain or punishment, but to really try to better myself and make the other side better. While I was on scout team, I was going to be the toughest person on it, the hardest person to block, the hardest person to defend. I think I played with a chip on my shoulder, knowing I wasn't the strongest or fastest on the team."

That attitude paid off for McLeod and the entire club his final two years. As a junior, Harvard finished 8-2 overall, 7-0 in the Ivy League, and ranked 21st in the final 2007 NCAA Division I FCS poll. In 2008, the Crimson were co-champions of the Ivy League with a 6-1 conference record and 9-1 overall ledger. McLeod covered kickoffs as a junior and then participated in all aspects of special teams as a senior (kickoffs, kickoff returns, and punt returns). For his efforts, he received Harvard's Buz Crain Award, given to the player considered "the most inspirational leader on the team."

McLeod hung up his shoulder pads in 2008, but the lessons learned as a walk-on keep him moving forward today. "You realize there are going to be challenges, but you're prepared to deal with the adversity. You don't give yourself an internal ultimatum like, *If one more bad thing happens, then I'm just going to give up*. It's more like not having a 'give up' sense in your vocabulary. Being a walk-on and not being the strongest guy on the team has prepared me for places where I feel like I'm not the best at something when I get in that room. That's not going to deter me from being able to deliver to the best of my ability."

McLeod graduated with a degree in Government (with a minor in Psychology and a language citation in Spanish) in 2009 before earning his law degree with a focus on labor and employment from New York University in 2017. Today he's an associate at the prestigious Proskauer Rose law firm. Prior to joining Proskauer, he interned at the PGA TOUR and worked as a litigation paralegal at Goldman Sachs. During law school, McLeod worked as a labor relations law clerk for the NFL, served as a staff editor of the NYU Journal of Intellectual Property and Entertainment Law, and was President of the Student Lawyer Athletic Program.

McLeod says his philosophy of choosing the best path, not the easiest path, helped him get where he is today. After being accepted into the law schools at both NYU and the University of Virginia, McLeod had a choice to make – similar to his William & Mary/Harvard options. "I turned down a better scholarship opportunity at UVa to do law in New York, realizing that if my focus was going to be on labor and employment, a lot of the employment work was going to be in New York. Instead of going back home to Virginia, I chose to move to a big city I didn't know at all. Then, during law school, I had to decide between two law firms. One seemed to have a greater opportunity financially up front. But I asked myself, *What do I ultimately want to do? What law field do I want to work in? Where do I see myself in 10 years?* Going through that process again made the decision easier."

CHAPTER 18

"Everyone Is Important"

David Carney
Southern Illinois, Basketball
Owner, VIP Foliage & Landscapes

When a manager is asked where he or she developed their leadership style, they often cite a combination of inspirational sources. David Carney says his four years as a men's basketball walk-on at Division I Southern Illinois were clearly the catalyst to his developing the voice and the connections that have helped him successfully build his own award-winning landscaping business.

Coming out of Tell City (Ind.) High School in 1998, the sharpshooting Carney was recruited only by Division III schools. Being 5-foot-10 and 160 pounds tends to limit your basketball opportunities, even if you're named All-Southwest Indiana and Big 8 Conference first team. Carney took a self-described "leap of faith" and walked on at Southern Illinois to play for future University of Illinois and Kansas State head coach Bruce Weber. Carney credits Weber for shaping him into a leader. "Even though I wasn't one of the main guys, he taught me to be more vocal because I could see things from where I sat," Carney said. "Like when we were in a specific defense, one of the players might not think it's working well or they're having trouble with the scheme itself. They might tell me, and then I could go to coach and say, *So-and-so doesn't think we need to go over the top with this. He thinks it's going to be better going under. Maybe you could address that during a time-out.*"

Carney didn't earn the right to give the coaching staff advice because of a superior athletic career at SIU. From 1998-2003 he scored just 15 points across 38 games as a Saluki, but he was encouraged by Weber and assistant Matt Painter, who has been named Big 10 Coach of the Year at Purdue multiple times, to speak up. "They always said I had a really good grasp for how basketball should be played and seeing things that other guys couldn't," Carney recalled. "They didn't ask me for advice all the time, but they certainly wanted me to speak up if I did see something."

Weber and the staff guided the soft-spoken Carney out of his natural comfort zone. "They pulled that out of me for sure. I was extremely reserved my first couple years at school. It took time for me to come out of my shell." The coaches did this even though they didn't expect Carney or the other walk-ons to see meaningful playing time. "They included everybody. They made you feel welcomed. When we had team meetings, our voices were just as important as the starting five's voices. At the team banquet my senior year, Coach Weber said over the years I had become the biggest smart-ass on the team and that I had really come out of my shell."

Southern Illinois experienced unprecedented success during Carney's time there, winning consecutive Missouri Valley Conference regular season championships his junior and senior seasons (2002 and 2003) and qualifying twice for the NCAA tournament, including a run to the Sweet 16 in 2002 with wins over Texas Tech and Georgia. Carney said the team culture established by the coaches – and upheld by the players – was key to that winning formula. Carney shared a story from a preseason pick-up game as an example of how he fought for a strong culture. "One year we had a couple bad apples on the team. This guy steals the ball, and I'm running down on his right-hand side, right next to him from mid-court all the way to the bucket. He goes up for lay-up, he misses it, and he calls foul. I said, *Hell, no. No. That's not our style. We're going the other way.* So, I take the ball and grab it to go the other way. On the very next play, he grabs the ball real fast out of the net, and I guess he doesn't think I'm paying attention, and from about ten feet away, he throws it as hard as he can. You know how a softball pitcher throws the ball underhand? He throws it underhand towards at me. He was trying to hit me, but I was paying attention and I caught the ball. And then I took it and I just threw it as hard as I could at his head. We got up at each other. Thankfully, the guys broke it up because he could have demolished me. I guess he probably didn't think that I would stand up for myself because of my stature and he was a 6-foot-3 jet."

After four years as a walk-on, including a redshirt season, Carney was rewarded with a scholarship and recognition as team co-captain his senior campaign. Carney said toughness and fairness are two traits the SIU staff emphasized, and he applies those today as a business owner. "They used to get on me to practice as hard as I could. *Get your ass in gear. You're not paying attention.* When you're not doing what you're supposed to be doing in practice, they definitely let you know. I was pushing the starting point guard, so they needed the most out of me they could get. Since I wasn't going to be playing in the games, it allowed me to step back and see how coaches dealt with players. Now I can use those things with my employees in how I should handle this situation with this guy versus someone else. It taught me more than anything how to work with individuals. How to treat them. How to get the most out of them. How to lift them up if they're down. How to encourage. How to be stern if it needs it without being demeaning.

"Depending on the time of year, I have four to 15 employees, and everybody is treated equally as important. There's a saying that goes, *Everyone is important, but no one is necessary.* Every single one of the coaches treated each player the same. They were equally as hard on them. I hold everybody accountable the same. You have to be here on time or suffer the consequences. Look professional. Act professional. Work as hard as the next guy. Don't slack off. I make sure they know, *You might be making more money than this guy, but I treat him equally.*"

Carney majored in plant and soil science at Southern Illinois, but that formal education was only one part that helped launch his business, Carney said. "Today I have a greenhouse and nursery and the whole nine yards of landscaping, but my first landscaping job was actually for Coach Weber when he got the job at Illinois after my senior year. I've also done landscaping for Coach Painter up at

Purdue. There are some neat things that otherwise wouldn't have happened if I didn't walk on."

CHAPTER 19

"The Pressure Of Potential Failure Just Made Me Stronger"

Sam Wyche
Furman, Football
Motivational Speaker; NFL Player, Coach, & Broadcaster

Sam Wyche's success in the NFL has been well documented:
- player for eight seasons
- assistant coach for four seasons, including a victory in Super Bowl XVI as the San Francisco 49ers passing game director
- head coach for 12 years with the Cincinnati Bengals and Tampa Bay Buccaneers, leading the Bengals to Super Bowl XXIII
- renowned innovator, introducing the no-huddle offense to the league
- broadcast analyst for NBC and CBS five seasons

But NFL fans don't know that Wyche's walk-on experience and relentless mindset served as the foundation for his success. In fact, you can say he doubled his walk-on experience first as an unrecruited, undersized quarterback at Furman University and then as an undrafted free agent with the Bengals.

Wyche played football, basketball, and golf at Atlanta's North Fulton High School, but the gridiron was his favorite. As a senior in 1961, he started on defense but was only third string at quarterback, stuck behind a fellow senior and his brother Bubba, a sophomore. "My parents didn't have a lot of money and they couldn't afford daycare for two kids, so my younger brother, who's 15 months younger than I am, and the better athlete, he went to daycare and then started school on time. I started early and was a year behind physically with everybody. Having your little brother ahead of you at quarterback, that was very embarrassing for a young teenager to have to swallow. But I was a pretty good tackler, and I knew I wanted to continue to play football in college."

Wyche dreamed of playing at Georgia Tech but because they showed no interest, nor did any other school for that matter, Wyche scheduled a visit to Furman, a tiny but blossoming college in Greenville, S.C., about a 300-mile round trip from his home. "One Saturday morning, my mother and I, in a 1960 Chevrolet Bel Air, drove from Atlanta to Greenville. This was before they had Interstate 85, so we were on two-lane roads all the way. We got lost a couple of times, going through these small towns. I had an appointment with the head coach, Bob King. Well, I thought I had an appointment. We went to what is now called the Old Gym just before 9 o'clock, which was our meeting time, and the gym was locked up. We sat there on the steps for probably half an hour. Finally, somebody came by and asked if they could help us. We told them we're waiting on Bob King, and they said, *Well, he's playing golf. I just saw him on the course.* He went and got Bob, told him he had somebody waiting to talk to him – I guess he'd forgotten about us, which speaks a little bit to the importance of a walk-on, even in small colleges. Bob came over at the turn after nine holes on his golf cart. He spent about five minutes with me and that was it. He handed me a brochure, which was a black-and-white mimeograph, folded piece of paper in those days, and said, *Will you ride around campus and take a look at the campus?* So, we drove around campus, and Bob went back to finish his round of golf. It took only about 10 minutes because it was a brand-new campus. We could see where the practice fields were going to be, and I think they were more dirt than grass at that point. Then we headed back. We were in the car a lot longer than we were at Furman."

Wyche received plenty of playing time for the Paladins that fall at both quarterback and defensive back on the freshman team (freshmen were ineligible for varsity competition back then). His standout performance against Florida State's freshmen, which included future Pro Football Hall of Fame wide receiver Fred Biletnikoff, got the attention of the Furman varsity coaching staff. "Late in the game with the score tied 14-14, they tried to hit Biletnikoff on a post pattern. I undercut it, intercepted the ball, and ran it down to the one-yard line. Rumor has it – I'm not sure if it's just legend or if it actually happened this way – that the center caught me from behind because of all the zigzagging I did trying to score. Two quarterback sneaks later, we go into the end zone and beat Florida State 21-14. I think that, along with my growth spurt to where I was now 6-foot-4, 205 pounds, is what the coaches liked. Also, I had worked hard and I was a good practice player. I jumped in there, I was picking up stuff being on the scout team, and I was happy to do it.

"After the season, Bob King called me into his office and said, *We're going to have to give up a lot of our scholarships, and we're going to be called the 'Football for Fun Bunch,' with a lot of guys playing for free. But, one of the scholarships I have I want to offer to you.* That gave me a college education. Otherwise, there's no way my parents could have paid for it."

Wyche's father worked as a traveling salesman and his mother was a secretary, so there wasn't discretionary income for four years of college – or meal money for Sam. "If I didn't get that scholarship, I would have stayed in college, but I would have had to do it intermittently. I would have had to go out and get a job, work for a semester, and then maybe go to school for the next semester. I usually worked two summer jobs – I would do anything I could, I saved every penny. When I needed it, I sold blood every month for $15. I was a member of ROTC, so I got $15 a month for what was called laundry money. That gave me $30 a month and a little bit of dating money, although our dates were generally hanging around campus together because we just didn't have the money to do a lot of the other things. I stayed in Greenville and helped build the student union at Furman over the summer for two reasons. Number one, I needed the money, but also that kept me close to (future wife) Jane, who I was dating at that point. I was in love with her and I didn't want her going back home to all her old boyfriends."

Wyche became a school leader off the football field as well, volunteering for charity work and earning spots as the President of the Fellowship of Christian Athletes and President of the Furman junior class. "The school put me in a position where I had a chance to try out for a lot of those opportunities and feel the success of my efforts. That stuck with me all the way through my life. When I started playing and then coaching in the pros, it's so ingrained in you that you don't even think about it. Your attention to detail becomes even sharper, and the word *anticipation* becomes a primary motivator in everything you do, what time you get to work, how late you stay, and everything else."

Wyche certainly cherished the scholarship and the chances it afforded him to build a future. "I was just grateful to be there, to have an opportunity to finish college. I made that scholarship through hard work – and I actually enjoyed the challenge. I took it on as a question of my manhood in my mind. I was as fearful of flunking out as I was about making the football team as a freshman. It would have been such a blow to my ego to not be able to make it as a college student academically. I made good grades, but I worried about every class I took. In Spanish, we had an excellent teacher, but she was tough as nails. If you walked in that class, there was no more English being spoken, it was all Spanish. I used to sit in the stairwell of the dorm to find a quiet place and try to memorize my Spanish for the next day. I knew I wouldn't have time to stop and check my notes in class because everything was in Spanish.

"So, I went through the fear of not making football, the fear of not making it academically and what, in my mind, would have been a disgrace to come home and say, *I didn't make it*, partly because my brother Bubba was having such good success at the University of Tennessee on a full scholarship. I was competing with him as much as I was competing with my circumstances. We were very competitive growing up. We didn't say, *Pass the salt*. We said, *You better give me the salt or I'm coming across the table right now*. Having to go back and face Mom and Dad and Bubba and my high school friends, I'd have to admit I wasn't good enough. That was a motivation for me rather than tearing down my confidence. My confidence grew at every stage. The work is confidence in one respect, but it is a realization of what hard work will bring if you just stick with it. Along the way, the pressure of potential failure just made me stronger."

Wyche applied that pressure to himself as early as the spring before he enrolled at Furman. Frank Jurnigan, Wyche's golf coach and football coach at North Fulton, give him a frank assessment of what he would be facing at the next level. "I can remember sitting on the bank of the driving range and saying to him, *Coach, I'm going to play college football.* Coach sincerely said – and I don't blame him for saying this – he said, *Sam, don't get your hopes up on that. You're not going to play college football. You know, there are a lot of other players out there that are better than you. They're going to be the ones who move up to the next level.* Well, he couldn't have motivated me more. I said, *Yes, I am. By golly, yes, I am.*"

Wyche backed up his words and was the Paladins' starting quarterback for his junior and senior seasons. His final year was injury-plagued as he broke the pointer finger on his right hand (his throwing hand) the first game of the season vs. Davidson. That limited his abilities – and the looks he would get from pro scouts. "I threw a pass, and my hand came down on somebody's helmet and broke right on the knuckle. They put it back in place and taped it to my middle finger, and I played the rest of the game and the rest of the season with three fingers and a thumb. I got the nickname of 'Three-Fingered Sam.' I was able to grip the ball, adjust it, and throw passes when necessary. Then, with four minutes to play in my senior season in Charleston against the Citadel, I drop back to pass, one player grabs me by the top of my shoulder pads, and when I bend over, somebody else hits me from behind. It's a legal hit, but it broke three vertebrae and two transverse processes in my lower back. Before I hit the ground, I'm screaming because I knew I was hurt. They put me on a stretcher and took me off. Because it was my spine, you have a potential of being paralyzed if you move in the wrong way.

"They took me to the hospital in Charleston and eventually, because I was in real good shape, the muscles around the spine basically became a cast. They put a steel, riveted girdle on me, and that held my back straight. My professors at Furman allowed me to stand up in the back of the room and walk back and forth because I couldn't sit more than a couple of minutes before I had to get up. I graduated from Furman a damaged piece of goods with only three good fingers on my passing hand and broken bones in my lower back. My back healed beautifully, I graduated, and I had a chance to play in the Continental Football League."

Wyche followed Jane, an elementary school teacher, to Martins Ferry, Oh., landed a special education teaching job in the school district, and played across the river for the CFL's Wheeling (W.V.) Ironmen. Wyche and the team practiced two nights a week and played Sunday evenings, earning $180 per game. Seeing no future in that league or as a teacher, Wyche decided to use his business degree at Furman as a hospital administrator. But then football beckoned again. "A former Furman coach who was now at the University of South Carolina said they needed another graduate assistant. He said, *We'll pay for your education. You can get your MBA and help us with football. You'll be like a gofer coach, an assistant's assistant.*"

After years of dirty work at Furman, Wyche didn't hesitate to take the opportunity at Carolina. And then he caught a break by being paired with a future College Football Hall of Famer. "They assigned me to a young defensive backfield coach named Lou Holtz who was maybe the greatest recruiter I have ever been around anywhere. My job was to be his manservant, basically, and run plays in practice for the scout squad. Since I was only about 23 years old, I was still able to play, and still wanted to play. I'd be the scout team quarterback for whoever we played that week. I was watching and learning everything and getting better as a player. When the pro scouts started to come around looking at the South Carolina players during practice, I'd leap in front of them and almost elbow them out of the way. I would point and say, *See that telephone pole?* and I would throw a pass and hit the telephone pole. The scouts would then say, *What's your name again?*"

Wyche caught the eye of the Cincinnati Bengals, an AFL expansion team in 1968 who would then join the NFL in 1970.

Undrafted and unknown to most of the Bengals coaches and players, Wyche was back in walk-on mode scrambling to make an impression and, hopefully, the final roster for the first-year club. "We started with five quarterbacks in training camp, and of course I was the last one for every drill. I prayed every day I wouldn't get cut because I didn't want to have to go back to South Carolina and say that I only made it two days or two weeks of camp. One guy would get cut, they'd bring in another quarterback, and I was still there.

"I got a phone call from (assistant coach) Jackie Powers at South Carolina. He said, *Sam, we need to know, are you coming back, or do you think you're going to make the team? Because we've got to get another graduate assistant if you're not coming back.* I said, *Coach, how fast do you need to know?*, and he said in the next day or two. I told him I'd go ask (Bengals owner and head coach) Paul Brown that question because I don't know whether I'm just raw meat in case of an injury or if I'm a real prospect.

"I'm planning on talking to the coach who's won a bunch of NFL championships before the Super Bowl was in place. I'm pretty nervous about this. A free agent is like a professional walk-on. You're not drafted. Nobody spent any money on you. You're cheap labor. So, I'm a free agent asking a Hall of Fame coach, *Coach, do I have a chance to make this team? If I've got a chance, even if it's a long shot, I'm staying right here and I will give it my best shot. But if you're just keeping me around in case there's a couple of injuries and you need me to finish practice, I think I'd like to go on with my life's work.*

"He said, *Sam, I'll tell you what I'll do. We play the Houston Oilers coming up* (in the final preseason game), *and I'll start you. I'll give you a chance to take that first snap and answer your question after the game.* Well, I had a good game. Paul called me in the next day and said, *Looking at the film, you're not just raw meat. You have a chance to make this team. I'm not promising you will. No guarantees. But you have a chance.* I said, *That's all I want to know.* I called South Carolina and I told them thank you, but they better go get another guy."

Wyche was placed on the Bengals practice squad to start the year, meaning he would work out with the team and attend meetings during the week but not suit up on game days. "I still had no life. We lived on a very minimal amount of money. We were just surviving in an apartment with a couple of chairs and rental furniture." Between 1968-76, Wyche played 47 games for Cincinnati, Washington, Detroit, and St. Louis, completing 116 passes for 1,748 yards and 12 touchdowns. Wyche then embarked on that well-documented coaching career that took him from San Francisco to Cincinnati to Tampa to Buffalo with a pair of visits to the Super Bowl.

Wyche said he was never tempted to take an easier road or give up on his dream for college football and then the pros. "One way or the other, however long it took, that was my mindset. I thought everybody thought that way; obviously they don't. But I was going to make sure I did."

Author's Note: Sam Wyche passed away Jan. 2, 2020, three days short of his 75th birthday. Our condolences to Jane, Sam's family, friends, and many admirers.

CHAPTER 20

"Rejection Is Just An Opportunity"

Elimu Nelson
Syracuse, Basketball
Actor/Writer/Producer

One constant in Elimu Nelson's life – besides his unique look that sparked a career as a model-turned-actor/writer/producer – is converting rejections into triumphs.

Go back to his senior year at Milton (Mass.) High School in 1991. A standout in the classroom, on the soccer field, and in his favorite sport of basketball, Nelson was weighing his post-graduation academic and athletic options. During a recruiting visit to Brandeis University (Mass.), Nelson sat down with the basketball coach. "I remember him asking me, *If you could play any place, where would you play?* I said, *Sir, I have always wanted to play for Syracuse.* He launched in right there and said, *You won't be able to play there. You're not strong enough.* And then he gave me all these other reasons why I wouldn't be able to play there."

That same year during a tour for prospective students on the Syracuse campus, Nelson broke off from the group to visit the Manley Fieldhouse where the Orange basketball team practiced. He crossed paths there with Syracuse assistant coach Wayne Morgan. "I remember I had on a pair of shorts and sneakers, and I said to him, *Hey, how are you doing? My name is Elimu Nelson and I want to play here.* He looked me up and down and he said, *You're too skinny. You will never play here.* Well, I'm one of those people if you tell me I can't do something, I'm going to do it."

So Nelson enrolled at Syracuse that fall but instead of participating in team tryouts, he watched those sessions from the sidelines with a friend. Of course legendary Syracuse head coach Jim Boeheim was in the gymnasium as well, but Nelson didn't think they would meet. "As I was watching I thought, *I'm as good as any of these guys that are trying out.* When the tryout ends, Coach Boeheim is walking by us two freshmen in college. He looks at us and nods his head and says, *How are you doing?* I was blown away that he actually spoke to me. That's when I said to myself, *Next year I'm going to go try out.*"

Nelson learned that prior to tryouts and official practices, any student could participate in preseason conditioning and play pickup games with the Syracuse scholarship players – or at least *try* to get onto the court. "Four of my friends and I ran sprints with the team – we did everything we could do," Nelson said. "But for the games, the players were running it. What I learned very quickly is that if you're in a regular gym and you call 'next,' you get on the court. But in these games, these players are looking to get better for the upcoming season. So one team would lose, we'd call 'next', and they would say, *Naw – we're going to go ahead and run it again.* You have all these regular students that are dying to play but they're not."

Undaunted, Nelson kept showing up at the court and made good on his commitment to try out for the 1992-93 club. He didn't make the team, but this rejection came with some encouragement from 'Cuse assistant Bernie Fine – even if Nelson didn't see it that way at the time. "He told me, *Hey, if we need somebody to practice, we're going to call you.* I was pissed off because I didn't make the team. I wasn't thinking that this could turn out to be something good."

Nelson worked on his game and his strength and, in part because of his exposure during those tryouts, became accepted by the scholarship players the next preseason. "A couple of my friends are still with me and we're running those sprints, and then those games come again. This time instead of me sitting, the players say, *No, no, no. He's playing with us this year.* So now, my friends are on the sideline, but I'm playing all the time with these guys. I remember the first game I got caught under the basket and Luke Jackson dunked on me. He said, *Welcome to the team.* I was mad. I was getting elbowed and pushed by everybody." Future NBA first round draft pick John Wallace was the next to challenge Nelson, but this time he was ready. "Wallace was going up to dunk it, and I met him in the air up at the rim, blocked his shot, and my strength cut him down. I was kind of in the mix with everything after that."

When coaches got word of Nelson's preseason performance, that made his tryout that fall a formality. But for Nelson the moment was still emotional after such an uphill climb. "I remember going back to the locker room and looking at the locker with my name on it. I'm holding my jersey and a couple guys walked in and congratulated me. It hit me. *Wow! I did it!* When I walked back to the gym, I went over to Coach Morgan. I said, *Coach, do you remember me? I walked in here in my senior year of high school and you said I'd never play here.* He said, *Yeah, I do, and my apologies.* I remember how intense practices were. I'd come home and just pass out in my bed for three or four hours. Then I'd wake up and go back to do it again."

Nelson didn't view earning a roster spot as his finish line. His next goal was to earn quality playing time despite Boeheim's history of using walk-ons only as practice players. That meant for Nelson the 1993-94 season opener vs. Tennessee presented another goal – and another obstacle. "The day of the game I go into the training room to get my ankles taped. I put my ankle up on the table, and the trainer looks at me and says, *What are you doing? Walk-ons never play. You don't need your ankles taped. Get out of here.* In warm-ups we're shooting around and I'm taking shots. I forgot who pulled me to the side and said, *No – you make sure you pass it out to the starters. They have to get warm, not you.*"

With about two minutes to play in the first half, Boeheim signaled for Nelson to check in. "I was really nervous, but I made a defensive play then I passed the ball to Luke Jackson who was wide open, and he dunked it. At halftime after coach talked with us about adjustments, I walked back into the training room, put my foot on the table, looked at the trainer, and sort of smiled. He nodded to me and said, *I'm sorry, E, but walk-ons never play,* and then he taped me up."

Nelson saw action in nine games that junior season, playing a total of 40 minutes, scoring six points, and grabbing nine rebounds as Syracuse (23-9) advanced to the NCAA Sweet 16. The following season the Orange (20-10) lost to Arkansas in overtime in the second round of the NCAAs. That year Nelson played in eight games, registering 18 minutes and four points.

Nelson was now just one semester away from earning his degree, so many doubted he would return to the club for a final season which meant an extra semester of classes. They underestimated Nelson's passion and determination. "There was a moment Bernie (Fine) said to me, *We can talk to the boys over at (Division II) Le Moyne if you want. It's right down the street. You'll start. You'll play. We hate to see you sitting on the bench.* I was like, *Hell, no. I'm going to play here.* I didn't think it was out of the realm of possibility. Over the summer, I called Coach Boeheim and said, *I'm in shape, I'm going to come back, and I would love to play.* He said, *If anybody deserves a scholarship it's you.*"

That year Nelson not only had his schooling paid for, but he also played 50 minutes over 16 games, totaling 17 points, seven rebounds, two blocked shots, and a steal.

In the semifinals of the 1995 Rainbow Classic in Honolulu, Nelson experienced what he calls the highlight of his career. "We were beating them (Rhode Island) pretty good, and I got in the game with around four minutes to go. I remember warming up that day, practicing on those rims, and just making every shot I put up. It was like the rims were twice as big. When I get in, we run a play, and I wind up getting the ball on the right wing behind the three-point line and put it up. Swish. The bench goes nut and so does the entire arena. Next possession, I get the ball again, drive to the basket, and get fouled. I get to the foul line, and the entire arena is chanting *Nelson! Nelson! Nelson!* I made the first free throw. Because I had dreadlocks and maybe only three other players in the NCAA had them at that time, crowds all over would be interested. This crowd was yelling, *Shake your hair!* So in between foul shots I did just that, and the crowd went crazy. If there was footage of that, you would see me start to laugh at the foul line. I missed the next foul shot – four points now with about two minutes left in the game. I came down on the next possession, shook my defender, and pulled up for a jumper in the middle of the key – six points. Next possession, I drive by the same defender and hit a layup down the middle – eight points. The last possession, my point guard and friend David Patrick passed me the ball with maybe three seconds left, and the crowd begged me to shoot it, but I passed it.

"After the game I was sitting with my crew of bench players and we were laughing and eating McDonald's when the media came in. We were about to head to the locker room like usual because no one ever spoke to us when I got rushed by several outlets asking about my game. I did interviews and wound up coming into the locker room a little late. Coach B is giving his speech, looks at me, and says, *Elimu, did you have family out there tonight or what?* and he laughed. It was a compliment for sure. Right after, John Wallace turns around and gives me a pound and just looks at me. His look said it all."

Later that year, in a mid-season loss at West Virginia, Boeheim played Nelson in the first half again because the SU guards were struggling. "I had a steal and a couple rebounds, but I also forced a three and it didn't go in. We were losing, so at halftime we know we're all going to get yelled at. Coach walks in and shouts at me, *If I ever effing play you again, do not ever effing do that play! Other than that, good effing job.*" Syracuse (29-9) was the NCAA title runner-up that year, falling to Kentucky in the finals, 76-67, in East Rutherford, N.J.

Upon graduating with a degree to Speech Communications, Nelson tried to expand upon a modeling career he began during his undergrad days. "I took my little modeling book I had made in Syracuse, I moved in with a friend of mine and his mom in Harlem, and I went on every single open call in New York for six months. At almost every audition they asked if I could act. At one they said

I had the exact look they wanted for their TV show, but I hadn't taken any acting classes. So, my manager sat me down and said, *We're going to get you an acting coach and we're going to have him go over the scene with you. We have to put this on tape.* I went home and memorized my lines. The coach meets my manager and me to record the scene. I wish I could have seen the look on his face when he heard me doing my lines. I was awful, and I didn't get the part."

An ordinary person might have given up at that point, but Nelson seized upon the opportunity despite the negative feedback. "I decided if I'm going to be in television and film, I'm going out to L.A." That was more than 20 years ago. Nelson developed his acting and writing skills behind the scenes and via one audition at a time. "With acting and writing, it's a lot of hours that people don't see. It's like playing a lot of pick-up or you're in the gym by yourself putting in these hours that nobody sees. It's going to classes, working the muscles on your own. If you're fortunate enough to have a good agent getting you in for a lot of auditions, that helps you understand what falling on your face is like, and you learn how to turn out a room whether you're testing for a film versus a drama on TV or a sitcom. I'm constantly 'on the grind' of this profession, and it's all-encompassing. That's something I transfer from basketball – the dedication and the amount of practice. From when I came in as a walk-on to where I ended up being as a scholarship player skill-wise, it was like night and day. That was from a lot of practice and doing things the correct way.

"When you play at the Division I level, the thing that immediately jumps out at you is the intensity. It's not just fun. It's a need for something much deeper and much more important. Something is always motivating them and always moving them. In this profession, there have been countless projects that I can tell you about where I thought I was the best actor and I didn't get the job. It definitely hurt, but it toughens your skin. Hollywood is so competitive because there's at least five of us trying out for every role. The intensity in this industry comes from rejection. But, to me, rejection is just an opportunity. After you're told 'no,' you need to focus your energy to keep yourself in shape and go to class. Then you study. Then you get more auditions. Then you study for those.

You go and you nail it and then you don't get it. It doesn't matter what any of them say. It just matters what you believe because eventually the right thing is going to find you. If I had listened to what the industry has told me, then I would have been crushed."

Instead, Nelson has flourished in ultracompetitive Hollywood. His TV credits include *Modern Family, Castle, House of Lies, Criminal Minds, Hit the Floor, The Shield, Private Practice, The Young & The Restless, The Rookie, Now We're Talking, Tommy,* and *Station 19.* Among his credits for film acting are *Love Don't Cost a Thing, #Truth, Gates of Darkness,* the independent film *Things Never Said,* the horror movie *Bleed,* and the Lifetime movie *Dear Secret Santa.* He also wrote, produced, and co-starred in the short film *Doorways* which showed at the 2012 Cannes Film Festival.

"Acting is very much a direct result of my basketball career. I look at it as a microcosm of playing for Syracuse. Starting back in high school, that was my intention. Even when I was 12, I always wanted to play for Syracuse. So, when I finally got there, it had been years of me intending this and working for it. For my career, it was years of me intending to get where I wanted to go. I had to keep swinging, stand up long enough, ride out the tough times, and trust it was going to work out.

"Like anything in life, you work, work, work at something, then you see the result. If I'm working on my jump shot enough, then my jump shot will get better. You control the things that you can control. So, if I'm studying, which I constantly am, if I'm staying in shape, then I'll be working. I've learned to let it go as long as I'm prepared. That's when your journey becomes more fun. Once your journey becomes fun, things start flowing for you."

CHAPTER 21

"There's Nothing Better Than Beating The Odds"

Blue Kinander Kelly
University of Tulsa, Golf
Vice President, Electri-Flex

Why would the University of Tulsa, a national power in women's golf, show interest in a high school senior who admitted she was only just learning what tournaments she should be entering? And why would that kid from Chicago want to leave the Windy City to study and golf on the plains of Oklahoma? Furthermore, why would she turn down scholarship offers from multiple other schools, including the nearby University of Illinois, to *pay* to walk on at Tulsa?

"Yeah, that's what my dad wanted to know," recalled Blue Kinander Kelly, who did all of the above – plus win an NCAA national championship – before returning home to help steer the Kinander family business towards a successful future.

Kinander Kelly was recruited to Tulsa by Dale McNamara, a coaching legend who formed the Golden Hurricane program in 1974 and led them to the first of four national titles just six years later. "I met Dale at a driving range in Florida by accident," Kinander Kelly said. "She was recruiting one of my friends I was competing alongside. She was intrigued by my personality, and I was certainly intrigued by what she and the Tulsa program were all about. I thought she would help me grow as a person. So, when I went back home, I told my parents, *I'm going to Tulsa.*"

In 1986, Kinander Kelly visited the school and bonded with her future teammates, but she saw a huge gap between her golf skills and the TU All-Americans. Tulsa had won national championships in 1980 and 1982 and was ranked #1 in the country for most of the 1985-86 season. "I was totally in over my head – I wasn't their caliber at all," Kinander Kelly said. "My odds of making it there were probably two out of 10. This was a team that was basically a breeding ground for the LPGA, and I had absolutely no right, no future being good enough to play in the LPGA. I had no résumé. I had no great victories nationally. I wasn't even a nationally recognized player. But I chose to compete alongside a group of golfers who were aspiring to be on tour. I was truly intrigued with what it was all about and how much hard work it was going to take.

"I knew if I worked hard enough and I allowed Dale to shape me into the player that she wanted me to be, it was going to happen. I know it's an overdone statement, but anything happens with hard work. If you're determined, if you have a good game plan, if you put in a lot of hard work, and you have the thought that you're not going to be denied, it will truly happen. You have to just keep working harder and keep digging and digging and digging."

Of course Kinander Kelly invested long hours on the practice range and putting green, but she took her development to the next level through cross-training and reading. "I always believed that books were helpful because they gave you a different platform to work from to be a better person and a better golfer. Reading really was a game-changer for me," she said. "I was also into building my strength: running, doing stairs, push-ups, sit-ups, swimming – all those things. That was really different compared to what most other golfers were doing back in the day. Then it was my blood, sweat, and tears on the golf course. I worked with a couple pros, and they really helped me with my swing. And I was usually the last one to leave practice. Whether I was sinking 50 two-foot putts or working on chipping, I was the last one to leave practice. I wanted to put everything possible towards it."

A byproduct of Kinander Kelly's extra effort and improvement was pushing her teammates to elevate their game as well. She didn't realize it at the time, but it was her first foray into servant leadership. "It did make my teammates more accountable because who wants to be beaten by a walk-on?" she said. "Here's this golfer from South Africa on an 80 percent scholarship, and here's this girl from Illinois who doesn't have her skills but is starting to catch up to her. If you're chasing them down and you're the underdog, that makes them work harder. Nobody wants to be beaten by the underdog."

Coach McNamara was so impressed with Kinander Kelly's development that she offered her scholarship money beginning with sophomore year. Kinander Kelly continued to improve, morphing from her underdog role into a consistent starter for the Golden Hurricanes. Tulsa experienced incredible success her final three years, winning the NCAA national championship in 1987-88, finishing as NCAA runner-up in 1988-89, and placing fifth in 1989-90. As a senior, Kinander Kelly placed first at the 1989 Pat Bradley Invitational.

"It was a marvelous four years – it really was," she said. "We traveled a tremendous amount. We were very successful as a team. I made a lot of really great friendships, and I'm still very close to my teammates and Dale. I knew in my heart that Dale was going to be a life-changer for me. The opportunity to be a part of her program was more of a life decision for me rather than thinking *I'm going to get X amount of dollars and take that*. It was a challenge I knew was going to change me for the rest of my life."

One year after graduating from Tulsa with a Liberal Arts degree in 1990, Kinander Kelly returned to the Chicago area to work for the family business, Electri-Flex, a manufacturer of flexible electrical conduits. Now a company Vice President, she drew from her walk-on lessons to help the company endure turbulent times. When Kinander Kelly rejected scholarship offers, she said there was some "chatter" questioning her decision, but she blocked it out. When her father, West Kinander Jr., who served as President of the family-owned company, passed away at age 50 in 1991, critics doubted Kinander Kelly and her two brothers could manage the organization.

"We heard that people were writing us off, saying the company grew under dad's leadership and that we weren't going to go anywhere. My brothers and myself banded together and said, *No, we're not going to hear that. We're going to fight this through. We're going to be determined. We're going to keep this family business. We're going to fight for our employees and work hard and develop our business into the next frontier.* And we have. We've now been in business over 60 years."

Kinander Kelly applies her walk-on lessons both professionally and personally. Her sons are excellent golfers, Tee-K earning a scholarship at Ohio State and Will doing the same at Florida Gulf Coast, thanks in part to their mom's guidance. "I always tell my boys that people are going to tell you you're not good enough, but don't ever listen to it. Don't ever settle for mediocre. Hold onto your dreams and focus on what you want to achieve. Don't listen to the background noises."

Kinander Kelly has helped lead Electri-Flex for 25+ years and was inducted into the Chicago Electric Association Hall of Fame in 2017, which pairs nicely with her NCAA championship team's induction into the Tulsa Athletic Hall of Fame in 2019. Reflecting on her professional career, she's grateful for the lessons learned from her walk-on experience. "If I hadn't done that, I don't think I would be as confident as I am now because there's nothing better than beating the odds. You always have that to lean on – knowing that you beat the odds and you achieved something that nobody thought you could. I think that's a forever lifetime peacefulness that I'll have. You always have that strength, that ammunition in your mind that, *I did it back then and I can beat the odds again.*"

CHAPTER 22

"I Vaulted Myself Into The Unknown"

J.T. Stephens

University of California, Basketball
Managing Director – Technology Investment Banking

If someone approached you on the street and asked, *Psst – wanna buy a watch?*, you'd probably walk past them without even making eye contact. Now imagine if that person had said, *Psst – wanna play basketball at Cal?* You'd think they were joking. That's an only slightly exaggerated version of how J.T. Stephens got his opportunity to walk on to the University of California men's basketball team.

As a sharpshooting high schooler coming off the bench at powerhouse St. Ignatius College Prep in San Francisco, Stephens wasn't recruited. He enrolled at USC (University of Southern California) as a 5-foot-11, 155-pound freshman and served as a manager and occasional practice player for the Trojans after receiving assurances from the coaches that if he grew a few inches (his father was a late bloomer) he had a shot at making the team as a walk-on the following year. That arrangement ended soon after USC parted ways with head coach Charlie Parker late in the 1995-96 season. So, when Stephens played in a well-known Bay Area basketball league that following summer, he was essentially a man without a team.

"I had grown a little bit and spent my freshman year at USC getting stronger and shooting 4,000-5,000 jumpers per week," Stephens recalls. "The additional inches and hard work paid off, and I ended

151

up getting noticed by the athletic director at Cal who was randomly in the stands at one of my games. He told me, *Listen, we're limited on the number of scholarships that we have because of the (coach Todd) Bozeman (NCAA probation) situation, and we need some players on our team. We saw you, and if you want to come to Cal, you can try out. We'll help you get into the school.* This was in August, and I knew that Cal started in a few weeks. I ended up going for it and got into the school three days after classes started. When I went to the tryouts in October, there were over 100 guys in the gym. We started scrimmaging and I was hitting my shots, playing good defense, diving on the floor – all the stuff that coaches care about. The coaches wanted 15 total players on their roster, and I ended up making the team along with a handful of other guys. The whole experience was incredibly exciting – and very surreal."

Stephens never saw extensive game action during his four years as a Golden Bear, but he credits Cal coach Ben Braun for creating a culture where every team member was significant. "He had this structure in practice where there was the starting team and then there was a second team of backups, and those guys would play each other. Then you had the team of walk-ons, and the walk-ons would play whichever team won. So our walk-on team was on the court playing significant minutes every day. It was super fun and competitive – each practice was the equivalent of playing a full game or more. I was playing with talented guys who would ultimately play at the next level, whether it was professionally overseas or in the NBA."

Or the NFL. Stephens recalled a funny yet harrowing encounter with Pro Football Hall of Fame tight end Tony Gonzalez, who played both football and basketball at Cal. During a practice drill, the 6-foot-1, 175-pound Stephens found himself matched up with the 6-foot-5, 240-pound Gonzalez. "Tony gets the ball, sizes me up and starts driving to the basket. I'm thinking, *He's going too fast, he's a little out of control, and this is going to be an easy charge.* But he was coming right at me like we were on the football field – probably thinking, *This guy is about to get run over.* I could see it in his eyes, but for some stupid reason I remember being committed to taking the charge. So, dribbling at full speed, the inevitable happens:

he runs me over. I remember being ready for the impact, but I really wasn't expecting the sheer force of it. He hit me so hard that instead of falling backwards and sliding along the hardwood, my legs came up off the ground and straight into the air. I was airborne flying backwards. It all happened so fast – me flying backwards and him stumbling over me to the ground – that I accidentally kicked him squarely in the nuts. He grimaces and crumbles to the ground like Goliath. Seconds later, he gets up and sprints over to me. I was like 15 feet away and dazed from the whole thing. He grabs me by the jersey, and yells, *I'm going to kick your ass for what you did!* Tony was an awesome guy and a phenomenal teammate, but in this case he was really mad. The coaches jump between us and say, *Hey, Tony, he just took a charge – you bowled the guy over. It was a clean charge!* Things settled down and practice resumed. But I think I'm the only guy that can say he kicked Tony Gonzalez in the nuts and lived to tell about it."

Stephens played hard each practice – even the early years when he wasn't always on Cal's travel team – and dedicated himself in the weight room and during the off-season. He gained 40 pounds to top out at 195 as a senior, and he spent summers honing his skills by coaching at basketball camps. Cal's coaches considered awarding him a scholarship as a senior for the 1999-2000 season, but foot surgery that sidelined him for five months during his junior season set Stephens back considerably. Undaunted, he returned from that injury and played his senior season, earning a spot on the travel squad for most trips.

Stephens said the top experience of his Cal career came at USC, his former school. "My grandparents, uncles, and cousins were living in L.A., and coach Braun had me travel for the UCLA and USC games so they could see me in uniform. That's the kind of guy he was. We were beating USC by over 20, and he puts me in for the last couple minutes. I end up hitting a shot right before the final buzzer from Steph Curry range. I shot it right in front of the Cal bench, and right behind the bench are the seats where my family and several of my USC friends were sitting. They all went crazy! That was the only three I hit during my college years. It was a big deal for me and one of my fondest memories. Just the fact that I got on the court in front of my family and friends validated all the hard work I had put in to get there."

After graduation, Stephens worked in the investment banking, e-commerce, and software sectors and earned an MBA at The Wharton School at the University of Pennsylvania. Today he's a managing director at UBS, leading the Internet and Consumer Software Practice after a near-decade run at RBC Capital Markets, where he rose from Associate to Director level. Stephens said his walk-on experience at Cal still influences him more than 20 years after his playing days ended.

"During college, I was at maximum overload at all times. My four years as a student-athlete at Cal required a huge amount of time and energy, and I took both my education and my basketball pretty seriously. I felt fortunate and blessed to get into Cal, so I figured I should make the best out of a world-class education. I typically woke up every morning at around seven, even after grueling practices. I'd start classes at eight, have practice or strength and conditioning in the afternoons and then do homework late into the evenings. It was a year-round commitment.

"The whole experience showed me that hard work really does pay off, and I would say that's been a driving force in my career to date. When I stood on center court in Haas Pavilion next to my parents on Senior Day, that moment probably represented the pinnacle of my athletic career. My walk-on experience at Cal, and all the trials and tribulations that came along with it, set the stage for my future and gave me a road map for how to approach the rest of my life. I knew I wasn't going to be a pro athlete, so instead I took the fundamentals I learned around teamwork, diversity, communication, dedication, and commitment and adopted them as the key operating principles to manage my life. To succeed at being a good father, raising a family, developing a career, maintaining friendships – whatever it may be – you need to appreciate that it's going to be a process and require a lot of hard work.

"I believe my experience as a student-athlete served me well by teaching me the importance of a consistent daily routine. Today I typically get up at six, help get my kids ready for school, eat breakfast, and then go to the office – or to the airport. A lot of times I work until ten, eleven, or twelve at night because I have one of those crazy finance jobs that you read about. People say, *I can't believe you never burn out.* I've thought a lot about this, and I think it's because I've effectively been working at this pace every day since I was 18 years old. You can do it if you get yourself in that walk-on mindset and you keep your mind and body trained."

Stephens said he's learned that kind of personal development is more important than the diplomas on his wall. He found immediate success in finance even though his undergrad degree is in English Literature. "I honestly had no business landing a job in investment banking out of college. When I graduated, it was the height of the tech bubble and investment banks were hiring undergraduates in droves to work on all the IPOs and M&A deals that were taking place. I certainly had limited technical knowledge compared to most everybody else in my class who were business, accounting, or math majors, but my firm was willing to give me a shot because I was a four-year varsity athlete. Then the tech bubble popped, and banks started reducing their workforces. My bank let go a lot of really smart people in my analyst class. But I was one of the guys that made the cut. To be honest with you, I think it was just because I worked harder than anybody else and was a quick learner. In basketball, or any sport for that matter, physical gifts are important but only last so long. In the professional world, if you work hard, learn as much as you can, and are a strategic thinker, you can pretty much compete with anybody. You should always be looking for that angle. You should always look for a new, efficient way to do something."

The walk-on experience not only benefited Stephens as an individual performer but as a leader. "Coach Braun and his staff demonstrated a strong sense of commitment to the walk-on group. We'd have a game coming up against Arizona, and the coaches would have the walk-ons learn their playbook and watch game film. Then as a group, we'd go into the gym before practice started, and we'd run through all the plays. There was a time when I knew the offenses for every Pac-10 team we played against. Coach gave us this unique responsibility to help the team win and, as a result of him entrusting us for a critical part of game preparation, we were accepted by the rest of the scholarship players as a core part of the team. You couldn't help but develop mutual respect for your coaches, teammates, and staff, and I think that is one of the reasons why we went to the Sweet 16 my freshman year and won the NIT my junior year. As I think about the way I work today, I have a lot of analysts, associates, vice presidents, and support staff that work on my team. I try to make sure that I treat all of them well. My reviews year-in and year-out are, *He's a great mentor* or *He's a good team player.* That's something I'm proud of and strive for every year. A team environment where everyone is valued and respected starts at the top."

But Stephens wouldn't have learned all those lessons if he had shrugged off the surprise summer offer to bolt USC for a chance to play at Cal. "I vaulted myself into the unknown. I dropped what I was doing to go pursue this crazy dream. It took a great amount of risk and a bunch of hard work, but it paid off.

"I specifically remember the second I got called by coach Braun and was told that I made the team at Cal. You know when you're having a near-death experience, there's that concept that your life flashes before your eyes? Imagine that same thing happening, but for your basketball career. I had these visions of dribbling a ball for the first time, going to the park as a little kid with my dad, playing on all these random courts and gyms around San Francisco, and all the great teammates and coaches I had in grammar school and high school. The hours and hours that I put into achieving my dream were 100% worth it."

CHAPTER 23

"Oh, Yes You Can!"

Charlie Grimes
Western Michigan, Track & Field
Collegiate Coach, Athletic Director, & Pastor

You know how the phrase "born with a silver spoon" represents a perpetually wealthy person – the privileged guy who always has the fancy cars, the latest fashion, and every luxury item you can think of? Charlie Grimes is *not* that guy. The only silver spoon that's part of his life is in his bowl of soup, and that's limited to when he visits a restaurant.

Grimes was so underfunded during his four years as a track and field walk-on at Western Michigan that he was thrilled to receive sneakers that were at least a decade old. "Coach (Jack) Shaw would give me what I call 'new old stock,'" Grimes said. "He would pull out a pair of shoes that he just found in a storage shed somewhere or in his equipment area, and say, *Hey, Grimes, what's your shoe size? Ten? Here.* I literally high jumped in these old Converse shoes that were – and this was during the early 90s – probably brand new back in 1975. So, our team colors were brown and gold and I would show up for a meet with these stupid red and white Converse shoes on."

Grimes said he mastered perseverance and resourcefulness during his walk-on experience, and his squeeze-every-drop-out-of-whatever-you've-been-blessed-with approach paid off across 22 years as a successful track and field coach and Athletic Director at Malone University, a private, Christian Division II college in Canton, Oh.

Grimes attended Western Michigan after starring athletically at tiny Gobles (Mich.) High School, located about 20 miles west of WMU's campus in Kalamazoo. A four-year varsity letter-winner in football, basketball, and track, Grimes twice earned his way to the Michigan state track championships. Coach Shaw learned about Grimes' all-around athletic ability and asked if he would consider enrolling in the school and training for the decathlon as a nonscholarship member of the team. "Being a child of the 70s, I identified with Bruce Jenner as a kid," Grimes said. "I idolized the Olympians and I thought, *Wow, this is the biggest challenge of my life!* Coach Shaw said, *We don't have anything for you except a chance.* That was the kind of thing that motivated me. That was all I needed to hear. I appreciated their interest in me. It's just nice to be asked to the dance, as they say."

Grimes said when he arrived on campus, coach Shaw was less than impressed with his abilities. "I really believe his intent for me was, once he saw me, to become a really good manager for the team," Grimes said. "He didn't really want to have any relationship with me and didn't have any plans for me as an athlete. At first I thought, *What did I get myself into here?* But coming from a small school where we had limited resources, for me to have access to an indoor track, a pole vault pit, hurdles, shot-puts and javelins, all of the tools of a track and field team, plus a training room to go ask questions about aches and pains and get treatment – those opportunities were really precious to me. I was grateful to have a sweat suit. Some of the other guys whose high schools provided those things took them for granted. But I didn't. I thought, *This is all I need.*"

Grimes trained with the scholarship athletes but wasn't participating in meets as a freshman, leading others to doubt his future at WMU. "I can remember visiting back home and what I experienced was that people would say, *Oh, that's cute. But you're not going to make it, of course. Nobody from Gobles does that.*" Even as Grimes improved his sophomore year and scored two points in the conference meet, the doubters persisted. Grimes chose to convert their words into fuel.

"I had an assistant coach say to me, *You probably ought to look at transferring someplace else because you work hard and you're going to be pretty good. Why don't you go somewhere they will appreciate you and utilize you?* What I heard from that was, *You've got a lot of potential.* I finally had some credibility from a college coach. I never took him up on transferring. I never investigated that. I never looked back. I was into a routine at that point in my career, and it was very exciting to have that kind of level of success. Whatever you call it, it's two points in the conference meet, but that was a lot more than some scholarship guys were getting. I was happy to be known for bringing persistence and dedication and loyalty every day, no matter what.

"Then this joke started to form – which I still took as a compliment – that I wasn't any good at any one thing so they put me in everything. *We're going to put Grimes in javelin. He's not going to win. He's not even going to be in the top four or five, but can he take seventh? Can he take eighth? Yeah, probably. Well, what about the long jump? Same thing. High jump? Same thing. Pole vault? Same thing. Running the relay? Same thing. The 400? The 1500? Thousand-meter indoors? Okay, put him in the long hurdle race. That's not even part of the decathlon, but okay.*

"Then in the third year, I start loving track so much that I said, *What about the triple jump?* There was only one guy on our team in the triple jump and he jumps 50 feet. Could I be the second guy? So, I tried the triple jump and I would go 44 feet. I realized I could place in the meet in the triple jump if they put me in there. So, I would go to these meets and would be in seven, eight, nine different events. That was just the open events, but I would end up with eighth place, seventh place, sixth place, fifth place – whatever I could do on that day. But when you add it all up over each event, I'd score seven or eight points in the meet. I thought that was pretty good for a kid that's just doing a little of everything."

Grimes wasn't earning any individual medals, but he was contributing whatever he could to the Broncos. "The heart of a walk-on is to be resourceful," he said. "You say to yourself, *This is what I have, and I'm going to make the best of what I have. I learned* persistence. The setbacks on a daily basis were temporary, and everything really came down to what are you going to do today? What are you going to do to make yourself a little bit better today than you were yesterday? If you can just live there, you'll be all right even if some coaches and other people are telling me that it's just not going to work. The early part of my college career, I must confess, I was motivated to prove other people wrong. My hometown didn't think I could make it. The coach didn't think I can make it. I'm going to make sure that they know that I can do this."

Grimes eventually won over the entire coaching staff with his efforts – including Shaw, a man who wasn't easy to please. "I can remember sitting in his office and him saying, *It's only certain types of guys I can coach, and you're that type of guy.* One day he had me work out with the throwers, then go lift weights, then work with the hurdlers, then I grabbed a pole and joined the pole vaulters for a severe workout. And then coach Shaw says, *Grimes, get over here and let's end today with your running workout.* I'm looking at four or five different workouts in one day and by the end of it I'm hanging over a garbage can throwing up. So, coach Shaw comes over to me, I'm spitting and sputtering, and he says, *Well, what did you have for lunch?* I looked at him and said, *I had nails.* He goes, *You're one tough S.O.B.*"

Grimes' extra efforts transformed him from an afterthought to a reliable contributor. He was a seven-time placewinner in the Mid-American Conference (MAC) indoor and outdoor track championships and set the University of Tennessee track record for the decathlon 1500 meter run. Additionally, he was twice honored by the MAC as an All-Conference Academic Award recipient.

Prior to Grimes' final year in the Western Michigan program, Shaw offered him a partial scholarship that would cover room and board for the year. "And I turned him down," Grimes said.

Wait – what? After investing hundreds of hours and breaking his body for the good of the team, Grimes turned down $3,000 of *free* money?

"I told him that I started this saga, this odyssey, on my own for my own reasons, and I'm going to finish it on my own for my own reasons. For the next seven years I paid my student loans back, but I don't regret that. I certainly don't. It was well worth it. I wouldn't change anything as far as that experience and what it means to me and my family, because today I can see the results."

After earning his bachelor's in Exercise Science from Western in 1993, Grimes served as a graduate assistant track coach at Eastern Michigan University. He received a master's in Exercise Physiology and Biomechanics in 1996 and jumped to NAIA member Malone the next year when he was named their head track and field coach. Grimes led that program to unprecedented heights, capturing 11 AMC (American Mideast Conference) championships and nine NCCAA (National Christian College Athletic Association) National Championships. In 2008, he was promoted to Athletic Director to oversee a staff of 60 coaches and administrators and serve nearly 500 student-athletes. In 2010, Grimes helped Malone complete its move from the NAIA into NCAA Division II.

Malone has an enrollment around 1,500 students – a far cry from Western Michigan's 23,000 – which means limited resources for Grimes, his coaches, and Pioneer student-athletes. But Grimes' walk-on experience prepared him for the role. "There is always somebody out there who has it better than us and, trust me, my coaches are always very quick to bring those situations to my attention. But this creates in us a discipline of being thankful, appreciating what we do have, and being resourceful with it. I've had to say to a coach, *Listen, there is famine in the land. Here is your budget. Here are your bags of food. That's it. You have to figure out how to get it done with this. I love you. I appreciate you. I'm your fan, but you had better figure out how to get* this *done with* that. *This is what we have, and there's no more. It's not like we have some evil administration sitting above us on a pot of gold and they just won't give it to us. There is no more money. That's it.*

"That was essentially my experience (at Western Michigan) showing up at a dorm room with two suitcases, a bag of clothes, and nothing else. If coach Shaw would have tried to give those old

Converses to a scholarship high jumper, the guy would have probably said, *I'm not doing this. I don't want those shoes.* There was no shame in it for me because I needed them. This plays out for me especially when I meet with students today. Students say to me, *My coach is harsh.* I say, *Okay, he says things that may hurt your feelings. You have to learn how to figure out how to put your cavalier armor on every day and go to practice for the right reasons. If you're only doing this because he's going to talk nice to you, then you're probably in the wrong place. We know that's not why you're playing.*

"And I bring them along saying, in essence, *Yes, you can. You can do this even if he's going to be kind of a hard guy to you. What will happen in life when you end up facing a hard guy? That person may be your boss. Then what are you going to do?* My walk-on experience under a hard guy for years is very helpful with this. By the end of the conversation, the student says, *Yeah, I can do this. I've proven to myself that I can.*"

In 2019, after 22 years in higher education, Grimes transitioned to become a pastor. He said coaching and teaching people in life isn't much different than he experienced in the university setting. He utilizes his experience in leadership every day leading and organizing, counseling and mentoring.

"When anyone says to me, *I can't do this. I don't have enough,* I respond, *Oh, yes you can! I know you can.* I've turned it into a positive to say, *This probably isn't really as bad as you think it is, and I know you're hurting, but you have more in you than you think! I know you're not feeling well. I know what that feels like. Trust me. You can do it.*"

CHAPTER 24

"Create An Opportunity"

Jon Harris
DePaul, Basketball
Founder & CEO, AthLife

Jon Harris stood under six-feet tall, weighed less than 150 pounds, and wasn't the best player on his basketball team at Paul V. Moore High School in Central Square, N.Y., near Syracuse. But Harris, a lifelong DePaul basketball fan – he rocked a Blue Demons royal blue Starter jacket (this was the early 90s after all) – was determined to attend the Chicago college and get involved with their legendary hoops program. Harris figured no scouting service was going to recommend him to the Division I powerhouse, so he took the initiative to call head coach Joey Meyer directly. Not surprisingly, the coach didn't answer; so Harris left him a message. Then, to everyone's surprise, Meyer called back.

"I was over at my neighbor's house," Harris recalled, "and my dad, who was a smoker and who had emphysema, literally ran over to us. He said, *Joey ... Meyer ... is on the phone for you.* I knew he definitely wouldn't have run over to play a joke on me. I ran home and told (Meyer) I had always been a fan of DePaul, your family, and what you guys stand for. I let him know that I had been accepted at DePaul, I want to be a coach, I want to come and learn from you, and I think I could learn a lot just being part of the program in any way I could. He said, *I hear it in your voice. I'm going to connect you with one of our assistants, and if you come to school here we'll figure a way to get you involved.* That's all I was promised."

And that's all Harris needed. He arrived on campus in the fall of 1991 and made a beeline to the men's basketball office to meet with assistant Jay Goedert. "He said, *We don't have an open manager position or anything. If you just want to learn to coach, you can tag along with us.* So, I showed up for everything in preseason, and in the first week of practice one of their star players got hurt. They needed a body for 'shell drill,' and since I was playing at the gym all the time and the coaches knew that I knew what I was doing, they threw me in the drill. I would run to the right spots – they didn't have to tell me what to do. The next day it was the same thing; there were a couple more drills, and I'm in there. Coach Jay grabs me after that practice and says, *You want to be a practice player with us? I can't promise you anything other than that, but you will probably learn a lot more that way.* I said, *Yes, I'm in.*"

In his newfound situation, Harris practiced patience and accelerated his initiative. "They didn't give me any normal repetitions because I wasn't integral to what they were doing," he said. "My role was, *Wait on the sideline until we need you.* So I did other things because I really wanted to learn the game. We had this video editing system, the AG-7500. It was this big hunk of metal just sitting there in the film room, and I learned how to break down tape after practice. By the time I got to be a junior, one coach would just hand me a stack of tapes. He would say, *Break down Cincinnati,* and I would come up with the whole thing. I would take the scout team, and coach would leave me with them. I'd run them through all the other team's plays because I knew all of them. I made the coaches' life easier."

Harris was moved to the active roster halfway through his freshman year, and during his four seasons in uniform (1991-95), he saw action in 16 games, registering four points, five rebounds, three assists, and two steals. One of his career highlights was making legendary broadcaster (and national championship coach at Marquette) Al McGuire eat his words on national television. Here's Harris' story: "My mom sold appliances at Sears, and during the summers I would work basketball camps during the day and at night I would go work at Sears, too. My junior year we were playing Georgetown on CBS on a Saturday afternoon, and the department she worked in was right across from the TVs. It was one of (Georgetown coach) John Thompson's worst losses ever (78-51). My mom watched the game with all the people who I worked with during the summer. Before the game, Al McGuire is in the elevator with me and one of my teammates. I said, *Hey, Al, make sure you say 'hi' to my mom today when I get in the game.* He said, *You're not getting in the game; you're going to be getting water for the guys.* I said, *No – we're going to beat these guys bad. We have a game plan.* So we blow them out and as they put me in the game, McGuire announces, *Here's Jon Harris. He said he was going to get in today, and I told him if he did I would say hello to his mother. So, hi, mom!* My Mom called me after the game and thought it was great."

Harris was never rewarded with meaningful playing time, but Meyer extended generosity to him in the form of a scholarship his senior year. "In my family I was one of six, so I didn't really have a lot growing up," Harris said. "Every year I'd get a pair of shoes for being on the team, and I remember calling my mom and saying, *Hey, mom, they gave me a pair of shoes.* She was so excited. As a walk-on I was always trying to figure out a way to pay for stuff. It's hard financially coming from not having a lot of money. Well, one day coach Meyer calls me in and he says, *We're going to offer you a scholarship.* I called my mom and said, *Hey, mom, do you remember that problem we were having with financial aid? I think I just solved it.* It was very emotional. It was very, very cool."

The walk-on experience continued to reward Harris well after he graduated from DePaul. Today Harris is the CEO of AthLife, a company he founded in 2004 to serve the education, career development, and life-skill needs of athletes. AthLife works with the NBA, NBA Legends Foundation, National Basketball Retired Players Association, NFL Players Association, The Trust (powered by the NFLPA), MLS (Major League Soccer), MLS Players Union, and the University of Virginia. AthLife has also worked with staff and student-athletes at more than 40 college athletic departments in the areas of education and life-skill development. In 2010, Harris established the AthLife Foundation that annually impacts more than 10,000 high school student-athletes at schools in need.

"If you're a former professional athlete, you have the opportunity to work with our team of advisers to help you with your transition to life after the sport. We ultimately try to help people find their passion. For some people, making a ton of money is their passion, and they don't really care what they do all day as long as they make enough money so they can smoke cigars and go to Vegas on the weekends. Some other athletes, they want to make sure they're doing something that they love.

"I've been able to tap into things that I'm very passionate about. When I was a walk-on, I was serviceable and I was scrappy. Whatever needed to be done, I would do it. That's now part of my DNA and our company. We were at an event this last weekend and I'm the head guy, but these tables needed to be moved and I grab a guy and we're moving these tables. What needs to be done, you get it done. I was of service then as a walk-on, and the work we do now, we're of service to those we do business with. I walked on at DePaul because I really wanted to go to a good school that was going to create an opportunity for me down the road."

Harris has done exactly that – and created opportunities for many others.

CHAPTER 25

"I Ran My Own Race"

Trent Dykes
University of Washington, Football
Corporate & Securities Attorney; Partner, DLA Piper LLP (US)

For most teenagers, taking a "long-term approach" means planning for next weekend. Trent Dykes had a radically more mature mindset when he walked on to the University of Washington football team as a quarterback in 1995. He was seeking an opportunity to launch his career, not to earn playing time. And he got exactly what he was aiming for.

Despite four years of lifting, running, memorizing playbooks, studying scouting reports, and getting roughed up on the practice field, Dykes never saw game action for the Huskies – not one play, not one second. He was and still is completely fine with that. "It was never to me about being 'Rudy' or anything like that," Dykes said. "Sure, I could have figured out a way to get on the field if I really wanted to, but I'm sure it would have come at an awful lot of sacrifice to other things. I don't think that would have optimized the end result, which ultimately was getting into law school and having a career that I enjoy."

A teammate of Dykes approached his walk-on QB status differently. "He was lower than me on the depth chart for the first year or two but he really wanted to get on the field," Dykes recalled. "He did everything he could do to get on the field, so he decided to be a holder for kicks. And he went out there and he worked with the kickers and long snappers every day before and after practice – in addition to his normal positional practices. His senior year he traveled with the team, and he would play in every game as a holder. He was smaller than me but passed me on the depth chart, and I thought that was great. His work ethic, strategy and determination, for what he wanted, was admirable. He wanted to play and became a holder – that's smart if you really want to get on the field. We had different endgames. I guess I ran my own race."

Unlike most Division I scholar-athletes, Dykes also served as an officer of a UW fraternity (he was recruitment chairman as a freshman, sophomore and junior and then president his senior year) for the purpose of developing his leadership skills and expanding his personal network. When he realized the fraternity responsibilities along with a full academic schedule and football was an overload, Dykes pondered quitting the team as a sophomore. But then he did what any good lawyer does: he made an argument. "Division I football is year-round and basically a full-time job. It was probably about 30 hours a week for us in-season," he said. "In the spring of my sophomore year, I talked about quitting with my position coach, but he (and my dad) talked me out of it, and we made a deal. I was helpful to the program because I knew the offenses pretty well, and they needed a scout team quarterback to give the defense a good look. What was killing me was all the extra film study the quarterbacks had to do. I told him if you keep bringing in scholarship players who are five inches or six inches taller than me, you don't need me watching film. So, I scaled it back and made the schedule work. My coach said, *Don't tell anyone you're doing this. I don't want a bunch of other players to do this.* It was a mutually beneficial relationship. They got something out of it, and I felt long-term there was a network value to this for me."

Dykes always viewed being a member of the team as a bonus – an opportunity he was fortunate to have. Washington was a national power in the early 1990s under coach Don James, winning three consecutive Pac-10 championships (1990-92) which included a perfect 12-0 season in 1991. But just prior to the 1993 season, the NCAA ruled that several UW players received improper benefits from boosters, so the Huskies received sanctions that included reduced scholarships. That opened the door for Dykes, a graduate of Sammamish High School in nearby Bellevue, Wash., and other walk-ons to fill out the roster. "Half of our recruiting class was guys like (future NFL QB and current NFL announcer) Brock Huard, and the other half were guys like me," Dykes said. "I was shocked I got invited as a walk-on – I honestly thought it was a mistake at the time. I started a couple games my senior year of high school in the second half of the season and had some okay moments, but I was not even the best quarterback on my high school team. And one of those games was when the Washington scout was scouting other players on my team. I think they probably saw that I had already been accepted at UW academically and figured *why not?*"

Dykes had received interest from Division II and III schools, but never considered them because of his long-term plan to use his UW connections to launch his career in the Seattle area. He also never expected Washington to give him athletic aid. "If they're giving me a scholarship, there are definitely problems with this program," Dykes laughed.

When Dykes first stepped onto the Washington practice field, he immediately experienced a frying-pan-into-the-fire moment. It was late summer 1995, and Dykes was asked to run the scout team against a UW defense that included All-American and future NFL All-Pro safety Lawyer Malloy. "I'm fresh out of high school – it's August and I graduated the end of June – and I'm trying to run this new offense. It's literally my first week, and I'm at the line calling a play. I'm in the middle of my snap count, and I see Lawyer walking towards the line of scrimmage. He starts to jog towards me, and I know he's got my snap count timed. I'm like, *Oh, crap! He's going to kill me!* Sure enough, as soon as I snap the ball, he's in on me. I barely got one step back from the center. And he just tapped me on the head. He didn't blow me up. He didn't try to kill me." (Another way of describing that story is that before Dykes became a successful lawyer, he was almost trampled on by a successful Lawyer.)

Dykes said he later talked with Malloy about that play, and the upperclassman's behavior left an impression on him. "There are people who conduct themselves in a classy way, and Lawyer was certainly one of them. He is a great human who also happened to be an all-American at football. He knew how to do things the right way. He set a good example. He was one of those people you wanted to be."

But not every UW starter followed Malloy's lead. And while it caused some grief for Dykes back then, he says the experience helped mold him for the professional world. "We're on the bus for the (1995) Sun Bowl in El Paso, and I'm studying for finals. One of the starting running backs, who will remain unnamed, grabs my book out of my hands. He yelled some profanities about me about being a nerd. He took my book, and he wouldn't give it back. I remember thinking, *Oh, my goodness. This is ridiculous. Why does this guy care? What is it about this person where they are so insecure that they would do this?* Well, a couple of the players stood up for me even though I didn't ask them to. One of the other running backs started railing on him. He said something like, *Just because you can't read, don't take it out on him.* You just sit there and you witness these things, and you see how people conduct themselves. And you think to yourself, *Okay, which person do I want to be?*"

Dykes said being thrust onto a team with a variety of personalities and capabilities helped him adjust to the working world after graduation. "One of my favorite guys on the team went on to get a Ph.D. in computer engineering form Berkeley after playing. Another guy who played just got released from jail and was there for being an accomplice to a drive-by. It's a really interesting mix trying to work with all those different types of people. They're from different cultures, different backgrounds, different socio-economic groups. Some are going to go to the NFL. Some are never even going to get in the game. It's probably one of the most diverse environments you're going to ever see. Now there aren't a whole lot of situations where I get in a room and I'm super uncomfortable."

After graduating cum laude from Washington with a concentration in finance, Dykes used postgraduate scholarships to earn his Juris Doctorate from the UW Law School in 2002. He then used that degree to get hired at a large law firm that later became DLA Piper, one of the world's largest law firms, where he became partner at age 32. Dykes has been named a Washington "Super Lawyer," a "Band

2" lawyer in the area of corporate law in Washington by Chambers & Partners (a recognition awarded to less than a dozen attorneys in his practice area and region), and was recognized by *The Legal 500 United States* in the venture capital and emerging companies practice area. He currently serves as DLA Piper's hiring partner for the Seattle office and is a member of the firm's National Leadership Group of the U.S. Emerging Growth and Venture Capital practice.

Dykes says he knows he could have traveled a less stressful path back at UW, but he's glad he didn't. He says a mindset to always persevere was key then and still is today. "At some point you do think to yourself, *Wow, life could be a lot easier if I didn't do this.* For me, there were points of deliberation and points of thoughtfulness, then the rest of it was just keeping your head down and getting stuff done. When I make a decision to do something, I just put my head down and move forward. Look up, figure out where I am, then put my head down again, and go. My family makes fun of me when we're in an airport and I'm carrying everyone's bags. I have my family's bags, and I just put my head down and say, *Let's just get to the car.* There's no reason to complain about the bags you're carrying. I'm aware that I have to get to the car, so talking and whining and strategizing doesn't seem like a real great plan at this time. Let's just get to the car. I guess that approach has worked for me."

CHAPTER 26

"It Takes Commitment And Grit To Get To The Other Side"

Alan Williams

Wake Forest, Basketball
Founder & Author, Teammates Matter; Author, Little Teammate
Co-President, BCW Food Products

Even if we devoted the next 50 pages to Alan Williams' walk-on experience at Wake Forest, you'd still be reading the abbreviated version of his story. In 2006, Williams authored *Walk-On: Life from the End of the Bench*, a 228-page book that details four years of his ups-and-downs. His book has since been rebranded *Teammates Matter*, the same name as Williams' outreach organization, and he even spun off a children's book in 2017 titled *Little Teammate*. A few of the quotes from Williams' walk-on book jump off the page:

- *As a walk-on I always knew I was only one visit to the coaches' office away from having my name taken off the roster.*
- *Being a walk-on was about practice; that is where we made our difference.*
- *Despite my unimpressive stat line, it had been an unbelievable experience.*
- *Sitting on the end of the bench made me realize that at different points in our lives we are all walk-ons.*

After a standout career at Briarcrest Christian School in Memphis, Tenn., Williams received scholarship interest from several small schools but opted to go big and accept an invited walk-on offer from head coach Dave Odom at Wake Forest. The adjustment wasn't easy. "In high school, I knew what it was like to hit the game-winning shot," Williams said. "I knew what it was like to play with a minute left in a tie game. I go to Wake Forest and my life takes a 180-degree turn. My freshman year was really a disaster in a lot of ways. The game was five times faster. It was challenging to even get playing time in practice. I remember being in the weight room and we had to do 10 push-ups with a 75-pound plate on your back. The strength coach would count to 10 really slowly and he'd say, *If anybody drops to the ground, you're all going again.* I can remember how humiliating it felt to be the guy who couldn't hold his position."

But the news after that season was even worse for Williams. "Coach calls me into his office and says, *Alan, I'm sorry, but we're not going to have a spot for you on next year's team.* I remember walking out of the office, down a stairwell that led to the parking lot, and I remember crying because for the first time in 14 years I was no longer part of a team. I decided I'm going to do whatever it takes to get my spot back on the roster. That was the beginning for me learning about perseverance. Perseverance isn't about working hard for one day or one week. It's really a process. I also learned about real confidence – being willing to get up out of bed every morning and give everything that you have even though you don't know what the result is going to be."

Since he was no longer part of the program, Williams wasn't allowed to work out with the Wake Forest team, so he was forced to run and lift on his own. But then Odom bolted Winston-Salem for the University of South Carolina. With no coach to keep him away from the team, Williams seized the opportunity as soon as he could for as long as he could. "Right after I heard the news, I'm back in the weight room with my teammates doing push-ups. I didn't care that they were hard. I just wanted to be in the weight room with the guys. A couple weeks later, the athletic director walks into the weight room and says, *Tonight, you're going to meet your new coach, Skip Prosser from Xavier. He's flying in with his staff. I want everybody to be in the Athletic Center at 8:30. This is for scholarship players only.* That was pretty much code for, *Alan, you don't need to be there.* Josh Howard (future ACC Player of the Year and NBA

All-Star) looked at me and said, *Come anyway.* I showed up and I hung on every word Coach Prosser said. He talked about the ABC's that he wanted Wake Forest basketball to be about: academics, basketball, conduct. He also said, *By the way, the first shooting workout is going to be tomorrow.*"

Williams knew this was his opportunity to win back his spot on the Demon Deacon roster. "Right before I get to shoot my very first shot in front of the new coaches, the coach kills the drill and says, *Alan, why don't you just be a passer today.* So, as my teammates did backdoor cuts, flare cuts, and curl cuts around trash cans, I was the designated passer. That's all I did that entire spring: pass to my teammates. But I was there, and I learned the value of showing up. That summer I stayed for one of the basketball camps. I just wanted to be everywhere. That was my strategy.

"The first day of my sophomore year I'm stronger, I'm quicker – I'm in the best shape of my life. Coach calls and says, *Alan, I need to see you in my office in 10 minutes.* I ran across campus, back up the stairwell where I was crying before, and walk to the big corner office where Coach Prosser is in his leather chair. He says, *Alan, I've got a major problem. We're going to have a walk-on but we need somebody that's 6-foot-6 or 6-foot-7, somebody that can bang with the big guys. There are too many guards.* That wasn't good for me being 6-foot-2, 175 pounds. I said, *Coach, you told us when you first came here that the gym was the best place to be. I'm not ready to give that up. Just let me work out with the team. Even if you cut me at the end of the pre-season, I'd be okay with that.* He said, *I appreciate your persistence, but my conscience as a coach just won't let me do that.*

"So, I walked back down that stairwell again, but I didn't believe the story was over for me. I just kept showing up. I watched what my teammates did in the weight room. I watched what they did on the track for their workouts, and I'd go do those workouts by myself at night. A month later near the post office I see a white notice taped to the wall and it said, *Walk-on tryouts 8:30 Thursday night. Must have had a physical in the past year.* Once again, I was going to show up. There were 43 other players trying out for the same spot.

About halfway through, all my teammates walked into the gym and they started to support what I was doing. I think they wanted to send a clear message to the coaches who had already made up their minds before the tryout."

Prosser and his staff relented, Williams made the team for that 2001-02 season, and he stayed on the club until graduating in 2004. He played only 59 total minutes at Wake, scoring 27 points on 9-for-21 shooting including a perfect 4-for-4 season as a junior. "If somebody pulled out a book before I started my career and said, *Read this and think about what you're going to go through. You're going to get cut from your team three different times. You're going to score one point your freshman year. You won't get the same gear that everybody else gets. You're going to play 59 minutes in four years. This is what you're signing up for.* There is no way I would have possibly signed up for that. But that's the beauty of life – we don't always know what's around the corner. Being a walk-on trains you to realize that things in life are not supposed to be easy. Getting through trials and getting through difficulties are one of the things that makes an experience meaningful.

"When I was at school, I met a businessman who was a walk-on and he told me, *There's a good chance what you're doing right now is the hardest thing that you go through in your life.* I found that statement profound because I'm thinking, *Gosh, my dad had cancer. There's a lot of things that could happen in somebody's life.* I think what he was saying was he's faced challenges in business, challenges with family, but he had never done anything tougher in his life than be a walk-on. I think that has proven to be true for me. I know the commitment that it took over those four years to endure that. I think that's what you learn as a walk-on. You learn that it takes commitment and grit to get to the other side."

It also takes support and encouragement from your teammates to help you keep moving forward. When giving motivational talks, Williams often retells the story of how an act of kindness by teammate Robert O'Kelley, one of the top shooters in Wake Forest and ACC history, helped lift his spirits. "We're about to begin a new season and Sarge, our equipment manager, walks into our locker room. He has this big brown box of black Nike travel bags. He passes a bag out to every player on the team, but he skips over my locker. I'm thinking, *Why didn't I get a bag? I've lifted every weight. I've been to all the workouts. I've run every mile.* I can remember that dejected feeling. I walked out of the locker room thinking it's bad enough I'm the guy who never gets to play – I just wanted to get the same gear like everybody else. When I walked back into the locker room and opened up my locker I didn't see my old beat up gym bag from high school. I saw another bag – it was a brand-new Nike travel bag just like my other teammates had received. I thought that maybe Sarge realized how much I wanted a bag. I didn't see my number on the bag, but I saw number four. Robert O'Kelley was number four. He was the captain of the team. He was the best player on the team. How long did it take him to put that bag in my locker? Probably 30 seconds. But sometimes it takes only 30 seconds to show someone that we love them and that we care about them. It was people like Robert O'Kelley that really kept me coming back.

"The best part about that story is that six or seven years after I was done playing, I was telling that story to about 300 middle school students in Memphis which is my hometown and Robert's. These students have no idea as I'm sharing this story about this black bag that Robert himself was in the audience. At the very end of the story I show them the black bag and I say, *There's Robert O'Kelley!* He stands up and he gets the biggest standing ovation that you've ever heard. He comes on stage, grabs the microphone from me, and he said with a smile, *I've changed my mind. I want my bag back.*"

Opposing fans weren't as supportive of Williams as his teammates. "Fans of the other team would call me 'Opie.' My strategy when I walked into an arena was to walk in with one of our best players because I felt no one would really pay any attention to me. At Maryland I walked in with (6-foot-9) Darius Songaila. The fans were giving him a hard time, then all of a sudden it got really quiet and one of them said, *Hey, Darius, is that your 12-year-old brother behind you?*"

Williams' books and speeches get plenty of attention, but his main vocation is serving as Co-President of BCW Food Products, a national service provider headquartered in Dallas. "When I think about what I learned as a walk-on translating into my professional life, I think about our food business where you have a sales cycle lasting sometimes 12-18 months. There's a lot of patience, a lot of grit, and a lot of perseverance that's required to endure that sales cycle. I call upon my experiences as a walk-on all the time to be able to see something through from start to finish, to be able to endure. I learned that just like those days I'd leave practice and walk down the stairwell and think I can't keep doing this because it was a really tough day, sometimes you're driving home from work and you think, *How did we move the needle today?*

"Most importantly you learn how to work with people. In our business it takes every single role, it takes everybody, for our business to be successful. For the rest of your life, a big part of your success will come from your ability to work, relate, and function as a member of a team. Do people want to work with you? Can you work with other people? As a walk-on, you learn to function and relate and adapt as a member of the team. You have no room as a walk-on. You have no choice but to be a servant. You don't get an opportunity to just focus on yourself as a walk-on. The world tries to convince us every day to focus on ourselves. I think there's a beautiful thing about having a season of your life where you are not allowed to focus on yourself. People speak so fondly about tough experiences because there's meaning in going beyond yourself. I look back at being a walk-on as one of the most humbling yet rewarding experiences of my life."

Williams is busy with his business and a growing family of his own, so why does he choose to invest time in Teammates Matter and writing books to help others? Why doesn't he just relax and watch more television or play games on his phone? "There's such a high commitment level that's required to be a walk-on that it just doesn't go away after you do that for four years. It's something that's reinforced in my life almost every day. I think the messaging around my walk-on experience is important, and I want young people to hear it.

"Everybody has had a bench in their life. Everybody has had a challenge. I think we're all walk-ons in some way. I was speaking at a high school assembly and afterwards a girl comes up to me and she said, *I don't play a sport but your message really resonated with me. I felt those things you were talking about where you said you didn't feel noticed. When you said that everybody has a role to play, that really resonated with me.* It just makes me want to keep reinforcing this message that teamwork is important."

CHAPTER 27

"You're Not Entitled To A Damn Thing"

Rob Frozena
Marquette, Basketball
Securities Trader

Robert Frost recommended taking "the road less traveled," but even he could not have foreseen that Rob Frozena attending a barbeque get-together would lead to four years of Division I basketball followed by a career in the securities industry.

Back in 2007, Frozena, a three-sport star at St. Mary Central High School in Neenah, Wisc., was a first-semester freshman at Marquette University with no plans to continue competitive athletics despite a stellar schoolboy career. Frozena was all-conference in football, baseball, and basketball, earning honorable mention all-state laurels in hoops. After averaging 24.0 points per game his senior season, he ranked seventh on St. Mary's all-time scoring list with 1,226 points. But because he always considered sports a pastime – and because he received a full-tuition academic scholarship to Marquette – Frozena declined interest from Division III schools and planned to focus on his grades in college.

Until that barbeque.

"A pretty experienced high school basketball coach told me I should try out for the team at Marquette," Frozena said. "I considered it, but once I got to school, I thought *I'm not going to try out.* Basketball had only been a hobby for me from the time I was a kid playing. Marquette held a basketball barbeque welcoming new students in September and, I don't know why, but for some reason the urge came over me and I decided to go. When I got there, I walked straight up to (head) coach (Tom) Crean and I introduced myself. I said, *Hey, coach Crean. I'm Rob Frozena. I'm interested in walking on.* He was like, *That's wonderful. Give your information to one of our graduate assistants.* I'm thinking nothing will come of it because how many hundreds of other guys did that as well?"

But, just days later, Frozena was invited to try out with three other walk-on hopefuls. Frozena called that session "one of the most miserable workouts I've ever been through in my entire life," but he performed well enough to receive a callback afterward to run more drills in early October. "The coaches said after that, *If we're interested, we'll give you a call.* A couple of weeks went by and I hadn't heard anything. I figured nothing was happening because their season had already started. But one day I was about to leave my dorm room to go home because I had a job back home in the fall, and my school phone rang. It was one of the assistants saying, *Coach wants you down here right away. Some guys got hurt, and we need you to get a physical.* They had a game the next day, but I couldn't go with them because I hadn't been through the NCAA clearinghouse yet. I had no aspirations to play Division I basketball, so I never went through the actual clearinghouse. It was a two- to three-week process, but once I was cleared, I started practicing. That's how it all started. It was just the most bizarre thing ever."

When Frozena finally navigated the NCAA's red tape and was handed a uniform, he was excited to spread the news. "The first person I called was my girlfriend at the time – she's now my wife. I had called her two or three times, and she was apparently sleeping. One of her girlfriends who she was living with told her, *Rob keeps calling you.* She was like, *Whatever. It's probably not important,* so she never answered the phone. So, I called my parents and said I got them tickets for the game tomorrow because I'm going to be suiting up."

Frozena wore a Marquette uniform for four seasons (2007-11), remaining a team member even after Crean left MU for Indiana in 2008 and was replaced by Buzz Williams. Frozena appeared in 40 games (54 total minutes), registering 21 points, 17 rebounds, three assists, and three steals. But what he did off the court contributed more to the Golden Eagles than his spot minutes. Frozena relished the (literal) dirty work. "I'm never ashamed to admit this: no job can ever be beneath you. I can't even count the number of times I was at practice and a manager or two had class. I would have the towels. I would have the clipboards. I would have the water bottles. And if some guy fell, I would be the first on the floor to wipe up the sweat.

"I had a great example to follow my freshman year. Tommy Brice was a senior walk-on, and I learned from him that no job can be beneath you. You're not entitled to a damn thing. I think that attitude is what kept me around. When we flew as a team, we might land after 11:00 p.m. For all my four years, I'd be outside with the managers loading bags off the plane and putting them on the bus. I'm a Division I basketball player, but I'm not necessarily helping this team with my basketball ability. I have to help them in other ways."

As new recruits arrived in Milwaukee, Frozena expanded his responsibilities to include developing younger players. "Starting in my junior and senior year, I would work out extra after practice. When these freshmen come in, they don't have college-ready bodies and they may not be playing every day. So, we would have workout sessions and get in extra weight-room work together. Our strength coach said to me, *You really need to be in there with them*, so for my last two years after almost every practice we would go into the weight room for an extra half hour or 40 minutes and get some work in. I may not be a leader on the floor, leading my team with a game-winning shot with a second left on the clock, but there are other things you can do. One way I could lead some of those guys was by example."

You can see why on his television show Williams called Frozena "the best teammate in our program" and rewarded him with playing time whenever possible. When asked to share his favorite on-court highlight, Frozena recounted the story of his first collegiate basket and how his teammates reacted to his accomplishment. In the final minute of a 79-67 win vs. Seton Hall, Frozena hit a layup to put MU up by 17. "There were a bunch of future NBA players on our bench – Lazar Hayward, Jimmy Butler, Jerel McNeal, and Wesley Matthews. All these guys on the bench are going absolutely ballistic after I scored. They were jumping up and down and going nuts. My mom still has a picture from that."

Marquette made the NCAA tournament all four seasons during Frozena's tenure, and he received several individual awards along the way. He was named to the Big East All-Academic Team four consecutive years and received Marquette's Standard of Excellence Award for men's basketball in 2010. But don't think that Frozena's walk-on experience was smooth from start to finish. "I'd be lying if I said I didn't want to quit every single year. In September, we'd go through these absolutely hellish work-outs to get prepared for the season, and the coaches would test you mentally. I can't tell you the number of times I would call my parents and talk about quitting. But I think that's a natural part of growth. You have to overcome that mental battle. Once you go through it, you know what you're capable of."

Since graduating in 2011 with a degree in Finance and Marketing plus a minor in Mathematics, Frozena has worked as a securities trader in Milwaukee, taking the same approach to work as he did Marquette basketball. "When this job opportunity was presented to me, it was not the road I was thinking I was going to go on. I didn't know anything about how stocks and securities worked. But I said, *That's something I'd be willing to try.* It's like when I introduced myself to coach Crean. I just jumped into it. I didn't know if I was going to like this or not at first, but now I love it and I'll do this for a long time."

And just like he performed extra work in college, Frozena studied evenings and weekends to earn an MBA from Wisconsin-Whitewater with the goal of future-proofing his career. "You can't predict life, but the one thing I can control is how prepared I am. My MBA was in finance, but most of it was an emphasis in IT (information technology). I did that because you can see how the world is changing. Even the financial world, it's changing from the stereotypical days of guys on the floor or *Wolf of Wall Street.*

Everything runs through computers now, and I just feel like the jobs will be in IT in the future. I'll stay at this job as long as I can, but you just never know. If that day should come, I want to make sure I'm marketable to employers and I have the ability to transition into something else if I need to. I expect the world to be drastically different in five years. Everything I learn may not necessarily apply like it used to, but I'm doing what I can do. That's the only way I know how to prepare.

"There's no entitlement to anything whether you're a walk-on for the basketball team or you're in your professional career. Even if you think you are entitled to something, you're not."

CHAPTER 28

"I Believe In You"

John Brosnahan
William & Mary, Football
Financial Advisor

Wouldn't your work life improve if you received more encouragement and engaged in more candid conversations ... and if you had fewer meetings, emails, and PowerPoint slides? Longtime financial advisor John Brosnahan can't do much about the number of meetings he has to attend, but thanks to his experience as a walk-on football player at William & Mary, for years he's been committed to increase candor and encouragement in his work environment.

Brosnahan's accomplishments as a high school quarterback at J.E.B. Stuart High School in Falls Church, Va. were impressive: as a senior in 1984 he was team MVP, Northern Region Offensive Player of the Year, second team All-Met, and MVP in the Virginia State All-Star game. But because he stood just 5-foot-8½, Brosnahan didn't show up on the radar of college recruiters.

He decided to walk on at William & Mary, a Division I school in nearby Williamsburg, Va., to prove the doubters wrong, showing them he could play quarterback and earn a scholarship on the collegiate level. However, when he arrived on campus, the coaching staff labeled him a scout team H-back (a hybrid between a running back and a tight end), moved him to wide receiver for a time, and then tried him at H-back again. After two seasons as a member of The Tribe, the first being a redshirt year, Brosnahan hadn't moved beyond the scout team. Nobody else considered him a quarterback, and he was miles away from being considered a scholarship candidate.

In year number three he finally saw the field on special teams and as a reserve H-back, but the frustration from his limited role and no scholarship money was mounting. "I went to William & Mary to get a great education, but because of the time I was putting into football I wasn't doing great in school. The time you put in if you're a walk-on getting no money or you're on a full scholarship from day one is identical." So to make his time worth his investment, he worked up the courage after the 1986 season to sit down with head coach Jimmye Laycock and ask if he could receive some scholarship money. The short answer was no. Brosnahan didn't complain to Laycock, but when he was leaving the football office, he vented to the running backs coach and receivers coach. "I pretty much threw my hands up and said, *I'm done. I just can't do it.* Even as much as I felt in my mind I could, it was just too much time, too much effort, and it wasn't helping with school. I wouldn't say I stormed out, but they knew I wasn't excited."

Brosnahan recalls returning to his dorm room and going for run to clear his mind. "I threw on my running stuff, which is something I still do today to get rid of stress. I'll never forget what those two coaches did – Coach Cox and Coach Kepa. They tracked me down in their car several miles from campus. They explained the money situation in terms of what was there and what wasn't there for them to give out, and I understood the numbers. What I appreciated the most was the concern they showed me. That was one reason I stuck it out and decided to keep playing."

Someone else who motivated Brosnahan during this frustrating time was his father. "During that winter break I was home for two or three weeks, and I was talking about not going back to the team. My dad said something I'll never forget. He said, *I believe in you. I know what you can do. I've seen you growing. I believe in you.* He also put the idea in my head that I should go talk with coach Laycock about going into spring drills that next year and trying quarterback again."

So when the 21-year-old Brosnahan returned to campus for the second semester, he walked back into Laycock's office – the same place his scholarship request was rejected just weeks earlier – to ask if he could play the most important position on the team. He was understandably uneasy. "Talking to any of your coaches, especially your head coach, is something that lends to making you a little anxious anyhow. I knew it was kind of a last-ditch effort, because when I had asked him before about playing quarterback, he said, *No. My decision has been made.* But when I asked this time he said, *Yeah – the quarterback position's open. I'll give you a shot at it. But you don't have a leg up on anybody.*"

Brosnahan capitalized on the opportunity in a big way, vaulting from third-string H-back to first-string quarterback by the time the 1987 season started. Over the next two seasons, he completed 251 passes, totaling 2,970 yards and 25 touchdowns despite missing five games because of hand and knee injuries. As a senior, he was named co-captain and led The Tribe to a 6-4-1 mark, including a win in the Epson Ivy Bowl on January 8, 1989. And, because of the important role he was being asked to play, Brosnahan was awarded a full scholarship that covered his final two years of school.

None of that would have been possible if Brosnahan hadn't had the fortitude to ask for the quarterback job. "I'm certainly not the only person who's been in a situation like that, but not too many 20-year-olds have to go through that. It was definitely something I think that has helped me along the way during my work career – if not directly, certainly indirectly – having that conversation at such a young age."

Brosnahan is a successful financial advisor today, in part because he's willing to have hard discussions with teammates and clients. The interactions mirror the respectful conversations with coach Laycock and the respect his William & Mary teammates showed him. "We have all sorts of people on our team – junior people, administrators, marketing people – and you certainly need to make clear what you want out of them, but I also have to treat them with respect. The respect is ultra-important. For me, it's become more second nature at this point, but I do attribute a lot of it to my experience at William & Mary.

"Part of the reason I think I had success and was ultimately voted captain by my peers in my last year was because of what they saw me go through as a freshman and sophomore. Most of them were on a scholarship and I wasn't, but they respected that I kept showing up and how I worked. It wasn't a secret how that whole thing played out for me. I know for a fact there's been a direct correlation between what I did back then and what I've done in business helping other people with their work ethic and sticking to a goal – working through the ups and downs. You're an important part of the team whether you're the starting quarterback or you're a backup holder."

Additionally, Brosnahan encourages William & Mary football players today as an active member of the HEYFARL program, which provides scholarships to walk-on football players. HEYFARL, which stands for "Hundred Each Year For A Rising Letterman," asks former Tribe players to donate at least $100 a year to help a William & Mary walk-on receive a scholarship. According to the school, more than 800 former players make an annual gift to HEYFARL, and across 20+ years the group has raised more than $1 million and has awarded 61 full scholarships.

"For someone like myself who benefited from going through all the trials and tribulations and not having any scholarship money and then earning a scholarship, I certainly appreciate what these kids are going through," Brosnahan said. "I feel like I have to be involved and encourage them to keep working."

CHAPTER 29

"Life Takes Way Longer Than You Think"

Scott Novosel
Kansas, Basketball
Author/Speaker & Personal Trainer

During his brief collegiate basketball career at the University of Kansas, Scott Novosel totaled more turnovers (six) than points (four) and scored just one field goal … but does he have a story to tell about that experience! It's so compelling, Novosel parlayed his account into a speaking career and a children's book that's endorsed by KU legends Danny Manning ("Dreams do come true!") and Coach Bill Self ("Full of positive energy!").

Novosel grew up in Leawood, Kan., one hour due east of the University's campus in Lawrence, and he dreamed of someday playing for the Jayhawks in historic Allen Fieldhouse. He was a scrappy yet unremarkable player at Blue Valley North High School, meaning the best he could do after he enrolled at KU was earn a spot on their junior varsity team as a freshman. While teammates were promoted to the varsity during his three years playing JV, Novosel was overlooked. For his senior year, Novosel decided to give everything he had to make good on his final chance to achieve his boyhood dream.

"Each year I hoped I would get called up, but it hadn't happened," Novosel recalled. "Then I thought about persistence. This is Kansas. No one gets on that team on a fluke. I thought to myself, *You're going to work for this one. This is the big one.* I was determined there was no way I was going to let them not put me on the team. I was going to give them an offer they couldn't refuse: I'm committed to help the team any way I can."

Novosel had developed a friendship with star KU guard Rex Walters who would go on to become a two-time first-team all-Big 8 selection, a first-round draft pick of the New Jersey Nets, and play seven seasons in the NBA. "When I was on the JV team, I would stay after practice and shoot, and he would, too. Rex saw how hard I worked – that's how we befriended each other. The summer before my senior year (1994), I started training with him. We did shooting drills, ballhandling drills, running drills. Rex was the most die-hard athlete I ever saw in my entire life. I got so much better that summer it was unbelievable."

When students returned to campus in the fall, Novosel attempted to participate in preseason pick-up games with the scholarship players. "I would sit and wait literally two hours hoping to get into a pick-up game. They played at 10 o'clock at night, and the first couple of weeks I never got in. I just sat there and none of the guys on the floor would ever leave. Even if it was a 15-0 loss, they made me just sit there. Little by little Rex picked me on his team. Then I would get a shot every once in a while. Then I got more and more and more shots."

Even though his game markedly improved, Novosel decided he wouldn't let his playing do all the talking. He mailed a handwritten letter on notebook paper to KU head coach Roy Williams asking for a chance to be on the team. In that letter, Novosel said, "I promise to be Kansas' most inspirational player." Williams didn't respond to Novosel, but assistant Steve Robinson did. "He said, *Look, there's going to be a try out soon, so don't be bothering Coach Williams.* When I told Rex that, Rex told me, *This is not Coach Robinson's priority. This is your life. You have one last chance. You need to talk with Coach Williams if you want to be on this team.*

"So, one night we're playing pick-up, and Coach Williams looked in to see who all was there, then he walked to his car. I chased him out there. When I got to him, I couldn't even breathe. He said, *Settle down, son. Settle down. Take a deep breath.* We set up a meeting for the next morning. When I got there, Coach Robinson lashed out at me. But I ended up having a great talk with Coach Williams. He said, *I see what you've been doing. You've been working with the guys, and you seem to have a good rapport with them. I think that's going to help you.*"

Novosel still had to jump through hoops in order to play some hoops at KU. "During the open tryout, they rated everyone, then selected a couple guys to practice with the team for a week. We got uniforms for the exhibition game – no names on the back of the jersey – and they told us that we hadn't made the team yet. We just kept dressing out for practices and games, and they put our names on the back of our jerseys for the final game of the fall semester. I wished I made the team earlier than my senior year, but it was a dream to see it finally come true. Life takes way longer than you think."

Novosel saw action in 16 games that year, totaling 21 minutes, four points, three assists, and one steal (plus the six turnovers mentioned at the beginning of this chapter). His only career field goal was a left corner three in the closing moments of a Kansas home victory vs. East Tennessee State. But Novosel's career highlight occurred on Senior Night at Allen Fieldhouse, and it's the foundation of his children's book which is aptly titled *Fieldhouse*.

Kansas has a tradition of starting every senior on the roster for its final home game, but the coaching staff hinted Novosel might not start this game for two reasons. First, he had been a varsity member only one year and, more importantly, Oklahoma State was the opponent, and the winner of the game would be crowned Big 8 regular season champions.

"Before every game, Coach Williams listed the starting five of the other team on the board, and then, with us in the room, he would write next to their names which starter was guarding him. Randy Owens was their point guard, and when coach didn't put my name next to his, I thought, *Oh, shit, I'm not starting.* I was cussing to myself. I thought there was no way he was going to put me on Randy Rutherford who was 6-foot-3 and a superstar. Then he writes my name next to Rutherford, and I'll never forget everybody looking around and we all started smiling. Coach told me, *Just face guard him. Don't look at anybody else. Just do what we ask you to do, and you'll be fine.*"

Novosel was introduced to thunderous applause and executed during his two minutes of playing time. On the Jayhawks' opening possession, he caught the ball on the left wing, faked a pass high, then threw a perfect bounce pass to All-American center Greg Ostertag who scored on a righthanded half-hook shot to give Kansas an early lead. When Novosel was substituted from the game, he stopped at midcourt and twice thrust his right fist into the air which fired up the home crowd even more.

"I had been running all year and was in the best shape of my life, but when I came out of the game I could hardly breathe I was so emotional. I remember literally feeling like I was walking on air. It was a dream come true. It was amazing. I always thought I represented the normal student. I was the one kid who got the chance to wear 'Kansas' across his chest.

"That experience was incredible because it taught me so many lessons. Any time I get down, I think about when I was in an empty Allen Fieldhouse running by myself. I think, *Nothing can stop you from getting what you want.* Whether that's happiness or whether that's a career goal, there *is* a way, and you can find a way through the process to get close to where you want to be. That whole experience taught me to shoot for the stars and bring out the best in yourself. That's all you can ask. Everything else will fall in line. Even if it wasn't meant to be, you are on the path to bring out the best in yourself. And that's what matters most in everything."

Novosel's primary occupation since he left Lawrence in 1998 after earning a Master's in Sports Psychology is working as a certified personal trainer. He also lived in Japan seven years running a basketball academy and training program at the Tokyo American Club. When Novosel returned to the States, he was determined to turn his walk-on story into something bigger. While living in Chicago in 2015, he teamed up with illustrator Sam Sharpe to publish *Fieldhouse* which chronicles in cartoon format Novosel's path from Jayhawk wannabe to Senior Night starter. The book is available for purchase online and is part of Novosel's speaking appearances at elementary and middle schools.

"I tell kids there are three ingredients for dreams: challenges, a positive attitude, and teamwork. I talk about daily challenges. I ask, *What's one thing that you don't like eating that's healthy? After you eat that thing, you realize it's not that bad.* Those little challenges prepare you for bigger challenges later in life. Next I tell them everybody loves a positive attitude – you can never go wrong with a positive attitude. If your parents want you to do a chore, say *Yes, I'll do it. What's the toughest one? That's the one I want to tackle first.* That's going to develop you into a person who can transform vision into a reality later in life.

"The final ingredient is teamwork, which I call team 'teamwork karma.' In life, you always have your team members – family, a basketball team, friends. When you give everything you have to make them better, you're going to bring out the best in yourself. You're going to take yourself to places you never thought you could go."

CHAPTER 30

"Focus Every Day"

Bobby Raymond
University of Florida, Football
Owner, Brightway Insurance Agency

What after-class activity would you imagine the eventual leading scorer in SEC football for two seasons was engaged in his freshman year? If you're thinking practicing with the team or working with a strength and conditioning coach, you're way off. If you guessed selling appliances and electronics, you're not only correct, but apparently you're some sort of savant.

Bobby Raymond took the unusual path from microwave salesman to University of Florida all-time great following a diet of hard work and steady progress, two habits he continues today as the owner of an insurance agency in Jacksonville, Fla.

Raymond was an accomplished three-sport athlete at The Bolles School in Jacksonville, playing baseball, earning first-team all-conference honors two years in soccer, and holding down two positions in football. On the gridiron as a senior, he earned second team all-conference honors as a defensive back and was named all-city as a kicker – the only season he played that position. Raymond received scholarship offers to play soccer at a few small colleges, but he preferred to attend a big school like the University of Florida, which was about 90 minutes from home.

With no practices or games on his schedule, Raymond hoped to make some money between classes. "When I went to Florida, I figured my sports-playing days for school were over," he said. "I went to work almost full-time when I started my freshman year in Gainesville. As soon as I was out of class, I'd go to Consumers Warehouse to sell people TVs and microwaves and washers and dryers and car stereos. I always had cash in my pocket to do all the fun stuff you do as a freshman."

One of those activities at Florida was attending Gator football games at Ben Hill Griffin Stadium, affectionately known as "The Swamp." As Raymond watched the UF kicker warm up before a game, he got the itch to return to the field. "I thought to myself, *Gee, I think I can kick as good as that guy.* I didn't decide to do anything with that thought until late in the winter when I talked to my father, and he encouraged me to walk on. He made a phone call to the gentleman that was the president of the Gator Bowl which is in Jacksonville where I grew up, and then that gentleman made a call to (Florida head coach) Charley Pell asking him to take a look at me.

"I showed up for spring ball and missed the team's winter agilities which are just a killer. Agilities were really the shake-out for many walk-ons who came out for the team. You'd have trash cans all over the circuits they'd run, and guys would puke their brains out. When I showed up in the locker room in the spring, I can remember a lot of the guys looking at me and going, *Where in the heck did you come from? How did you get in here without going through winter agilities?*"

Raymond had caught a break, but the Gators didn't exactly roll out the red carpet for him. He was relegated to the junior varsity locker room and for the 1981 season had to sweat his way onto the roster. "It was no shoe-in, I'll tell you that. It was hard work. Brian Clark had already been a three-year starter, so all the other kickers knew nobody was going to beat him out. So, when I went out for the team, my goal was just to not get cut. I know I'm not going to win a starting position and I probably won't be the first backup. I wanted to work, and I figured I never focused on kicking and thought I could get really good at it."

Raymond honed his skills and hit the weights hard, adding 20 pounds of muscle. For the 1982 season, longtime backup Jim Gainey was a senior and likely to earn the starting position, but the second spot on the Gator kicking depth chart was wide open. "At one point in the spring there were eight guys kicking. A manager charted every single practice kick and wrote down the percentages and gave the stats to the coaches. Through that, I established myself as the backup to Jim. That's part of what you go through in the walk-on world. You just have to wait your turn – wait and keep working hard until you prove yourself."

Raymond traveled with the team that year but only saw action in the Blue Bonnet Bowl in Houston after Gainey injured his plant foot while working on a friend's truck. Raymond had gained game experience as the starting kicker for the Gator JV team, making every field goal he attempted. Raymond was consistent off the field as well, continuing a regimen of practice and strength training that set the stage for spectacular years as a junior and senior.

In 1983, he made 20-of-23 field goals and 29-of-31 extra points, leading the SEC in field goals made, field goal percentage (86.9%), and points (89). He actually beat out college football legend Bo Jackson of Auburn (84 points) for the SEC scoring crown. As a senior in 1984, Raymond built on his success, converting 23-of-26 field goals and 34-of-35 extra points. He led the conference again in field goals made, field goal percentage (88.5%), and points (103). By the time Raymond graduated with his Business Management degree, he ranked in the top three of several UF career categories including most field goals in a game (six twice), highest all-time field goal percentage (87.8%), and most field goals made (43), along with several single-season records.

"Frankly, I didn't know I could be that good, and I didn't really expect it. I just focused on the little things, and I made sure to focus every day in practice and during the off-season. I kicked as much as I could every summer. My family lived across the street from a golf course, and there were some spare areas out there where there was nice groomed golf course grass. I got permission from the club pros to go out there and practice. I'd go out there with a PVC pole, plant it in the ground, and just work with that. I'd attempt about a hundred kicks a day. I worked to get that starting job. Before my junior year,

I knew there would be a lot of guys hoping to beat me out, and some of them could kick the ball farther than me. I knew where I wanted my focus to be. My focus was to be accurate. If it was within my range, I was going to make it. I was deadly from 52 yards and in."

Raymond was also deadly serious about contributing any way he could to the Gators' success. He even turned down the school's scholarship offer for both his junior and senior seasons. "My parents had set aside money for me to go to school, and we felt like it would be more advantageous to the team if we didn't accept the scholarship. The team could use that money for someone who needed it more – get another recruit that they might not otherwise be able to get. To me, earning a starting job, making the travel team, dressing out for every game – those were the rewards. I just wanted to be part of the team and know I was contributing whether I was on scholarship or not."

Raymond doesn't split the uprights anymore – and he now uses golf courses for actual golfing – but the lessons he learned from his walk-on experience are applied daily at his company, Brightway Insurance Agency. "My attitude was and still is to always do the best I can every day. If my coach made me do a drill, even if I hated the drill, I worked at it as hard as I could. When we used to stretch before practice, I wanted to be the best stretcher and push my stretching as far as I could. It didn't matter what I was doing, whatever the coaches or the team had me doing, or whatever I was doing on my own, I've always had a focus of wanting to do it to the best of my ability.

"I'm in the insurance business and my goal is not to write more insurance and be the biggest producer. My goal is to do the best job that I can for my clients and take care of them. Each account that I work on, I do it to the best of my ability. If I give them good advice and make the best recommendations I can, good things will come out of that.

"In business, scary things happen. Even when you work as hard as you can, bad things happen. You can't let it get you down. You have to have the attitude that you're not always going to have success.

You're going to have ups and downs. If every day you're working to do the best you possibly can, that's all anybody can ask of themselves. And the times it doesn't work out, you know what? I lay my head down on the pillow every night and I sleep like a baby."

CHAPTER 31

"You're Going To Be More"

Jim Roddy

Gannon University, Basketball
Business Coach, Executive, Author,
Podcast Host, & Speaker/Moderator

Author's Note: If you've read every preceding word in this book, congratulations and thank you. You are well-versed in The Walk-On Method and are primed to achieve career and business success. But please delay conquering the world a few more minutes to read my first-person account which provides significant details about the walk-on experience and describes how The Walk-On Method has served as the catalyst for my career success – and will work for you, too.

Your dream growing up might have been to play basketball for the Celtics or Lakers, but mine was suiting up for Gannon University, a Division II powerhouse in my hometown of Erie, Pa. I was so committed that when a high school classmate I pursued for years told me she was free for a movie date an upcoming Saturday night, I replied immediately, *I can't. Gannon's playing Philly Textile Saturday. Maybe next weekend?* She was never free again.

I was a first-team all-league guard at Bethel Christian School, scoring 1,526 points for my career, including 24.8 ppg as a senior, but I received only a handful letters from Division III coaches. Though my stats were big, my school – and the rest of the teams in the Pennsylvania-Ohio Christian Athletic Association – were tiny. Bethel was so small that I graduated ranked third in my class academically but I wasn't in the top 10%. Believe it or not, the class of 1988's 15 students was the largest in school history. The only scouts who attended Bethel Christian games sold cookies door-to-door.

My freshman year we had just seven players on the varsity roster for many games (there was no JV team), and when our two seniors and a sophomore fouled out at Ashtabula (Oh.) Christian Academy, we finished the game with four on the floor. And won. For four years, I was the starting point guard with literally no backup. I checked out of a game only four times in my entire high school career: one foul out, one blowout, 30 seconds for an injury, and then I was briefly benched for feigning a yawn on the court as we were thrashing a rival. (My bad.)

I was a big fish in a wading pool so, to me, playing at Gannon looked like the Pacific Ocean. Most years the Knights advanced in the DII NCAA tournament, including the 1987 national championship game, and their players were older and taller than many Division I teams. Among head coach Tom Chapman's many stars were 6-foot-7 U.S. Army veteran Mitchell Smith, a lanky 27-year-old who could dunk from one step inside the foul line, and 6-foot-9 former steel mill worker John "Shanghai" Matthews, a sinewy 31-year-old who could jump flatfooted and touch the top of the white square on the backboard. At 5-foot-10 and 145 pounds, I was crazy to think I could keep up with athletes like that. But I was undaunted despite often being discouraged. Joey Del Sandro, a third grader at Bethel (the school was K-12), and his dad attended both Gannon games and my high school games, and they got word I planned to try out for the Gannon team. While my senior classmates and I were selling hot dogs during school lunch one day, Joey placed his order with me and then said, *I told my dad you said you were going to play at Gannon. He doesn't think you can.* "Really?" I replied, the smile disappearing from my face. *Yeah. He doesn't think you're good enough.*

The spring of my senior year, I called Coach Chapman from the Bethel office to tell him I wanted to try out for his team. I was petrified. In Erie, Chapman was larger than life, an affable, media-savvy coach who knew how to stroke the egos of his fans. He won the community over through his weekly "Tom Chapman Gannon Basketball Show" on local TV and frequent radio interviews, telling the Gannon fans they were his Sixth Man and the reason for the team's success. Before big games while the teams were warming up, Chapman would walk up the stairs through the 2,800-seat Hammermill Center pumping his right fist as the screaming sellout crowd (me included) rose to its feet. *Come on! We need you! We need you tonight!* he would bellow. When advance tickets for an NCAA tournament game at Gannon went on sale, hundreds showed up before the sun rose to secure a seat. Ever the showman, Chapman bought dozens of donuts and distributed them to the Gannon faithful. The local TV stations and newspaper photographers captured it all.

You can see why I was more nervous calling him than asking Miss America out on a date. My heart pounded as he picked up. I informed him I wanted to try out for the team and was inquiring what steps I needed to take. He said when school starts pick-up games take place at the Gannon Rec Center every weekday at 3:00, so I should show up and try to get on the court. Practices started October 15, and after several practices they would decide to keep a walk-on or not.

Now on Gannon's radar, I needed to prepare to take the biggest shot of my life. Each summer during high school, I would ride my 10-speed four miles west to McDowell High School, the biggest school in Erie County, and spend hours at Paul Goll Gymnasium facing the top high school players in that area. But after graduation I had to work to help pay for college, so I spent much of the summer of 1988 in customer service at the Erie Zoo, a 10-minute walk from my home. I would dribble a basketball to the zoo each day and for my 30-minute daily break, I'd order food at the zoo concession stand where I was working, sprint to a basketball court the next block over, get 15 minutes of intense shot work in, and then sprint back to eat my cheeseburger and fries. I'd be sure to eat secluded from others and then splash myself with water in the restroom because the smell of grease and sweat emanating from my pores wasn't co-worker friendly.

I commuted to Gannon which meant catching a city bus four blocks from my house followed by a 20-minute ride downtown. I rented a locker on campus to store my workout gear while I attended class, and I'd change in a restroom before running down to the Rec Center. Turns out not only did scholarship guys play pick-up but alums showed up as well. Every day I'd tell multiple guys I was there to play, and most every day I'd do nothing but sit on the sidelines and get shots up between games. I didn't chat with anybody, I never had "next," and I got on court maybe one game a week if the numbers worked in my favor or a few guys were feeling lazy. Some Fridays I would hang around campus after my classes through the afternoon only to show up to an empty Rec Center because they guys decided not to play that day.

When official practice started, everyone received maroon-and-gold reversable practice jerseys, team sneakers, and their own locker with a name plate. I had to bring my own gear and keep it in my gym bag. One other Gannon student was attempting to walk on, and he tried charming some of the players through friendly conversations. I didn't say a word to anybody off the court. My plan was to show up the earliest, play the hardest, follow directions, and not be a hindrance on the court. The Gannon coaches were deciding my fate, not the players.

I was fast, so my effort immediately appeared on the coaches' radar. In every sprint I finished first – and I touched every line every time. Because I commuted, I didn't have the option to hang out in my dorm or apartment before practice, so I would arrive at the gym early and walk upstairs to the men's basketball office to ask for the equipment room key from one of the assistants. The exception was Mondays and Wednesdays because the school had scheduled me in an Introduction to Liberal Arts class that ran until 3:10, a conflict with the 3:00 p.m. practice start. I informed the coaches about this from the get-go and they encouraged me to visit their office in the morning those days to review the practice plan and then arrive at the gym as soon as I could. So, for each Liberal Arts class, I wore my practice shirt and shorts underneath a sweatsuit, and once the clock hit 3:10, I darted for the gym. Running through the hall, down the stairs, and across campus wasn't cool, but that wasn't my focus.

During those October practices, the only attention I received from Coach Chapman was him mispronouncing my name when dividing the team for drills and barking at me when a pass glanced off my hands. One Monday in November when I stopped by the office for the pre-practice plan, no assistants were there – just Coach Chapman in his private office. I let him know the reason for my visit, and he said, *I wanted to talk with you anyway. Have a seat. Jimmy, we've decided to keep you on the team.* I have no recollection what he said after that and I don't recall touching a step on the way back down to street level. I immediately called my mom and then a teacher at Bethel who had offered me encouragement. I couldn't believe the news myself – my head was still spinning.

When my family watched that season's first "Tom Chapman Gannon Basketball Show," I sat on the edge of the couch hoping I'd get a mention. Host Steve Bohen and Chapman appeared to be heading to a break after reviewing the entire scholarship roster. But then the camera angle changed slightly – the sign of a segment being spliced in – and Bohen said, *And we can't forget about walk-on Jim Roddy* ... because I believe they had forgotten about walk-on Jim Roddy. Chapman said, *When I told him he made the team, he jumped over my desk and kissed me. Jimmy is the heart and soul of our team. And if the leg of my dining table ever needs replaced, I can use Jimmy because he's so skinny.* I jumped off the couch with joy – I was the butt of a Tom Chapman joke! Another bonus to making the team was receiving an official velour-style maroon tracksuit with white/gold stripes and GANNON on the chest. When my outfit was delivered at the end of one practice, I beamed ear-to-ear and laughed when Coach Chapman said, *I didn't know they came in children's sizes.*

I was also happy when the sports information director asked me to complete a bio form for the game program, but he informed me I would need to submit my own photo. The scholarship players had theirs taken before official practices started. Thank goodness I had started contributing to the *Gannon Knight* student newspaper as a sports writer because they were the only ones on campus with a decent camera and photo developing equipment. The game program had an amusing (to me) advertisement by a local bank that paid tribute to "Gannon's 11 special young men," unaware (I think) that I had filled a twelfth spot.

Being the walk-on meant I received whatever game jersey, shorts, and warm-up everybody else didn't want. I was given uniform #34, a decent number, but alarming to me because I knew the Gannon player who wore that jersey last year was 6-foot-4 and nearly 300-pound David "Motown" Morris. His unaltered uniform shirt was hanging in my locker when I arrived about 90 minutes before our home opener vs. Shepherd (W.V.) College. I slipped it on, and the openings for the arms nearly came down to my waist. My ribs were completely exposed and the top ballooned so much that two more of me could have fit inside. But the bigger problem was the warmup pants I received just before we took the floor as a team 20 minutes prior to tip-off. Written on the tag inside the pants was "43" which I surmised meant last year they belonged to Mitch Smith, the 6-foot-7 guy who was nothing but legs. Even when I pulled the pants up as high as I could, the cuffs still bunched around my feet. Complicating my situation further was the lack of a drawstring to make the 40-inch pants cinch around my 30-inch waist. When I asked the manager for alternatives, he brought me two safety pins. I inserted one on either hip and prayed they would hold.

Gannon's a Catholic school, but God wasn't listening to me that night. Our team warmup plan included these elements at the start: tall guys in back, short guys in front, the first four players carrying a basketball. Half the group would take a right turn and run a lap around the court counterclockwise while the others would hang left and run their lap clockwise. When we passed each other, we'd raise our left hands for high-fives, then meet at midcourt for a quick huddle before beginning layup lines. Being short, I'm holding a ball near the front of the line as we wait in the tunnel, my college debut just seconds away. As we run onto the floor I feel a "ping" on my left hip as one of the safety pins springs open. Ouch! I grab the pants with my left hand and pull the fabric and pin away from my body. Not even ten steps later, I feel another "ping" on my right hip. The other safety pin is now stabbing me, so I grab that area and pull it away, still holding the ball under my right elbow. I'm wishing I could stop the world from spinning, but unfortunately reality says I not only must keep running but in a moment I have to raise my left hand to high-five six teammates. I bit my lip and let the pin on the left hip do its stabbing. I immediately ditched my pants after our huddle so I could perform a layup without embarrassing myself further.

Starting with that first game, I saw my role as a cheerleader, occasional opponent heckler, and the designated guy on the end of the bench. As much as I wanted to hear what the coaches discussed during game action, I didn't want a scholarship guy to call home and say he sat at the end of the bench. The seat next to the manager and trainer was mine because for me any spot on that bench was a dream come true. I didn't play vs. Shepherd but Gannon ran away from Queens (N.Y.) College in our second game, and Chapman signaled for 6-foot-8 freshman Gregg Blair, a 22-year-old Navy veteran, and me to enter the game; my mouth suddenly became dry and sticky as I jogged to the scorer's table. Guards had been taught during our practices when catching the ball on the wing our first look should be to a big man posting up. If the defender is on the high side (with their back towards the foul line), we should pass the ball towards the bottom corner of the bankboard which would lead the big man to the basket. On my first touch against Queens, I caught the ball on the right wing, saw Gregg posting on the right block, his man on the high side, so I instinctively fired the pass where I was taught. Gregg caught the ball in stride and laid it in with his left hand.

Turning to run back on defense, I looked across the court at our bench and made eye contact with Coach Chapman. He pointed at me for a job well done, and I pointed back at him. When our team returned to the lockerroom, everyone was happy with the victory, but I was ecstatic that I actually played a minute for my dream team. Chapman gave his postgame speech, pausing at the end, taking one step towards the door, and then looked at me to say, *Oh, and Roddy, you can clean the shit out of your pants now.*

We played our first 12 games that season at home, thanks to our large crowds and ticket revenue share contracts drawn up by legendary Gannon athletic director Howard "Bud" Elwell. My only real conversation with Mr. Elwell that year happened about 45 minutes prior to a practice when I was the only person in our lockerroom. I was sitting on my stool tying my shoes with my back to the door when Mr. Elwell walked in and asked, *Where's a towel?* I responded that I didn't know but I could find one for him. He said, *What do you mean you don't know? I just gave you a stack of them five minutes ago!* Unaware of what he was referencing, I turned around with a perplexed look. *Oh,* he said, *I thought you were the manager.*

Road trips included bus excursions to Pennsylvania towns like Indiana and Johnstown plus to metropolitan areas like Philadelphia (to play Philadelphia Textile), the University at Buffalo, Long Island (Adelphi), and downtown Manhattan (Pace). That last one was the most memorable not only because it was my first visit to Times Square, but for the practice at Pace University the night before our game there. The starters were working on a new zone defense, so the scout team was their fodder. Maybe it was because the small Pace gymnasium, located in the basement of a building next to the Brooklyn Bridge, reminded me of the courts I played on at Bethel, but I kept finding gaps in the zone and knocking down three-pointers. One of the assistants walked behind me and whispered in my ear, *Stop doing that. If they can't stop you, they'll think they can't stop anybody with this defense.*

We finished the season 21-9 and just missed out on an NCAA berth, a disappointing season by Gannon standards. Coach Chapman scheduled one-on-one postseason meetings with every player, and his assessment of me was frank and filled with dry wit: *I've come to learn that a person's intelligence is often in direct opposite proportion to their athletic ability. Jimmy, you're a very smart guy.* I felt in a great spot with Coach Chapman because he valued what I brought to the team. He and other Gannon coaches were under pressure from the administration to produce teams with winning records *and* higher grade point averages, so my 3.5 GPA on a team of 12 helped raise his score. Looking back on it, he told me I made the team the day after first semester mid-term grades were released. That couldn't have been a coincidence.

My basketball world was rocked that spring when Chapman was announced as the new head coach at St. Bonaventure. His entire staff was leaving with him, except perhaps for graduate assistant John Reilly. Gannon hired Bob Dukiet who had totaled 199 wins over 10 years as a Division I head coach at St. Peter's (N.J.) and Marquette, the latter school dismissing him in 1989 after his second sub-.500 season. I was essentially starting all over again with a new coach who didn't know me, and I didn't know his attitude towards walkons. (Spoiler alert: it wasn't positive.)

Dukiet hired Reilly as his full-time assistant, so I had an ally in the coaches' office. Coach Reilly asked me to visit the office that summer to help stuff envelopes and give me the opportunity to engage with Coach Dukiet. As I'm folding recruiting letters, Dukiet walks out of his office, shakes my hand, and fires this question at me: *Who are the three guys on the team that you would go to war with? Who would you want on the battlefield with you?* It was clear to me he was bringing a new level of intensity to the program. Dukiet also more than hinted walk-ons weren't his thing so I shouldn't expect to be on the roster that season. I finished my conversation with him saying, *I just want Gannon to win a national championship. If you think the best chance of that happening is with me on the team, that would be great. And if you think there's a better chance of that happening without me ... I just want Gannon to win a national championship.*

I recall walking down the steps from the office thinking to myself while my heart rate accelerated, *Oh my gosh – what did I just do? Did I just give him permission to cut me?* Dukiet instituted a preseason conditioning program which included a gratuitous amount of full court sprinting, my specialty. One time we ran so hard that 6-foot-10, 30-year old sophomore James "Big Daddy" Henderson ran off the court to vomit in the nearby restroom. Dukiet waited for Big Daddy to return to the court and greeted him by saying, *Congratulations, James – you broke a barrier!* One other student was trying to walk on the team, and Dukiet would regularly lump him and me together with criticism. *Jimmy and Kelly, you're missing a lot of shots. You're holding us back!* I didn't take that as a positive sign.

I honestly don't recall being told I made the team. I just kept showing up, the other guy stopped, and when the new uniforms were delivered, there was one for me. But here's an interesting twist – and it shows how fortune favors the bold and the persistent. Our home opener that year, in our new gold jerseys, was against outmanned Division III Elmira (N.Y.) College. I played 13 minutes, which would turn out to be by far the most single-game playing time of my career, and scored my first collegiate field goal, a pull-up right wing jumper in the final minutes. After the game, I was informed my uniform number would have to change because #13 had been retired to honor Glen Summors, regarded by most Gannon fans as the school's greatest player of all-time after averaging 19.2 points and 19.1 rebounds a game for his career. I figured I would get a different jersey altogether, but instead the school took mine to the Erie Sports Store and had a maroon 4 screenprinted over the 1. The fonts weren't the same, but since I was going to wear a shooting shirt over my jersey most of the season, the mismatch really didn't matter to anyone.

I quizzed our manager why the coaches had ordered #13 in the first place. He said it was the request of a junior college transfer who was expelled from Gannon for an on-campus fight before our official practices began. I paused and asked a follow-up: *If he hadn't been thrown out, what uniform would I have worn?* The manager looked away and down understanding the answer was more uncomfortable than my question. If that fight hadn't occurred, I might not have been a member of the team and my walk-on experience might have been nothing but a one-year wonder. Even though I had a roster spot that season, I still had more convincing to do.

One more note from that Elmira game: We handled them so thoroughly from the outset that I played the last two minutes of the first half. Nervous energy caused me to expend myself to the point I was borderline hyperventilating when we returned to our lockerroom for halftime. As we quietly waited for Coach Dukiet, a teammate asked me if I was all right. I responded seriously, *Yeah. I just never thought I'd be breathing hard at halftime,* which caused the rest of my teammates to laugh ... just as Coach Dukiet walked in. *You think this game is over?*, he shouted. *You're laughing now? This game isn't over!* We won going away, 85-47.

I had a moment in practice that season where my ego was damaged worse than an ACL tear. Coach Dukiet loved running a one-on-one full court drill, but it wasn't particularly helpful to my 7-foot-3 teammate Akol Tong who, the rare times he played, operated near the basket as a post player. Akol's weakness was his hands, so usually during one-on-one full court he and I would work on a side basket with me throwing him passes at multiple speeds and angles. But for some reason one practice Akol and I were both in the one-on-one full court drill, and I was matched against Gannon alum Roland Shannonhouse, a 6-foot-1 guard who ranked among the quickest and strongest defenders in school history. My job was to drive around him and get to the basket but, after trying in vain for nearly 20 seconds, I couldn't even get past *midcourt*. A frustrated Dukiet shooed me off the floor; I had to hold back tears I was so humiliated.

Our team's season was stellar, even surpassing the standards of many Gannon fans as we won the Mideast Collegiate Conference regular season, MCC tournament championship, and 1990 NCAA East Region, advancing to the Division II Elite 8 in Springfield, Mass. We finished 24-8, but the season wasn't a breeze. In half of our wins, we rallied from a late deficit to send the game into overtime or win in regulation by two possessions or fewer. Against Division III Allegheny (Pa.) College, we squandered a 31-point lead and found ourselves down one with under a minute to play before a clutch jumper gave us an 81-80 win. At crosstown rival Mercyhurst, who occupied the basement of the MCC, we came back from 15 down with eight minutes to play to win, 69-64. Against Le Moyne and their coach John Bielein, who would later find fame at West Virginia, Michigan, and the NBA's Cleveland Cavaliers, we eked out an MCC semifinal win, 55-53. I recall during a timeout that game with the score tied inside the final two minutes, our team was excited and confident, not nervous at all. We had played on the edge so many times that season, the pressure cooker was our comfort zone.

In the NCAA regional finals, a 72-63 victory at home over East Stroudsburg, we had the game sealed in the final minute. As the seconds ticked off the clock, for some reason I stood up on the bench with my forearms resting on top my head, in total disbelief that it wasn't just Gannon going to the Elite 8 but this was happening with *me* on the team. Our season ended the next round at the hands of Morehouse (Ala.) College, 75-69, after we fell behind 18-0. We roared back to take a lead in the second half but couldn't complete our comeback after three starters fouled out. As Coach Dukiet delivered his final speech of the year, I sobbed into the towel I had waved over my head most of the season.

That was the greatest team I had ever been a part of. We weren't ultra-athletic or more physical than our opponents. But every member of that team was egoless, sacrificing for the good of the whole. I don't remember one person complaining about playing time or not getting enough shots. I'm also confident we outworked every other team in the country. Several days that year, we had shooting drills scheduled for 6:00-7:30 a.m., but those often turned into competitive practices that butted up against 8:00 a.m. classes. Then we'd be back in the gym for our official practice from 3:00-6:00, the scholarship players rushing to take a shower and get to the cafeteria before it closed. One day before a 6:00 a.m. workout, I had a test and paper to finish, so I stayed all night at the newspaper office getting prepared and sleeping on the couch. When a couple fellow staffers heard about my early-morning basketball responsibilities, they said, *Why don't you just skip? Just tell them everything you had to do and that you don't feel well.* That was blasphemy to me. Walk-ons don't call in sick; they fight through whatever is in their way.

My walk-on experience was already benefitting me professionally. Erie was awarded an expansion franchise in the World Basketball League in 1990, and Gannon Sports Information Director Rick Love had connections with the league office. He knew my work ethic through both basketball and my role as the *Gannon Knight*'s Sports Editor and recommended me for a summer internship as the Erie Wave's Public Relations Assistant. I worked for the team part-time until school ended in May and then full-time until the WBL season ended in August. The position started as unpaid, but I knew I needed to make money that summer to help pay for school. So I used the first few weeks in the spring to become trusted with several jobs inside the PR department and the office. Once I proved myself as vital to the organization, I informed my boss and the General Manager that if they wanted to keep me around, I'd have to pull in about $150 a week. If they said no, I'd have to quit to go back to the zoo. The next day I got the thumbs up from the Wave and made sure I was the first person in the office – and often the last to leave – most every day.

There was no drama for me prior to my junior season at Gannon. Coach Dukiet valued my intensity and relentlessness in practice. He even asked me to work his basketball camp as a counselor, and I jumped at that opportunity immediately. He and Coach Reilly also understood that I could be trusted achieve high grades on my own, so they excused me from the team study hall so I could balance my classes, Sports Editor duties, and my Wave job in the spring. I hadn't talked them into anything; I built their trust through my actions.

That carried over into the athletic department. Even though my spot on the roster was secure, I still arrived first for practice every day. My routine was to get dressed, hit the restroom, stretch out, and then get up as many shots as I could. One day I'm already out on the floor when Mr. Elwell announces today is random drug test day, so everyone had to pee in a cup before practice. I told him I'd give it my best but I had just used the bathroom. He said, *Heck, you don't even drink beer, Jimmy. Don't worry about it.*

The 1990-91 Gannon roster was full of freshmen, many of them from the top Catholic high schools in Pennsylvania and one from the Croatian army. When the media guide was published, one of them read my bio, saw I averaged 24 points per game, and asked, *Who the hell did you play against?* Three of them shared a dorm room and asked me to show them one of my high school game films to watch between our team meal and when we had to report to the gym for that night's game. I brought in a VHS tape from a game my senior year at Southridge Christian Academy in Conneaut, Oh. Their religious beliefs required the players to dress modestly, so their uniform tops were short-sleeved shirts and their bottoms were long pants. If that didn't strike my freshmen teammates as unusual, the 19 points I scored in the third quarter did. I couldn't miss – slashing for layups, drilling a three off an inbounds play, and swishing a contested baseline jumper with two men on me. Nick Rovis, the Croatian, was on his bed slapping his pillow and laughing so hard tears were streaming down his face. It proved to them I wasn't inflating my stats – and it made them understand what a giant leap it was for me to play at Gannon.

Our team slipped to 17-13 that season, and I missed two late December games after breaking my thumb in practice. I was required to attend practice, but I couldn't participate. So immediately after class I would run laps at the Rec Center to stay in shape. I was still a week away from returning (doctor's orders) watching practice from the sidelines when Coach Dukiet approached me in the middle of a scrimmage to ask in a panicked tone, *Jimmy – when are you coming back? We need your energy!* Two days later I ditched my plastic cast, asked the trainer to heavily bandage my thumb, and I was back on the scout team defending our starting point guard.

We lost six of our final eight games, including a 90-64 drubbing on a Saturday night at Pace, the only loss I ever played in across 27 career games. One week later we were routed at Philly Textile, 70-50, and the deficit was more than 20 points at halftime. Usually for halftime, the players get a drink after entering the lockerroom, hit the restroom, and wait a minute or two before the coaches talk and illustrate on the chalkboard. But for this game, Dukiet started talking – er, yelling – before we even sat down. *We're getting killed again! What are we down – 20? 30? Like anything I say now is going to make a difference.* Then he walked out. Junior forward Mike Crawford asked, *Should we go back out and shoot now?* and we all decided that wouldn't be a good look for the team. So, we waited until there were five minutes left in halftime before jogging back onto the court.

I was fired up for my senior season because I had everything lined up academically, professionally, and athletically. Because I carried 18 credits in two prior semesters, I only needed 15 credits each semester in 1991-92 to graduate. That lighter load was imperative because the Erie Wave had promoted me to Public Relations Director even though I was just 21 years old and still a full-time student. So while my classmates were pondering their job opportunities, I knew exactly what I was doing after graduation – and combining writing and basketball was a dream vocation for me.

I even produced a moment during the Gannon basketball camp that summer where I saved Coach Reilly some money when the scholarship players couldn't. All week long the kids, middle schoolers and younger, had played "Knockout," a competitive drill that begins with players single-file at the free throw line. The first two players have a basketball, and each player shoots until they score – Shooter A first, then Shooter B. If Shooter B scores before Shooter A, Shooter A is out and Shooter B goes to the end of the line to wait until it's their turn again. If Shooter A scores before Shooter B, they both join the end of the line. When campers challenged the counselors (five Gannon scholarship players and me) to a game of Knockout, Reilly not only obliged, he put a wager on it. He said if one of the campers won the game, he'd buy all of them ice cream. The kids shrieked with delight as we lined up with one counselor behind every camper – and they cheered louder as two counselors were eliminated. Then another. Then another. Then one more. I was the last man standing (literally) between four hot-shooting kids and ice cream for everyone. Above the din, I could hear Coach Reilly imploring me, *Come on, Jimmy! I don't have the money!* I made nearly every shot, and the few I missed I quickly rebounded before I could get knocked out. It's kind of sad that one of my college highlights is outgunning a bunch of 12-year-olds, but I had to take what I could get.

I recall our first preseason workout that year because Gannon had recruited freshman Bronze Simpson, a 6-foot-5 forward who was so fast on the track he ran in the Junior Olympics in high school. I wanted to see how I would compare against a world-class speedster, hopeful I could maintain my streak of winning every sprint. We all stood on the baseline as our coach said we would run an "8," four times baseline-to-baseline full court. My strategy was to concentrate 100% on my strides the first three laps and then look to see how close I was to Bronze. With one lap left, I looked to my right to see how close Bronze and I were ... and he was crossing midcourt facing me, a few strides away from *finishing*. My winning streak was over – permanently over – but I kept running as hard I could the rest of that year to at least beat everyone else.

Bronze redshirted that year along with two talented transfers, Matt Flannery from Alvernia (Pa.) College and Scott Kornick from American International (Mass.). They were my teammates on the scout team all season, and with them in the lineup we would beat the first team often in scrimmages. Heading into our annual Maroon/Gold intrasquad scrimmage, I was more confident than nervous I could play well in front of my family and the several hundred Gannon fans who attended this game. With only six other players on the Gold team, I figured I would receive more minutes than ever during my Gannon career. When our new assistant coach didn't play me at all in the first half, I thought he was testing a few of the scholarship players' endurance. I got loose at halftime because I knew I'd be going in soon. Five minutes went by, then 10, then 15. With five minutes left, I still hadn't checked in and our coach was focused more on winning the game than ensuring I saw the floor. My heart was pounding because what I anticipated to be a dream evening was on the brink of becoming my worst nightmare. The buzzer sounded with me still on the bench.

Being a walk-on, I never expected the program to feel like it owed me anything, but after nearly four years of busting my tail and following every order, I thought giving me a couple minutes *my senior year in an intrasquad scrimmage* wasn't asking too much. I was steaming with anger and on the verge of tears by the time we got to the lockerroom. I sat on my stool and stared at the floor. A fellow senior who occupied the locker next to me and had played for Maroon patted me on the back and said, *That's messed up.* The coaches were taking longer than normal to talk with us, so we started getting undressed, until Coach Dukiet finally walked in. He had let the assistants run their respective teams that night as he paced back and forth during the game. He started saying, *Jimmy, I'm sorry about that. We'll make it up to you.* I appreciated he validated my perspective, but I also thought, *How?* My moment had passed. There would be no more Maroon/Gold scrimmages for me and possibly no more chances at playing time beyond mopping up at the end of a blowout.

A week later, we hosted a second exhibition game vs. a team of Gannon alumni, a seemingly formidable foe because past teams were so talented. But their conditioning was, shall we say, less than optimal, so we opened up a big second half lead. Coach Dukiet subbed me in along with some scholarship players with a few minutes left, and I played with confidence and abandon. I flew around the floor on defense, and when I had the ball in transition, I flipped a no-look, underhand pass to set up a teammate, a move I hadn't made since high school. Later after an alumni miss, I caught a long outlet pass on a bounce, dribbled once, and pulled up to drill a left-wing three-pointer. Afterwards a friend of mine who was shooting video for the Gannon TV station gave me a tape with every possession I played that game. At the end, he had a loop of my three, including the public address announcer blaring, *Threeeeee! For Jimmyyyyy Roddyyyyy!*

After scoring four points my first three seasons, I "exploded" for 10 as a senior. In a 105-63 walloping of Daemen (N.Y.), I drove for a righthanded layup to score Gannon's 100th point. I penetrated with the intent to pass to a teammate, but the defender guarding him never turned around, so I obliged. Ten days later we squared off with East Stroudsburg in a key regional contest. With Stroud 7-0 and us 6-1, the result of the game could have NCAA selection implications in March. Coach Dukiet was superstitious that players who received pregame media coverage would perform poorly, so he requested the player featured on the cover for the game program be me. The accompanying story inside said "with several important games coming up on the Gannon schedule, Jim Roddy isn't likely to see any playing time." That's kind of brutal but they weren't exactly exposing a secret.

Stroudsburg came out flat, and we jumped them right away, stretching the lead to over 40 points before I was inserted into the lineup. My teammates and the fans wanted me to score, so when a Stroud player shot a free throw with six seconds to play and the score

98-53, my teammates motioned me to stand at midcourt where they could throw me the ball make or miss. I caught a long pass in front of the scorer's table and immediately dribbled down the right side of the floor with a Stroud player on my left shoulder. We got to the basket with two seconds on the clock, but I knew if I shot a layup normally it would get blocked. So, I kept my body between the defender and the ball, scooping it one-handed off-balance, my momentum carrying me over the baseline where I fell on my back and slid a few feet. I heard the buzzer, looked up at the rim through the plexiglass bankboard and could see the ball still spinning around the cylinder like a roulette wheel at a Vegas casino. The ball finally fell through the net and, because I was still on my back, I thrust my arms and legs in the air in jubilation. Since this happened near the Gannon bench, my teammates were only steps away and stormed the court to congratulate me. Instead of helping me to my feet, senior forward Derrick Price lifted me off the ground and carried me across the court on his shoulders to shake hands with the Stroudsburg players. One of the Gannon statisticians started calling me "the 100-point man."

Our strong start continued through the end of the calendar year, capped off by a win at the buzzer of our holiday tournament over eventual DII national champion Virginia Union, 54-51. Everyone expected us to return to the NCAA tournament, but a self-inflicted injury helped knock us out of the running. Our starting center, a talented 6-foot-8 freshman, let his emotions get the best of him and punched a window in his dorm, sidelining him for a week. We lost by one to Edinboro (Pa.) and then by five at NAIA Westminster (Pa.), causing us to tumble down the regional rankings. With his hand heavily bandaged, that freshman sat by me at the end of the bench for both those games. Instead of cheering, he did a lot of complaining about Coach Dukiet's play calls and substitutions. I couldn't take it anymore. The guys at the end of the bench were supposed to lift their teammates up, not endlessly gripe. When we called a timeout late at Westminster, he started grumbling again. I said to him in no uncertain terms, *You of all people have no room to question someone else's judgment!* He was stunned – and so was I. The short, skinny walk-on who was happy to sweep the floor before practice was telling a much taller scholarship player to put a sock in it. For the remainder of that game, he did.

On a Saturday in February, we were scheduled to play at local rival Mercyhurst, so the team met that morning to load into vans for our shootaround in their gym, about a 10-minute drive. Coach Dukiet pulled up in his car and became impatient as we waited for our transportation. When told the vans were only a couple blocks away, Dukiet announced he was leaving and told me to ride with him. When I closed my door he said, *Jimmy, what do you want to do after you graduate?* This was unusual. Coach Dukiet one time benched a guy for asking on the day of a game if he was allowed to grow a beard that winter; game days required 100% concentration. I answered that I was very happy working in for the Wave and if I could make it to an NBA PR department someday, that would be incredible. He replied, *That's good, but you're going to be more. You can do more than public relations. I think someday you're going to own your own pro basketball team. And if you ever do buy a team, I'll coach for you.* What a difference four years had made. I had gone from intimidated to look directly at the Gannon coach to him offering to work for me down the road. I took it as an incredible compliment that my behavior as a walk-on over the years earned this level of respect.

Our second-to-last game of the season was a home against Pitt-Johnstown (Pa.), a Division II school that had won at DI Youngstown State earlier that year. We were on the bubble for an NCAA selection, so a loss to UPJ would be fatal to our playoff hopes. Our practice the day before was sluggish (as February practices can be) despite Coach Dukiet's incessant encouragement. So he stopped practice, called me over, and put his whistle around my neck. He said, *Take a quick break and afterwards Jimmy's going to run practice.* I thought he was joking, but when he felt the water break had gone on long enough he asked me to blow the whistle. As I mentioned before, if the coach asks me to do something, consider it done. I don't recall what I said to the team as they gathered around but a minute later I was standing on the baseline telling defenders to stay in front of their man and jump to the ball when it's passed. This wasn't just a five-minute diversion; I coached the team for the rest of practice.

The Johnstown game was a near repeat of East Stroudsburg, Gannon racing out to a 30-point lead and never looking back. Coach Dukiet subbed in all the scholarship players and with two minutes left I was the only one who hadn't seen action. I then heard in real life something that had only happened in my dreams: the Gannon crowd was chanting *Roddy! Roddy! Roddy!* Coach Dukiet heard the fans, walked towards me at the end of the bench with a smile on his face, and instead of pointing at me to go in, he extended his arms to his right towards the scorer's table, like a maître d' directing a guest to his table.

We were nearing 100 points, and I was hopeful to hit that milestone again. With a minute to play, I sneaked behind my defender under the basket and attempted a reverse layup I've made countless times before, even with my eyes closed. But I left this one short, and the crowd groaned as UPJ grabbed the rebound. I started retreating to play defense, but two Johnstown players collided with each other, and the ball popped out to me near the free throw line. I immediately drove to the basket where my layup was goaltended. After the referee blew the whistle and counted the basket, I jumped for joy behind the basket because my shot put us past the century mark again. With play halted, I ran back on defense near the sidelines where the fans have front row seats, and one of them reached out to high five me. Then another, and another, and another. I exchanged high fives with the entire front row until I got to midcourt and the ball was in play.

The pattern after each game was coach speaking to our team then the Gannon Sports Information Director stepping in to announce which player the media wanted to interview. After Dukiet began his interviews, I started unlacing my shoes as usual until SID Bob Shreve announced, *I need Jimmy Roddy!* Many of my teammates cheered and I couldn't contain my smile. When I stepped into the hallway with the print reporters and TV cameras, it was a strange feeling to have the spotlight on me. Before I could answer my first question, Coach Dukiet stepped in and announced that my running practice made the difference and he might have me run the team the rest of the season – and then he planted a big kiss on my cheek. Did I mention there were TV cameras filming all this?

For every college basketball program, the last home game is Senior Day, and many coaches play all their seniors the opening minutes of the game. Coach Dukiet didn't embrace that philosophy – and we were in a fight for the NCAAs – so I took my seat at the end of the bench after all the seniors received pre-game recognition. The contest against Mercyhurst was close, so my Senior Day present was another stat sheet listing next to my name the letters DNP: Did Not Play.

Despite our 22-6 record and rallying to win nine of our final 10 (the only loss by two to John Bielein at Le Moyne), we were not selected for the NCAAs. Our team watched the selection show via a satellite feed in the basement of the Gannon library, and my head dropped to the table when our name wasn't listed among the four clubs for the East Regionals. It was an abrupt end to an unexpected four-year college basketball ride. I pleaded with Coach Reilly that we should inquire about the ECAC (East Coast Athletic Conference) Tournament, a four-team consolation event for Division II teams in the northeast, but he said Gannon doesn't play in sub-NCAA tournaments.

I thought all I had left now were my memories and my meager statistics like scoring 14 points for my entire career. What I didn't realize back then was that the walk-on experience was ideal training for my professional career.

My work life had been jump-started with the Erie Wave, but the summer after my graduation the team ceased operations and the World Basketball League folded soon after. In need of a job, I jumped at the opportunity to work for the Career Concepts employment agency interviewing temporary workers and assigning them to shops and warehouses in Erie County. The company owner was Chuck Campagne, a longtime Gannon booster and season ticket holder whose seats were directly across from the Gannon bench. I told people Chuck hired me because we became comfortable sitting across from each other for four straight years – and that he stood up more during games than I did.

After a year at Career, I took my first of several Big Shots from a professional perspective. Let's view two of those through The Walk-On Method framework: first Owner/Publisher of startup *SportsLook* Magazine and then President of national business-to-business publisher Jameson Publishing. My tenure at Jameson includes authoring the book *Hire Like You Just Beat* Cancer and being selected Chairman of the Board for the Retail Solutions Providers Association (RSPA). I won't dig into details of my current duties as Business Coach, Executive, Podcast Host, and Speaker/Moderator because I feel like I've talked about myself too much already.

Owner/Publisher, SportsLook Magazine

Step 1: Take a Big Shot
Anybody can make a layup

With just $6,000 in my savings account, I left Career Concepts to launch my own monthly sports magazine at age 23. I rented the smallest, cheapest, mouse-free office I could find in the back of an office/industrial park – a windowless 12 by 12 that vibrated when freight trains passed – and I went to work. I knew little about printing, circulation, distribution, accounting, or sales but I could produce content because of my experience with the Gannon newspaper and the Wave. And I saw a niche in the market for sports coverage in Northwestern Pa. because the *Erie Daily Times'* sports section had become lethargic, their writers only covering games and ripping stories from the Associated Press, rarely going behind the scenes to pen feature stories on local athletes.

Taking on the paper as a bootstrapping sole proprietor was David vs. Goliath. The Times Publishing Co. employed dozens in the editorial and sales departments alone; my freelance writers included my mom, my older brother, and acquaintances who agreed to a rate of $25 per story. The *SportsLook* sales team was me and a stack of black-and-white business cards (they were cheaper than color). The

Times had a fleet of nearly 100 little red cars they flooded the city with; I had a 1992 maroon stick-shift Geo Prizm. But I was determined to take the paper head on. *SportsLook*'s tagline even threw shade at the Times: "Because Erie's sports are more than just a box score."

Step 2: Make a Passion Statement
Prepare with Passion, Practice with Passion, then Play with Passion

SportsLook was outgunned from a resource standpoint; however, our small but mighty team had a passion advantage. For the Times, covering local sports was a job to them, and they seemed genuinely excited only when writing from the press box at a Pirates or Browns game. Meanwhile, I was fired up to feature the top girls basketball player for the North East High School Grape Pickers (yes, that's their real nickname) on the *SportsLook* cover. I also relished the opportunity to appear as a regular guest on local sports talk radio and local TV sports shows, and I wore my *SportsLook* jacket and T-shirts everywhere. We were thrilled to create the magazine plan each month, track down athletic directors, coaches, and athletes, write evenings and weekends, and positively impact Erie sports. Never once did a freelancer ask me for a pay increase, and we were happy to exchange ideas to improve the magazine.

Step 3: Run Uphill
Takes longer, makes you stronger

On non-deadline weeks, I was putting in 55-60 hours at work, but when the magazine needed to be put to bed and distributed, my week expanded to 70+ hours. To accommodate that schedule, I moved out of the office park and rented an apartment so I could sleep for a few hours when on deadline and get back to my desk ASAP. When the paper was pasted up (this was before digital desktop publishing was mainstream) and ready to be dropped at the printer, I would drive the hard copy to my mother so she could proof the headlines. While she did that, usually in the middle of the night, I chugged two 12 oz. Cokes – I called them my "insurance policy" – to help me stay awake during the 90-minute round trip drive to the printer.

I never thought of myself as a salesperson, but I was excited to promote the paper. One of the largest advertisers in Erie was H. Jack Langer, known through his ubiquitous radio and television ads as "The Doctor of Plumbing." After a few issues were published, I called Langer asking for an appointment and he obliged. Dressed in a suit, tie, trench coat, and wing-tipped shoes – but still plagued by my early 20s looks – I showed up at Langer's and rang the buzzer at the front of his shop. When Jack answered the door, I introduced myself and reminded him of our scheduled appointment. He looked at me from head-to-toe and then asked wryly, *School get out early today, son?* I got the sale.

Step 4: No Fuss, All MUS
Maximize Unique Strengths

For four years I was a full-time student, a walk-on basketball player, and either writing for the student newspaper or working for the Erie Wave PR department, so my time management skills were forged under fire. That translated into me following through on every commitment and never missing a printing deadline for *SportsLook*. I recall talking with the General Manager of our printer after publishing several issues with them and he marveled that we were on time every time. *Do other people not do that?* I asked naively. He replied that *SportsLook* was one of the few publications they could count on to arrive to the press shop on time and meet all their specs.

I also wasn't afraid to Take a Big Shot with special issues and features. We named pre-season all-star teams for local men's and women's college basketball, published keepsake magazines for area high school state champions and runners-up, named male and female high school athletes of the year, and had the guts to select the Top 50 Erie-area high school athletes of all-time, ranking them in order then naming an honor roll. One writer at the Times disagreed with some of our choices and trashed the issue in a Sunday column. The community came to *SportsLook*'s defense, flooding talk radio lines with their appreciation of our efforts. I received calls from distribution points asking if I could bring them more issues, but we were all out. Instead of getting upset at the Times' criticism, we welcomed the attention and made the next issue, our special high school and college football edition, one of our top sales months ever.

Step 5: Make Them Throw You Out of the Gym
Never, ever, ever, ever, ever, ever, ever quit

My transition from *SportsLook* to Jameson Publishing is a perfect opportunity to clarify this step. Before I moved out of the office park, Corry Publishing (which later changed its name to Jameson) moved in. Co-owner Terry Peterson was thrilled to have another publisher in the building and asked me to go to lunch with him to talk work every month or so. Even after I moved offices, the lunches continued. During one get-together, Terry said his company needed a Managing Editor to keep production of their national technology magazines on schedule and supervise the editorial team, and he asked if I would consider it. I felt I had figured out local publishing and decided to Take a Big Shot with national publications. Instead of traveling from Albion to Waterford to Harborcreek for work, I'd attend trade shows in New York City, Chicago, and Las Vegas. I accepted the job offer when it came.

So did I technically quit *SportsLook*? Yes. But I didn't quit on my career goals. That's what Make Them Throw You Out of the Gym is all about. Don't stop until you get what *you* came for.

President, Jameson Publishing; Author, Hire Like You Just Beat Cancer; and Chairman of the Board, Retail Solutions Providers Association (RSPA)

Step 1: Take a Big Shot
Anybody can make a layup

My five-and-a-half years publishing *SportsLook* proved to be more valuable than an MBA – and with less debt, too. Over the course of 17 years at Jameson, I progressed from Managing Editor to Operations Manager then to President/General Manager for the final 11 years. I was part of a team that led the acquisition of a web-based publisher and was a member of their steering committee as well.

None of this was planned on my part; I advanced by falling on a series of grenades. When I saw a problem or one was presented to me, I pounced on it. For example, our sales team was experiencing turnover, and because our operations hiring was successful, I started interviewing prospective sales reps. When our sister company struggled with consistent operations, I spent two days a week with their team doing some supervising, some coaching, and some evangelizing of best practices. When a key trade association in our space was undergoing a significant transition – which presented a potential opportunity for our top-producing magazine – I hopped on planes and phone lines to meet the right people, offer assistance, and influence industry leaders.

I was also broadcasting Gannon basketball games on the side, which didn't impact my bank account much (I made $25 per game) but it improved my communication skills. So, when trade shows in our industry were seeking speakers and moderators, I raised my hand. Positive feedback from those engagements led to more associations and advertisers asking if I would speak at their conferences, which boosted Jameson's brand and market status.

From a product standpoint, we kept an eye on our competition, but they weren't our only measuring stick. We served our readers and advertisers, listening to their perspectives and bouncing our ideas off them. In our flagship magazine, *Business Solutions*, we launched a Best Vendors issue with integrity as our guiding principle, not pay-for-play like our competition did. The list of top vendors would be determined via a reader survey, so I reached out to the Penn State branch campus in Erie to learn best practices from a statistician who specialized in surveys. The issue was a hit from a financial and publicity standpoint. Our 40,000 subscribers appreciated the guidance and even the vendors who didn't make the list admired our even-handed process and appreciated us sharing survey feedback to help them improve their company.

I was bold with hiring as well. Yes, I followed our disciplined and detailed hiring process, but I placed my bets on the character of the potential candidate, not the length of their resume. I presented a candidate for Production Manager to one of the owners (who approved all hiring decisions), and he bristled that I would want to hire Niki Hykes for that position because she was only in her mid-20s. But Niki possessed many of the walk-on traits discussed throughout this book, and I insisted that we give her a chance. During her near-decade tenure, Niki revolutionized our production department, was promoted to Managing Editor then Operations Manager, and proved to be one of the finest leaders in company history. Years later when we were launching an events division, I took a chance on another 20-something candidate, Abby Sorensen. Others suspected that because Abby was a millennial, she would likely leave the job soon after we hired her and wouldn't commit to our cause. A former Division III golfer who exhibited many walk-on traits, Abby rolled up her sleeves, integrated with our sales and operations teams, and transformed our conferences into a growing and profitable product line.

Step 2: Make a Passion Statement
Prepare with Passion, Practice with Passion, then Play with Passion

The editorial team's primary goal was to produce a high-quality magazine that would build our brand and entice more advertisers. But early in my career errors kept showing up, stories were informative but not always compelling, and the staff was stressed scrambling from deadline to deadline. Everyone agreed with the end goal, but our preparation process was flawed. Among the steps we took:

- Instead of assigning stories six weeks prior to their due date, we assigned them 12 weeks out. This enabled writers to contact feature subjects early and effectively work around travel schedules.
- We instituted one-on-one meetings with writers to ensure their stories were on schedule. Meetings concluded with specific takeaways and firm deadlines. Writers who proved they could stay on track met with me less frequently.
- We launched a monthly writer critique meeting to accelerate the staff's learning. Every writer and editorial department manager would read our published feature stories and compare each against the standards outlined in our style manual. We even developed a scorecard to help everyone

align their thinking. During a 90-minute lunch (we'd order pizza for everyone), writers would briefly explain their writing process, including obstacles and shortcomings, and stories were discussed candidly. We made the meetings fun by voting for the best story and presenting a trophy and $100 to the winning editor. New editors zoomed up the learning curve while veterans improved their work instead of stagnating.

- We developed a four-stage proofing system that I won't describe in detail, but it ferreted out almost every mistake.

After executing this system for several quarters, we began consistently producing high quality, error-free magazines. We never relaxed or relented on our process. We sought to make incremental improvements every quarter. The systems made the process smoother, but the team was never in cruise control, always preparing with a purpose.

Step 3: Run Uphill
Takes longer, makes you stronger

Our company grew every year during my first 10 on staff until the Great Recession of 2008-09. We had recently moved into a larger office to accommodate our growth and hired new employees to handle the expanded workload, but as the international financial crisis worsened, large contracts were cancelled. We hoped the situation would turn around quickly, but when that didn't happen, our steering committee made the decision to lay off employees.

I had terminated people before due to their performance, but furloughing employees who had done everything you had asked of them – or had just started with the company a couple months earlier – was even more gut-wrenching. I had been company President for about two years at this point, so it was my job to deliver the bad news in termination meetings and then gather our surviving staff to update them on our actions. I can recall my heart pounding and my voice fluttering as I read from my notes in front of our team. I couldn't help but notice one of our production managers angrily staring back at me; the rest of the team was in shock. These layoffs were an awful surprise.

Until that point, we had communicated only company wins with our team, so no wonder they felt blindsided. After that meeting I committed to share the unvarnished truth with everyone so they would never be stunned by bad news again – and so they could help the management team right the ship. Through one-on-ones, department meetings, email updates, and all-hands Q&A sessions, they understood the need to do more with less. As the recession worsened, we were forced to conduct two more rounds of employee layoffs, and the people who stayed took a hit financially. With our revenue off nearly 33%, the take-home pay of most sales employees dropped by $10,000-$40,000. Operations employees went for more than two years without pay raises. Managers lost their overtime pay. On top of that, for the first time in company history, we stopped our dollar-for-dollar 401(k) match. For one year, 11 months, and nine days. (Yes, I was counting.) You'd think employees wouldn't have been able to work with all the complaining going on around them or that many of them would have quit to avoid this difficult time. But that's not what happened.

Our employees innovated and positioned each of our products to take advantage of sectors in their industries. In 2010, we grew our sales 20%, enabling us to turn on pay raises and our 401(k) match. We began hiring again because we had more customers to take care of. It was a monumental accomplishment in a tumultuous time. Leaning into the challenge made us all better.

Step 4: No Fuss, All MUS
Maximize Unique Strengths

As mentioned earlier, Coach Chapman informed me I made the Gannon team the day after mid-term grades were announced. I'm sure he computed that I raised the team GPA by 0.1 or 0.15, and thought to himself, *That will help me. Let's add him to the roster.* Everybody else was taller, stronger, and more skilled than me, but my unique strength provided value to my boss.

231

I followed that philosophy at Jameson. Instead of being a cookie-cutter Operations Manager or President, I continued to write occasionally for the magazines and their websites and I embraced emerging social media channels. Additionally, my interview skills were staying sharp with our high volume of hiring. To ensure pre-employment best practices throughout our organization, I helped create a training program for our hiring managers which consisted of classroom work, role playing, and a thick three-ring binder that detailed our successful process. It was well received, but I kept wondering if there was a more accessible and memorable way to present this material.

I decided to write a hiring book that weaved our best practices with my personal stories. That's where I utilized a unique strength: surviving cancer. Nothing captures attention like the "Big C"; I had it, beat it, and was going to use it. *Hire Like You Just Beat Cancer* offered "hiring lessons, interview best practices, and recruiting strategies for managers from a cancer-surviving executive." Here's an excerpt that explains the title:

Since I had success with hiring on the editorial and production side of our business, the owners asked me to help interview and hire sales employees. After a couple sales candidates asked, "Why am I talking with an editor?" the owners changed my title to Operations Manager. It lacked the fanfare you see in the movies when someone is promoted, but it was a move up. Then I got cancer.

I was only 32 years old. I had to tell my teenage brother that if surgery showed that my colon cancer had spread to other organs, I might not be around through the end of his basketball season. As you can imagine, we were both scared and shared a long cry. I also had to tell my boss and co-workers that even if things went well, I was going to be out of commission for two months after surgery. And, due to chemotherapy treatments, I would work only part time for most of the next year. If things didn't go well, the team would move on without me.

Before my diagnosis, I'd thought I understood the importance of hiring top-notch people. But it took being forced to step away from my co-workers for an extended period of time (with one of the options being stepping away forever) for me to realize that the people you hire truly make or break your business. It doesn't matter if you have the best product, best systems, best location, or a spotless reputation. Your situation will change eventually. When that happens, who's going to make the right adjustments to your business? Your people.

Combining my writing skills, my hiring knowledge, and my unique perspective surviving cancer resulted in a book (plus speaking opportunities, media exposure, podcast interviews, and more) nobody else on the planet could have published.

Step 5: Make Them Throw You Out of the Gym
Never, ever, ever, ever, ever, ever, ever quit

The Retail Solutions Providers Association (RSPA) was one of largest and the most important organizations in Jameson's industry and, back in 2006, many of their members despised our company. Seeking to displace the retail IT industry's #1 magazine, a zealous former employee of ours had written caustic letters to RSPA board members. Years later I was shown copies of the letters, and they were akin to a punch in the face on paper. The first RSPA trade show I attended was in Reno, Nev., and I saw firsthand that our competition was kicking our butt. Most obvious was that nearly every exhibitor booth showcased a placard of that company's advertisement in our competitor's magazine. More subtle was that their staff was friends with many other attendees while we were viewed as interlopers. We weren't invited to any private functions and certainly nobody was asking us to hang out with them for drinks.

It reminded me of my days at the Gannon Rec Center where I showed up hoping to play but nobody wanted me on their team – unless they needed a tenth player to keep a game going. We decided to engage with the RSPA staff and members, ask them what they needed, and then help in those areas. We weren't requesting anything in return, just the opportunity to lend a hand. They were lacking volunteers for several committees, so we signed up, showed up every meeting, and offered to execute takeaways. The RSPA wanted more exposure, so we published their association news in our magazine and on our website, then we brainstormed how we could best cover their conferences. This was the early days of online video (before you could stream live from your smartphone), so we purchased Flip cameras for our editors and scheduled appointments with as many exhibitors as we could to record a demonstration of their product. At RSPA's RetailNOW show in Las Vegas, a vendor was making a major announcement the first evening of the three-day event. My role that night, after a 12-hour day on my feet, was to record the announcement then hustle back to my hotel room to work with Chief Editor Mike Monocello editing and launching videos we shot that day. This announcement was supposed to take place at 8:00 p.m. local time, but by 10 o'clock they still hadn't stepped to the podium. I knew I had plenty of work to do, but I was committed to capture this video, especially since our competition was nowhere to be found. I squeezed my way to the front of the crowd, sat on the floor of this Vegas nightclub (gross), and shot what we came for. The announcement was a business model change for our industry, and we were the only ones who had it.

I raced back to the hotel room where Mike was already busy writing summaries, editing video, and uploading final clips to our website. Our internet connection was slow, so we couldn't move very quickly, but he and I were committed to launching and emailing links to all our videos by the time RetailNOW attendees woke up the next morning. We worked without looking at the clock but realized how late it was when I received an email from a co-worker who had arrived for work early back home in the Eastern time zone. After a couple hours of sleep, we attended the show's Day 2 general session energized. Attendees who had received our email were approaching us to say what an amazing job we had done and how informative the videos were. The RSPA's show manager approached me to say, *Your newsletter was great. I'm learning things about my own show from you guys!*

Our servant's attitude continued which opened multiple opportunities for us. I was asked to become Chairperson the RSPA Marketing Committee, present educational breakout sessions, and moderate breakout panels at next year's RetailNOW. Eventually I was asked to moderate at the RetailNOW general session in front of nearly 2,000 attendees and chair the Vendor Working Group Committee. Meanwhile, our competitor experienced staff turnover, and we gladly filled the gap with editorial coverage of the industry, featuring many of the RSPA's most successful members. When the RSPA announced their Awards of Excellence, we were thrilled to win second place in our category and then even happier the next year when we began a near-decade streak of first place finishes.

In 2010, I was asked to run for the RSPA board and beat out five industry veterans vying for the one open seat. In four years, our magazine had gone from outcasts to award winners and board members. We did it because of our team's commitment to serve and because Mike and I never missed a welcome reception or closing party and we never went to bed early during an industry event. We followed the advice of former RSPA Chairperson Mark Olson who told us, "You can sleep when you get to the old folks' home!" We even printed custom T-shirts for RSPA members displaying Mark's picture and quote.

In 2015, I was asked to Chair the RSPA Board and immediately accepted. It was the ultimate position of service to the organization and the industry. That summer at RetailNOW, we not only won first place in our category but were flabbergasted to be announced as the winner of the RSPA's prestigious Gold Medallion Award, presented to the industry's top overall vendor. Our small team was selected over several multibillion-dollar Fortune 500 companies.

After years of relentless focused effort, we had transformed from underdog to extraordinary.

And so can you.

The Walk-On Method
To Career & Business Success

Step 1: Take a Big Shot
Anybody can make a layup

Step 2: Make a Passion Statement
*Prepare with Passion, Practice with Passion,
then Play with Passion*

Step 3: Run Uphill
Takes longer, makes you stronger

Step 4: No Fuss, All MUS
Maximize Unique Strengths

Step 5: Make Them Throw You Out of the Gym
Never, ever, ever, ever, ever, ever, ever quit

All 5 Steps Are Within Your Power

43 Walk-On Workplace Do's and Don'ts

This chart will help you translate lessons learned from *The Walk-On Method* into actions that will accelerate your career progress. I chose **43 Walk-On Workplace Do's and Don'ts** to commemorate when my #13 uniform at Gannon had a maroon 4 screen-printed over the 1 because #13 was already retired. The fonts weren't the same, but since I was going to wear a shooting shirt over my jersey most of the season, the mismatch really didn't matter.

Walk-On's Do's	Walk-On's Don'ts
Sets personal goals that exceed others' expectations, then executes. Takes initiative.	Does only what they're told, or less.
Steps outside their Comfort Zone and into their Courage Zone. Learns new skills; accepts daunting challenges; has hard conversations (without being harsh).	Takes permanent residence in their Comfort Zone.
Acts with urgency. Rearranges their schedule to ensure problems and important issues are addressed as soon as possible.	Works at their own pace. Hopes the problem disappears on its own or that someone else takes care of it.

Works quickly and with purpose always, as though their boss is sitting behind them every moment of every day. Self-disciplined.	Coasts when their boss isn't looking.
Creates a winning culture by setting the pace for effort, focus, and harmony. Generates enthusiasm and commitment in others.	Disrupts the culture by placing their wants above the organization and the mission.
"You can sleep when you get to the old folks' home!"	Hits the snooze button, skips the morning workout and morning reading, then rushes to start the day.
Begins work early; works late and weekends when necessary. Work isn't over until the job is complete.	Sneaks in late; sneaks out early. The clock is the judge of when work is done.
Makes as many efforts as necessary to achieve the outcome. Sends multiple emails, makes multiple phone calls, and leaves multiple voice mails when necessary. Practices persistence.	"I sent her an email and I didn't hear back."
No matter their tenure or title, gets their hands dirty, working elbow-to-elbow with colleagues.	Considers some jobs beneath them.
Consumes digital content (podcasts, websites, newsletters, etc.) and reads books with lessons and best practices that can be applied at work.	"Learning was for back when I was in school!"

Seeks out new systems, ideas, and techniques to improve their effectiveness – without being asked.	"I'm good."
Shares what they learn.	Hoards knowledge in hopes of gaining an advantage.
Addresses bad habits. Does not excuse shortcomings. Instead, they seek to expand their knowledge and improve their skills.	"I am what I am."
Seeks to improve the greater good. Makes sacrifices (of time, resources, recognition, etc.) to help the team achieve its goal. Serves others.	Their core question is, *What's in it for me?*
Exhibits "Productive Paranoia." Understands that conditions can change unexpectedly, violently, and fast, so they prepare for that situation. (Term and concept by business author Jim Collins.)	Comfortable in the status quo.
They are an Energy Elevator, lifting the spirits of everyone they encounter. When asked, *How are you?* they reply with words such as *awesome, fantastic,* and *wonderful.*	They are a Soul Sucker, deflating everyone they encounter. They reply with words and phrases such as, *okay, I've been better, same stuff different day,* and *don't get me started.*

Volunteers for additional work. Frequently asks, *How can I help?* When work spikes for a teammate or client, they are happy to help.	During a labor or time crunch when a teammate or client needs help, stares at their shoes, hoping others will step up.
Volunteers to have their work reviewed by a supervisor, peer, subordinate, or client well before the deadline. Asks for honest feedback to ensure the final product meets or exceeds expectations. Embraces accountability.	Assumes their work will be "good enough" and believes comments from others wastes time.
Volunteers for industry associations, lending their time and expertise for the sake of the community.	Uses industry associations only to obtain leads and increase their sales totals.
Applies critical thinking when making decisions. Asks questions and conducts research to fully understand specifics of the situation. Is humble enough to understand their perspective might not capture the full picture.	Takes a guess based on what they know. Announces half-baked conclusions.
Maintains emotional control – in good times, bad times, and when there's a crisis. When work spikes and becomes overwhelming, they don't get overwhelmed. When bad news gets delivered, they act constructively.	Freaks out – or shuts down.
Leads when necessary; follows when necessary. Understands and embraces their role on the team.	Shrinks when courage is called for; gripes about decisions made by others.

Assumes positive intent from others.	Expects to get jerked around.
Cooperates.	Counteracts.
Compliments.	Complains.
Humble.	Arrogant.
Shares "job well done" notes with co-workers and clients – unsolicited.	Complains about co-workers and clients – unsolicited.
Deflects credit, accepts blame. Speaks up when they fall short of a goal or made a mistake.	Brags. Outsources blame. Offers excuses or points fingers when outcomes are not achieved.
Doesn't pester their boss for a raise.	Pesters their boss for a raise. Rolls eyes when boss explains why not. Repeats this process next meeting.
Loyal to their team and their organization. Doesn't bail at the first sign of trouble. Works through difficult situations.	Looks out for #1.
Answers truthfully, even if the truth exposes a failing of theirs.	Stretches facts or provides incomplete answers to cover up their failings.
Expresses gratitude: says "thank you" to clients, co-workers at all levels of the organization, suppliers, restaurant servers, airline attendants, ride share drivers, maintenance workers – everyone.	Stays silent when being served because they expect to be catered to.

Listens 80% of the time; talks 20% of the time. Speaks to benefit the listener.	When others are talking, looks for a pause to interject their opinion.
Holds the door open for others, even when they're in a rush. Keeps their head on a swivel so they notice if anyone else needs the door held open.	Opens door. Walks through.
Answers emails promptly. If a request can't be fulfilled in a timely manner, acknowledges receipt of the email.	Allows emails to pile up, leaving the sender wondering if the message went through.
Ends emails writing, *If you have questions, suggestions, or need more information, please let me know,* followed by an email signature with complete contact information.	Because they are not open to questions/suggestions/changes, ends emails abruptly.
Double-checks work to ensure it's accurate and high quality before presenting.	Embraces the Hide-and-Go-Seek Method with projects and presentations: *Ready or not, here I come!*
Runs spellcheck every time.	Maybe they'll run spellcheck, maybe they win't.
Consistently meets (and beats) deadlines. Finishes projects early understanding that an emergency may arise closer to the deadline. If a deadline might be missed, contacts affected individuals in advance to alert them. Establishes a reputation of punctuality.	Completes work at their own pace. Comfortable throwing things together last minute. When confronted about a missed deadline, lists other projects that occupied their time.

Stops to pick up debris on the office or shop floor – even just one paper clip.	Keeps walking.
Spends company money wisely, like it's their own. Does not see work travel as an opportunity to expense pricey meals.	"I've got the company card!"
Submits an accurate expense report in a timely manner.	Makes operations personnel track them down to report expenses.
Seeks clarity when discussing expectations and takeaways. Draws closure on who will complete what by when.	Assumes.

All 43 Actions Are Within Your Power

ABOUT THE AUTHOR

Since 1999, Jim Roddy has educated business and non-profit leaders (and future leaders) through books, national magazine articles, podcasts, and presentations at national conferences. Jim is one of the most popular speakers in the technology industry because of a presentation style that is "infotaining" – a combination of informational and entertaining. Jim is regularly requested to moderate keynote panel discussions featuring executives from companies such as HP, NCR, IBM, and successful software startups. He has presented from coast-to-coast throughout North America (Hawaii, San Diego, Las Vegas, Chicago, Austin, Toronto, Orlando, Philadelphia, New York, Boston and more) as well as internationally (Aruba, Bahamas, Virgin Islands, and more).

Jim is author of *The Walk-On Method to Career & Business Success* and *Hire Like You Just Beat Cancer*. He's been featured as a guest on the Read To Lead podcast and has been published by Entrepreneur and Nasdaq. Jim has interviewed best-selling business authors Chip Heath (*Made To Stick, Switch, Decisive*) and Michael Gerber (*The E-Myth*), hosting with Mr. Gerber a series of webinars and podcasts that attracted 1,000+ executives.

Jim is a graduate of Gannon University in Erie, Pa., where he was a walk-on member of the men's basketball team for four years and sports editor of the student newspaper for three years. Jim resides in Erie with his wife, Barbara, and daughter, Evelyn.

For more information on Jim, visit:
www. JimRoddyCBA.com

To hire Jim as a keynote speaker, contact:
Jim@JimRoddyCBA.com

Follow Jim on Twitter:
www.Twitter.com/Jim_Roddy

Connect with Jim on LinkedIn:
www.LinkedIn.com/in/JimRoddy1

Follow *The Walk-On Method* on Facebook:
www.Facebook.com/TheWalkOnMethod

To order bulk copies of *The Walk-On Method*, email:
Contact@JimRoddyCBA.com